EARLY HISTORY

OF

CLEVELAND,

OHIO,

INCLUDING ORIGINAL PAPERS AND OTHER MATTER RELATING TO THE ADJACENT COUNTRY.

WITH

BIOGRAPHICAL NOTICES

OF THE

PIONEERS AND SURVEYORS.

BY COL. CHA'S WHITTLESEY.

CLEVELAND, O.
1867.

FAIRBANKS, BENEDICT & CO., PRINTERS,
HERALD OFFICE CLEVELAND.

PREFACE.

THE materials for this work have been accumulating many years, but were far from complete, when Judge BARR turned over to me, his historical collections without reservation. He has been engaged with much assiduity more than a quarter of a century, in reclaiming the personal history of the pioneers; a labor which I trust their descendants will appreciate. The extent of the obligations I am under to him will appear frequently in this volume.

I am also indebted to a number of other gentlemen, particularly to General L. V. BIERCE and the Hon. F. WADSWORTH, of Akron, to Messrs. H. A. SMITH, Prof. J. P. KIRTLAND, JACOB PERKINS, SAMUEL WILLIAMSON, and the late JAMES S. CLARKE, Mrs. ASHBEL W. WALWORTH, and Mrs. Dr. LONG, all of Cleveland. The heirs of General MOSES CLEAVELAND, and JOHN MILTON HOLLEY, of Connecticut; the surviving sons of Governor HUNTINGTON, of Painesville, and Judge WITHERELL, of Detroit, have done me essential service.

Many documents relating to later periods, and to other parts of the Reserve have been procured; which will at some future period be required for historical purposes. I am more ambitious to preserve history, than to write it, and have therefore freely transcribed from papers, letters, verbal statements, and casual publications, relating to the early times. The originals are certainly more authentic, and more entertaining, than a reproduction would be, in the language of another. This plan necessarily involves some repetition, and defies strict chronological arrangement, but possesses more life, freshness and variety.

My prospectus included only the "Early History of Cleveland," but with a mental reservation, had the subscription warranted me in the undertaking, to enlarge the work, and include what relates to the more recent progress of the city. This I have not been enabled to do. What concerns commercial matters, in later times; to railways, local improvements, institutions, general improvements, and general statistics, could not have been inserted, and do justice to those heroic pioneers, who laid the foundation of our prosperity. What refers to banks, churches, newspapers, trade, benevolent societies, manufactories, and the city authorities, is on record, and therefore not in danger of being lost.

In 1810, the county was organized, since when all judicial matters are to be found in the recorded proceedings of the various courts. The "Village of Cleaveland," was incorporated in 1814, and its municipal record is in existence. A weekly newspaper called the *Cleaveland Gazette and Commercial Advertiser*, was issued in August, 1818. Since that time there are unbroken files, of weekly or daily papers for reference.

But for the more remote periods, it has been more difficult to obtain reliable information. Works relating to the early French and English occupation on lake Erie, and especially the southern shore, are rare, and in respect to this region, their contents are very meagre. The papers of the Connecticut Land Company and their surveyors, have been only partially transferred to Ohio. Perhaps many of them are no longer to be found in Connecticut, and such as exist are so much scattered as to be in practice inaccessible.

The personal history of the first settlers and surveyors, has been partially procured. My principal object has been to secure from oblivion, what relates to them. Since they are no longer with us, to speak of themselves; what they accomplished, and what they suffered, was to be sought for in traditions, private letters, and transient publications. In carrying out this design, it was necessary to insert much that occurred outside of the city limits, in other parts of the Reserve. The history of the city and country, previous to the war of 1812 is so intimately connected, that it should be written as one.

C. W

CLEVELAND, January, 1867.

CONTENTS.

ILLUSTRATIONS.

EXPLANATION OF THE VIEWS.

1.—CLEVELAND, FROM THE WEST SIDE.—*a*, Erie House, on the canal.—*b*, Old Bethel Church, on the side hill, in line with the Court House.—*c*, Mouth of Ohio Canal, in line with the Stone Church.—*d*, End of Superior Lane, on the River.—*e*, Mandrake Street.—*f*, Stone Flouring Mill and Light House.—*g*, Mouth of the River.

2.—ST. CLAIR STREET, LOOKING EAST.—*a*, Court House.—*b*, Stone Church.—*c*, Trinity Church, corner of Seneca Street.—*d*, Academy.

3.—PUBLIC SQUARE, LOOKING WEST.—*a*, Trinity Church.—*b*, Governor Wood's Office.—*c*, Light House.—*d*, Cleveland Hotel.—*e*, Commercial Bank and Market, Bank Street.—*l*, Stone Residence of Dr. Long, corner of Superior and Seneca.

4.—EUCLID STREET, LOOKING WEST.—*a*, Residence of Hon. J. W. Allen, on Public Square.—*b*, Stone Church and Trinity.—*c*, Court House.

5.—STOCKLEY'S PIER.—*a*, Light House.—*b*, Ashtabula Rail Road Shop.

6.—COLUMBUS STREET BRIDGE, from Detroit Street.

STOCKLEYS PIER FROM THE GOVERNMENT PIER, 1850.

I. BRAINERD DEL.

b a

PRE-ADAMITE HISTORY.

History, under a strict definition, should include nothing more than the record of human transactions, but I here venture to introduce an article which relates principally to natural science.

The wells, springs, cisterns, and sewers; the general improvement of our streets; the protection of the lake shore and the state of our harbor, are all influenced by the geological structure beneath us. I imagine, also, that it will be interesting to look briefly at the cause of the most recent geological changes.

On the gravelly plain which was selected by the surveyors in 1796 as the site of a future city, there are numerous low, sandy ridges, which are parallel to the shore of the lake. These ridges were the first roads of the pioneers on their way to the west. They appear to have been formed beneath the surface of the water at a remote period, when the lakes had a much higher level than now. On all sea coasts long, narrow sand-bars are known to form, a short distance from the shore and parallel with it. Their position is indicated to the navigator by the outer line of breakers. The formation upon which this city rests is geologically the most recent of all, except the alluvium.

There are trees, sticks, and leaves imbedded in it, which have not yet perished; but in reference to the period of written history its era is very ancient. It was formed after the earth had assumed substantially its present surface, in a topographical sense. Geological investigations show conclusively, that since the era of the coal, the chalk formations, and even the tertiary beds, there was in the northern hemisphere, north of about 40°, a period of universal ice; as there is now in Greenland.

As that frozen age was disappearing the more ancient and solid rocks of the Carboniferous, Devonian and Silurian ages, on which the universal glacier rested and moved; were ground down, scoured and polished. The crushed and pulverized materials of the rocks form what is commonly called earth, as distinguishable from indurated strata. In the northern hemisphere, the ice movement was toward the south, which carried the fragments of rocks and their mixed debris, in the form of dirt, always towards the equator.

In this way we have here pieces of rocks designated as "boulders" or lost rocks; which were originally in place on the shores of lake Superior or Hudson's Bay. Our soil is composed of the disintegrated particles of these rocks, mingled with the crushed portions of strata nearer home. The surface formation on which the city stands belongs to the close of the ice period when the glacial masses were disappearing, and the waters were assuming their present level over the land. It is sometimes called "post-tertiary," or "quaternary," but more often "northern drift." There are in it no rocky beds, although it is frequently stratified, and laminated. The waters from which, by a joint action with moving ice, it was transported and deposited, were throughout the upper lake country wholly *fresh*. Numerous shells have been found in it, all of which belong to fresh, and none to sea water. Nearer the ocean, the shells of the drift are of marine origin. Throughout all the region of the upper lakes, there are numberless trees, logs, sticks, branches and leaves scattered through the drift formation. It is composed of red, blue and dun colored clay, on which rests coarse sand, gravel and boulders.

By an analysis of the laminated blue clay taken from the foot of Ontario street, made some years since, it was found to contain:

Silex and Alumina,	77.50
Carbonate of lime,	6.00
Carbonate of magnesia,	9.50
Sulphide of iron,	3.50
Vegetable matter and loss,	3.50
	100.00

An analysis of the red laminated clay of lake Superior gave a similar result, except in regard to the red oxide of iron which exceeds that of the lake Erie clay, and which is the cause of its red color.

The drift clays always contain alkalies, sometimes in sufficient quantities to prevent their being used for the purpose of making brick.

Sometimes it changes to a compact hard-pan, composed of clay and fragments of rocks. There are boulders and pebbles of northern rocks throughout the whole mass. In many places it is not stratified, but mixed and confused like the moraines of Alpine glaciers now being formed. There are places in the valleys of the upper lakes where the drift is 600 and 800 feet thick, but here, it is probably nowhere more than 150 feet, down to the underlying rock. When lake Erie receded to its present level, its ancient bed was partly inclined like the rim of a basin sloping towards the water.

The mouths of the rivers were farther out than now, the lake was smaller in size and its shore line quite different. Where the shore was composed of marly clays, as it is along much of its outline, the waves made rapid inroads upon it and the soft materials were dispersed by currents that exist in all bodies of water. There is a tradition that when the French first coasted along the south shore of lake Erie, the Indians remembered when there was no outlet at the present mouth of the Cuyahoga river.

It discharged at the old mouth one mile west, and the point of the bluff extending westerly from the light house then interposed between the river and the lake. A mound, the remains of this point is represented in the sketch made by Capt. Gaylord in the year 1800. It remained at nearly the same height when I first saw it in 1827.

Operating upon such material as the blue marly clay, the encroachments of the lake were rapid. On the Canada shore opposite Cleveland the formation is the same and its destruction equally rapid. The remains of soldiers who were buried near the crest of the bank in the war of 1812 were in 1836 found to be at the water's edge. As the lake gained upon the shore its banks became higher, owing to the inclination of the land towards the water. The surface of the lake has a fluctuation of level which during a period of nineteen years, from 1819 to 1838, amounted to six feet and nine inches. When the water of the lake is high it has more erosive action upon the shore than when it is low. By the above analysis the blue clay deposite is shown to be principally fine sand, with merely clay enough to cement it. It also contains lime enough to give it a marly character.

When soaked with water the mass which in a dry state is compact and hard, becomes soft and yielding like quicksand.

The plan and profile which is here inserted, explains the mode of encroachment.

Profile of the *Blue Clay*, along Bank Street, Cleveland, Ohio, showing the land slips and mode of encroachment.

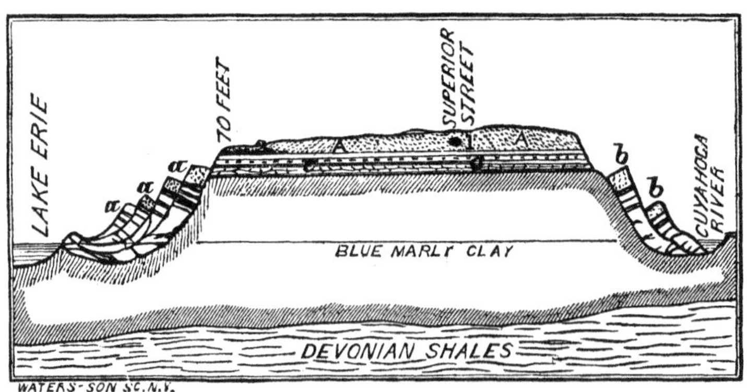

NOTES FOR THE MAP.

a, *a*, *a*, Ancient position of the river and shore line.

b, *b*, *b*, Position of river and shore line, 1796.

c, *c*, *c*, Lagoons old river bed, ✪ springs.

d, Outlier of the Bluffs, *e*, *e*, *e*, *e*.

e, *e*, *e*, Clay bluffs and slides—ancient and modern.

✱, Perry Monument, in Public Square.

h, *i*, Imaginary shore line at the close of 1000 years, without artificial protection.

NOTES FOR THE PROFILE ON BANK STREET.

A, *A*, Sand and gravel stratum.

a, *a*, *a*, Slide of October, 1849.

b, *b*, Older slides on the River side.

c, *c*, Layers of clay and sand.

1, Bones and grinder of an elephant.

2, Position of trees sticks and leaves.

There is in the clay very little tenacity in a dry state and thus when the waves have dissolved and carried away the foot of the bank it breaks down by its own weight. A long narrow strip of land at the crest, suddenly drops 10, 20 or 30 feet, pushing the previous slips, *a*, *a*, *a*, before it into the lake. The shore line is temporarily carried forward and a bar of clay rises above the water level. At the top of the impervious clay bed the surface water which has settled through the sandy stratum, *A*, *A*, exudes everywhere in the form of springs. This water follows the crevices of the slides continually carrying the materials into the lake. The waves act rapidly upon the foot of the slope, softening and carrying away the part which was forced up from its bed. If the lake surface falls away, a sand beach is formed, consisting of coarse littoral materials, acting as a protection to the clay and quicksand. Thus for a time the shore line remains unchanged; but a series of storms or a rise in the water, renews the undermining process, and new slides occur.

When the city was surveyed the shore line was laid down by measurement on the town plat. A reduced copy of this survey made from the original which bears date, Cleveland, Oct. 1st 1796, is also inserted among the illustrations.

The plan shows what changes have occurred since the lake assumed its present general level.

During the high water of 1838, the advance of the lake waters upon the town site, was so rapid that the corporation took measures to protect it. By comparing the surveys of 1796 and 1842 there had been a general encroachment of *two hundred and five* (205) feet. In 1806 or 1807, AMOS SPAFFORD sent his hired man, with a yoke of oxen to plow a patch of ground on the margin of the lake, which must have been not far from the Marine Hospital. At noon, the man chained his team to a tree, fed them, and went home to dinner. Returning in the afternoon, his oxen were no where to be seen. Proceeding to the edge of the bank, the man discovered them still attached to the tree, quietly chewing their cuds, but the ground on which they stood had sank between twenty and thirty feet, carrying with it some of the new furrows, the trees and the oxen. Thus a belt of land about twelve and one half (12½) rods in width was lost, along the entire front of the city. In one hundred years this would at the same rate have amounted to twenty-seven (27) rods. It would, in about five hundred years, have undermined the PERRY monument. Before the close of a thousand years that part of the town north of Huron Street would have disappeared. The supposed new shore line and mouth of the river is shown by the line h, i, on the plan.

As the ancient surface of the lake went down, the Cuyahoga river cut a deep channel in the drift clay, with steep banks from which numberless springs issued. The ever shifting channels of streams undermine their banks continually, but in a different manner and with less regularity than the lake waters. On the river side the same slides have occurred, but not as many in number for the encroachment is not as rapid. Only one has been known since the settlement of the city, which took place near the foot of Light-House street, about the year 1808. Evidences of ancient slips were, however, abundant on both banks throughout the city. There were the same succession of benches or terraces, on the river as on the lake side. Wherever excavations took place for the grade of streets, the extent and exact outline of the old slides were as apparent as those of 1849, which were observed and sketched at the time. By means of heavy piling and stone on the lake front, the advance of the water has been wholly stopped. By taking up the springs that issue at the surface of the clay, and grading the bank to an angle of about 15°, a smooth grassy slope is obtained, adapted for a park of exquisite beauty. Grinders of the elephant and mastodon are common in the superficial materials, which cover the indurated rocks of the west. A grinder is said to have been found in blue marly clay on the West Side many years since. Remains of the elephas primigenius, the mastodon, megatherium, megalonyx, the horse, beaver, and some other animals, characterize the drift period. They existed prior to that geological era, and through it to the alluvium, in which their bones are also found. They became extinct after the earth had taken its present condition. The elephant, whose bones were discovered a few years since, in digging the coal vaults of the Merchants Bank, was about twelve feet below the natural surface. Another grinder of an extinct elephant was brought to light in the grade of Champlain street, which was about fifteen feet beneath the surface. It was secured by Dr. E. STERLING, and is now in the possession of Prof. NEWBERRY. This grinder had been worn by transportation, partially into the form of a rolled boulder; but the outlines are not wholly destroyed and the internal structure remains easily recognizable.

Pieces of buried timber, sometimes whole trees with numerous leaves, also characterize the northern drift. Layers of this ancient vegetation extend beneath the entire city. The wells from which water was originally procured, were sunk through the sand and gravel bed, *A*, *A*, to one of the impervious layers, *c*, *c*, where water is always found. It was frequently impure and even offensive, from the rotten layer which lies at the surface of the clay. There is more or less of it, distributed in thin dark layers through the clay, but it has collected in larger quantities at its surface. A white cedar, twenty (20) feet in length and six (6) inches in diameter, was taken up by the late John Wills, at the depth of eighteen (18) feet, in grading the bank at the Marine Hospital. The roots and some of the branches remained, and its strength was not wholly gone. There were several shorter pieces of ancient drift wood, found at about the same depth, which show the wearing action of the ancient surf upon a sand beach, like pieces of floodwood upon the present shore. Among the leaves in the mucky layers are cedar, spruce, and pine; and these are the most common kinds of timber, found in the drift material at other places.

To persons who have not become familiar, by observation, with the changes that have occurred on our planet, the assertion that there has been a period when this region was enveloped in ice, from 2,000 to 3,000 feet in thickness may appear monstrous.

To those who have examined the evidences which exist, in more than half the counties of this State, in support of such a conclusion; the proof is as conclusive as it is, that in Switzerland, the glaciers of the Alps, at one time reached down into the valley of the Rhone.

The slight changes of temperature which occur there now, affect the extent of the glaciers. A few degrees rise in the thermometer; diminishes the area of the ice fields; and a few degrees of depression enlarges it.

In ancient times, Alpine glaciers extended across the valley at Geneva lake, carrying boulders of rocks from the summit of the Range, which were dropped in the low ground, when the ice disappeared.

Beneath the present glaciers, the rocks are polished, ground and striated, by the projecting points of boulders; firmly held in the ice, as it moves towards the lower levels. The rocks in districts from which the ice has disappeared, and where there are now cultivated farms and cities, are worn and striated in the same manner.

Greenland has within a few years been closely observed by Dr. Rink, a Danish naturalist and by Dr. Hayes, of the American expedition under Dr. Kane. There, a large part of a continent is found to sustain a vast glacier; which has a slow but resistless motion outward toward the ocean. The cause of this motion, constitutes one of the most brilliant discoveries of Agassiz. In Greenland, there is, in places, a fringe of territory next the sea, not invaded by ice; which is variable in its extent, like that at the foot of the Alps. About 200 years since, the Moravians had mission establishments on the eastern coast of Greenland, which are now buried under snow and ice. The temperature of that country is becoming lower. The great central field of universal frost, is gaining upon the territory where vegetation exists. Towards the northern part, glaciers come to the sea, with a front of more than a thousand feet high; scratching and grinding the rocks precisely as they do in Switzerland. They push themselves along the bottom of the ocean, until there is buoyancy enough to cause them to float, when they are broken into large blocks, and range the sea, in the form of ice bergs.

It is only necessary to bring the temperature of Greenland down to our latitude, and the same results would follow. The moisture of the air derived from the ocean, would be deposited upon the earth in the form of snow, instead of rain. It would thus accumulate, century after century, filling up the valleys, rising to the tops of the mountains, effectually preventing the growth of trees, and plants, and thus gradually driving men and animals from the country.

Throughout the western States and Canada, are lines etched upon the rocks, the same as are seen in Greenland and on the Alps; produced by the movement of glaciers. They may be seen in hundreds of places in Ohio, when the rocky surface is cleared of its earthy covering. They are very common in the cellars at Sandusky, and on Kelly's Island, where the lime rock is thoroughly polished, having marked grooves, warped surfaces, and channels parallel to each other.

On the summit of Coal Hill in Tallmadge, Summit County, Ohio, at an elevation of 625 feet above Lake Erie, and 1189 above the Ocean, the coarse grit of the coal series is smoothed and scratched over a space of several rods.

At the old grindstone quarries in Euclid, Cuyahoga County, they are very distinct and straight, bearing about South 20° East by needle.

There is a good exposure of glacial etchings on the sand rock, near the North line of Austintown, Mahoning County, in the North and South center road.

The most southerly point in Ohio where they have been observed; is at Light's quarry, seven miles North of Dayton, their bearing being South 26° East. For the benefit of those who have no opportunity to examine the work of the ancient ice gravers, I insert a reduced copy from the fac simile of a polished slab of limerock, near the Light House at Sheboygan, Wisconsin. The waters of Lake Michigan, are there wearing away a bluff of red clay, of about the same height as the blue clay deposite at Cleveland; but the rock on which it rests is nearly level with the water. A belt of this scratched rock, several rods in width, recently uncovered, extends along the shore at the foot of the clay bluff, beneath which the ice etchings extend. About three miles in the interior, the Sheboygan River has cut a channel in the same red clay down to the rock, which has a depth about the same as the valley of the Cuyahoga, within the city limits. Where the rock projects beyond the clay, it is smoothed, and worn away by attrition, precisely as at the Light House, and the lines have the same direction. If the covering of clay, from the Sheboygan River to the lake shore was all cleared away, there would be several thousand acres of this polished rock exposed, of which this is intended to be a fac simile.

NORTH.

The most conspicuous lines are due north-east and south-west, but as usual, there is more than one set. Such is the condition of the strata over the States bordering upon the lakes and the St. Lawrence. During the progress of the various geological surveys in the Northern States, and in Canada, many hundreds of observations have been made, upon the direction of these lines.

Where there are hard spots in the rocks, able to resist the grinding process better than the surrounding parts; a narrow ridge is left on the southerly side, like the snow which forms in the lee of a pebble in a driving storm. The northern faces of mountains, and of rocky eminences, are abraded, while the southern faces are not. But the most conclusive evidence that the movement was from North to South, is found in the transportation of fragments of northern rocks to points always southerly from their position in situ. The boulders of Ohio are principally trap, gneiss, granite, breccia, and conglomerate; from strata that are in place on the shores of Lake Superior, and which exist in no other direction. The movement was modified by the topography of the country, pursuing in general, the course of the great valleys, such as those of the Kennebec, the Connecticut, and the Hudson Rivers.

In New England, the ice marks are found at an elevation of 3000 feet above the sea, which is higher than the highest land in the western states.

In the valley of the St. Lawrence, the course of the movement was south-easterly until the east end of Lake Ontario is reached. At Buffalo, it was South 30° West. On Lake Superior it had the same general bearing, except in the minor valleys, or where mountains turned it aside temporarily. The opening between Lake Huron and Lake Michigan, at the Straits of Mackinaw, gave it a westerly direction, as far as the mouth of Green Bay. On the summit of the Iron Mountains of Marquette County, Michigan; of the Copper Range of Point Kewenaw, and the Mesabi Range in Minnesota, the markings are as distinct as they are at Lake Erie; and their bearing is uniformly south-westerly. How the change of temperature, of the glacier epoch was brought about is a question still under discussion. Such changes have occurred much earlier in the history of the earth, and are probably due to astronomical causes; involving immense periods of time. During the era of the coal, a tropical climate existed as far North as Melville Island, in the Arctic Sea.

The origin of motion in such wide spread fields of ice, is thought to be understood. Agassiz spent several seasons in the Alps observing the movements there. He has demonstrated that the expansion which arises from freezing at the center of the mass, finds relief only towards the edges, and consequently, on the side which is thawing, there must be motion. This is very small but irresistable, and continuing for thousands of years in one direction, produces monstrous results.

If an ice field enveloped the northern hemisphere, its thawing edge would be on the side of the equator. Consequently, the movement would be southerly, and would be greatest along the front, where dissolution was taking place. But the lines of equal temperature, are not coincident with parallels of latitude.

Across this continent and through Europe, they are oblique, bearing to the North as we proceed westward.

This was probably the case, at and before the age of ice. Thus the southerly edge of the continental ice field, would not bear East and West, but north-westerly and south-easterly, modified by the elevation of the country. In that case, the motion would be at right angles to the Isothermal lines, or from north-east to south-west. There is an exception to this, in the bearing of the stria across the westerly part of Lake Erie, but here the Southern limit of the boulders of northern rocks, forms a curve, and is nearly parallel with the southerly shore of the lake.

Such is supposed to be the manner in which the beds of clay, sand and gravel were formed, on which the city of Cleveland rests.

PRE-HISTORIC INHABITANTS.

Throughout thé southern half of Ohio, there are remains of earth works constructed by a people of whom we have neither history or tradition. All we know of them, is what may be deduced from the character of these ruins. Some of them are in groups occupying several hundred acres. They consist of mounds, lines of embankments, either single, double or treble; sometimes with ditches, but more often without. When without ditches, they resemble a turnpike, but such was not their original design. They are both straight and curved, generally forming an enclosed figure, approaching to mathematical regularity; such as a rectangle, octagon, circle or ellipse. A partial enclosure in the form of a horse shoe, or a segment of some regular figure is common. Although mounds and banks of earth, are as nearly imperishable as any structure raised by man, they are more or less obliterated by rains, frosts and other atmospheric agencies.

Some of the parallels require close examination to detect, and especially to follow them; through cultivated fields, herbage, and the undergrowth of western forests.

Ditches and pits are sooner obliterated than works in relief. On these ruins, the timber is of the same size and character, as it is around them. Trees 400 years old have been cut down, whose roots were fixed upon the top of embankments, where the remains of previous generations of trees, were also visible.

There is evidence to show that the race of red men, whom Columbus, De Soto and John Smith, encountered on this Continent, had then been here fifteen or twenty centuries. The Aborigines had no knowledge, and no received traditions of their predecessors; which they must have had, if the race of the mounds were their ancestors. Everything which remains of the mound builders, indicates a people of higher cultivation than that of the Indians. The more ancient race were industrious, cultivating the soil; not wandering hunters. They erected mounds of earth, which are in some instances from sixty to seventy feet high, with a circumference at the base of seven hundred and eight hundred feet. These are still quite imposing piles, rising nearly to the tops of ancient trees, among which they stand.

A single fortification on the bluffs of the Little Miami, called "Fort Ancient," in Warren county,

Ohio, has a parapet which in some places is eighteen feet high, and fifty feet thick at the base. The entire work, is computed to contain six hundred thousand cubic yards of embankment, and would allow of twenty thousand men for its defence. Near Newark there is a circle, one-fourth of a mile in diameter, where the bank is at the highest point, twenty-six feet above the bottom of the ditch. This people has left numerous ruins, not only over the southern half of this State, but throughout the low lands of Kentucky, Western Tennessee, Southern Indiana, Illinois, Missouri, Arkansas, Texas and Mexico. The large cities, if we may judge by their position, were selected on the same principle by which our fathers selected theirs. Extensive ruins were once visible, on or near the sites of Cincinnati, Marietta, Portsmouth, Chillicothe, Circleville, Dayton and Newark.

They were contiguous to large tracts of good land upon valuable water courses. The same people worked the copper mines of Lake Superior. Many of their mounds, are monuments raised to the dead, where valuable relics were placed; consisting of beads and shells and plates of native copper and silver.

Their tools are of copper, which appears to be the only metal they had for implements. They forged of it spears, arrow heads, axes, chisels, spades and gouges in its native state, never having been melted or refined. Their tools are found, not only with the ashes of their dead, but on the surface, in the vicinity of their works. Very good cutting tools were made of stone, of which great numbers have been found. The race of red men had also stone axes, knives, spear and arrow heads, but did not possess implements made of copper, with the exception of some very rude knives, found among the tribes inhabiting Lake Superior. Here the Chippewas have sometimes fashioned an awkward knife, or an instrument for dressing skins, from nuggets of native copper which they found in the gravel. The style and finish of their rough knives, enables one at once to separate them, from the more perfect work of the mound builders. This difference of mechanical perfection, aptly distinguishes the civilization of the two races.

The North American Indian relied principally upon flint, which the race of the mounds used very sparingly.

As implements of wood soon perish, we have little trace of them, although they must have been numerous. Some of the wooden shovels and bowls, which they used in the mines of Lake Superior, have been preserved beneath the water and rubbish of old mines. A part of the decayed handle of a copper spear, was found in the same situation. In the north eastern part of Ohio, in the county of Geauga, a war club of Nicaragua wood, was discovered early in the settlement of that region. This might have belonged to either of the races, which preceded white men on this soil. Wooden ornaments and implements, not being so precious, were not buried with the dead. If they had been, there are cases where something would remain of them. Threads of hempen cloth, and timber forming a sort of coffin or vault, have, in some cases, resisted decomposition. So has their ornaments of shell, bone and stone; and their pipes, grotesquely carved with images of animals. All these relics, show a condition advanced beyond the people, called by us the Aborigines, who were the second, perhaps the third, race which preceded us.

Along the south shores of Lake Erie and Lake Ontario, are numerous ancient works; but of a character different from those on the waters of the Ohio. There were two of them within the limits of the city of Cleveland. A low mound was visible within the last twenty years, on the lot at the south east corner of Erie and Euclid streets. But the mounds, embankments and ditches, throughout the lake country are insignificant in size, in comparison with those in the southern part of the State.

Most of those in New York and the northern part of Ohio, are fortifications; while a large part of those farther south were not designed for the purposes of war. Many of the latter had reference to religious ceremonies and sacrifices, probably of human beings.

There is a wide belt of country through central Ohio which is nearly destitute of ancient works, as though there was a neutral tract, not occupied by the ancient races. Those on the waters running northerly into the lake, are generally in strong natural positions. They may still be seen on the Maumee river, above Toledo, and on the Sandusky, Huron and Black rivers. A group of these enclosures existed at the forks of Huron river, where the road crosses, about a mile and a half west of Norwalk. As a sample of ancient forts in the lake country, I insert plans of some of those which are not yet destroyed.

ANCIENT FORT, NEWBURG.

This consists of a double line of breast works with ditches across the narrow part of a peninsula, between two gullies, situated about three miles south-easterly from the city, on the right of the road to Newburg, on land heretofore owned by the late Dr. H. A. Ackley. The position thus protected against an assault, is a very strong one, where the attacking party should not have projectiles of long range.

On three sides of this promontory, the land is abrupt and slippery. It is very difficult of ascent, even without artificial obstructions. Across the ravine, on all sides, the land is upon a level with the enclosed space. The depth of the gully is from fifty to seventy feet. About eighty rods to the east, upon the level plain, is a mound ten feet high and sixty feet in diameter. At the west end of the inner wall is a place for a gateway or passage, to the interior.

Ancient Fort, Newburg.

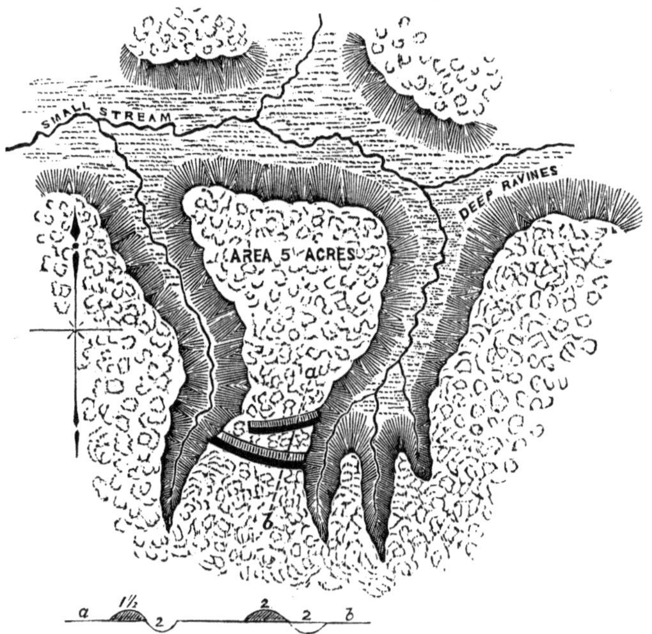

The height of the embankment across the neck is two feet, and the enclosed area contains about five acres. Perpetual springs of water issue from the sides of the ravine, at the surface of the blue clay, as they do at Cleveland.

About six miles from the lake, on the eastern bluffs of the Cuyahoga river, is a similar work that has but one line of embankment, with a ditch. The bluffs are higher, but not quite as inaccessible as on the Ackley farm. About the middle is an unexcavated space across the ditch, but the breast work has no gap for an entrance.

Two miles farther up the river, on the same side, is a third work, in the same style, similarly located, but enclosing about twice as much space. The general figure of the enclosure is very much like the one on Ackley's premises. Two small branches head near each other at the upper end of two ravines, from one hundred to one hundred and fifty feet deep. Across the neck are two parallels, which have been nearly obliterated by cultivation. The inner parallel does not appear to have been as high as the outer one, and between them was a broad, but not a very deep ditch. A conspicuous ditch was made on the outer side of the outer wall, from which, no doubt, the earth was taken for the embankment. There are no gateways in either of the walls.

A much stronger and more elaborate fortified position, exists in Northfield, Summit County, on the river bluffs, two miles west of the center.

A road leading west from the center to the river, passes along a very narrow ridge, or "hogs back," between two gullies, only wide enough for a highway. Before reaching the river bluffs, this neck of land expands right and left, where there is a level space of about two acres, elevated near two hundred

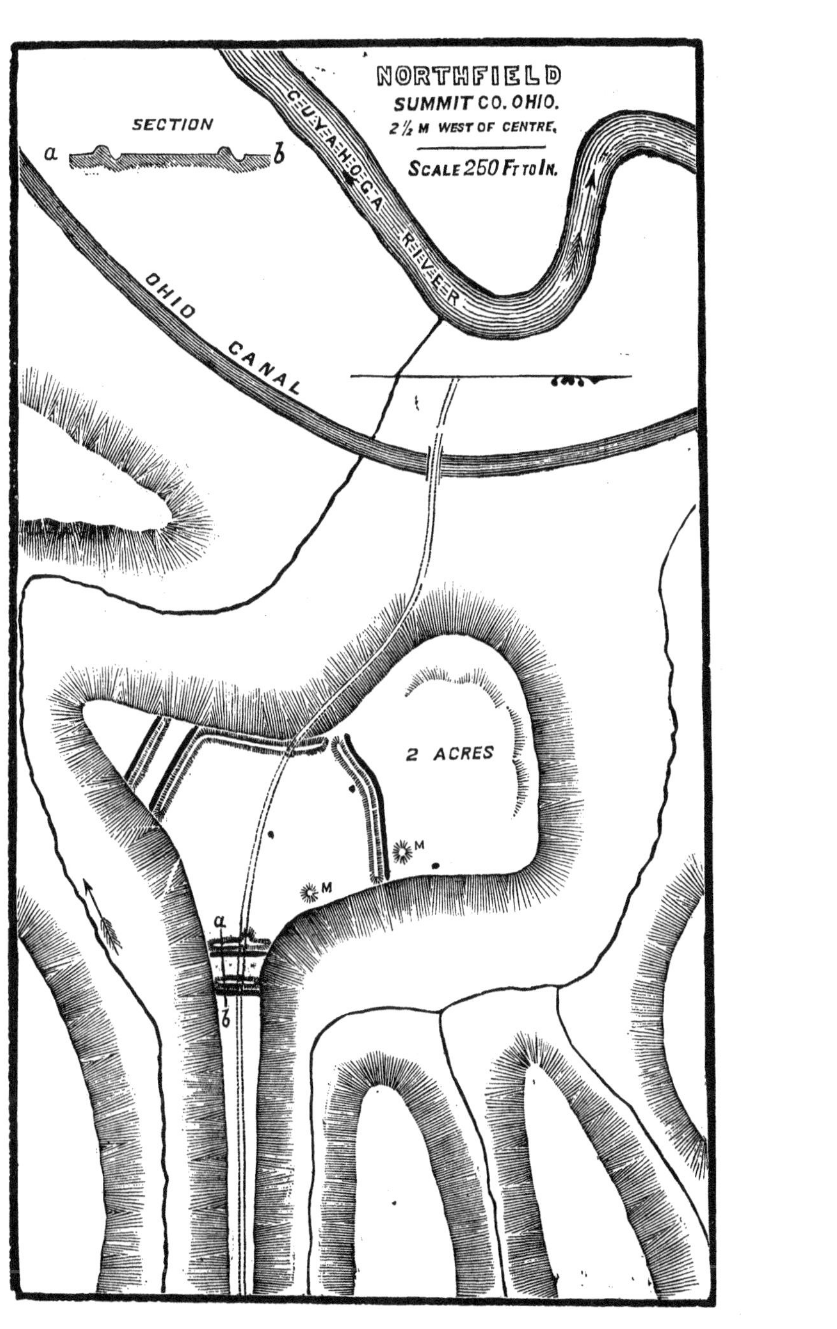
NORTHFIELD
SUMMIT CO. OHIO.
2½ M WEST OF CENTRE.
SCALE 250 FT TO IN.
SECTION
a
b
CUYAHOGA RIVER
OHIO CANAL
2 ACRES
M
M
a
b

feet above the canal and river. Where this area begins to widen out on the land side, there are two lines of banks, with exterior ditches, which are forty feet apart, and extend across the neck, without entrances or gateways. From the top of the breast work to the bottom of the ditch, is now from four to five feet. Mr. Milton Arthur, the owner of the land stated, that before the land was cultivated, a man standing on the ditch could not look over the wall. On all sides, the flat land is bounded by gullies, eighty to one hundred feet deep, except where it is joined to the ridge.

There is permanent water in the ravines. The earth of the bluffs is so steep that it is subject to slides. It is remarkable that there is, within this area, another set of lines on the side towards the river, reducing the fortified area to about one-half the space, whose edges are at the bluffs. Two projecting points are cut off by these lines, and left outside the works. In this way, much of the natural strength of the position is lost. At these places, there are pits, which the early settlers of Northfield say were filled with water, and were stoned around like wells. There are also two low mounds, *m*, *m*, on the east side. Where the bluff is not as steep as it is elsewhere, there is a parapet thrown up at the crest. A part of the earth on the north and west side, was taken from the inside, which indicates a state of siege, or at least some pressing haste when this part of the line was finished. Perhaps their enemies had gained a foot-hold in the level space outside the lines.

On the west side of the river is another ancient fortification, opposite this, and it is stated there is in the township of Independence, on the bluffs, north of Tinker's creek, near its mouth, another work of the same character. There are no doubt others which are known to the inhabitants not yet surveyed or described.

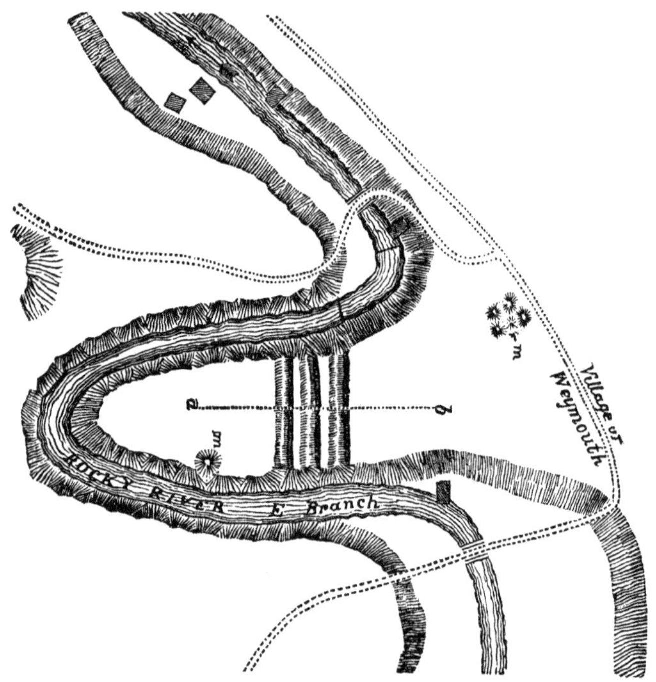

Enlarged profile on the line a, b.

A short distance east of the village of Weymouth, in a bend of the Rocky River, is a fortified point of land, with three lines of banks and ditches. From the outer to the middle one is forty-two feet, and thence to the inner parallel, thirty-eight feet. In 1850, the outer and the inner lines were in the best condition. From the top of the outer wall to the bottom of the ditch, is five feet; of the middle one four feet, and the inside parallel six feet. The excavations for the ditches reached to the slate. This ground was selected by the first white settlers, for a burying ground, but was abandoned because the soil is not deep enough for graves. Around the bend in the river is a deep channel, with vertical rocky walls, thirty to fifty feet high. It is therefore, a very defensible position.

The length of this peninsula is three hundred feet, from the inner parapet to the extreme front, and the distance across the base, one hundred feet. There are no openings or gateways through the parallels, and no breaks in the ditches. The engineer who planned the works, must have provided for passing over the embankment, into the enclosed space, by wooden steps, that have perished. Near the village of Weymouth are five small mounds, *m*, and within the fortress, one.

One-half mile east of the center of Granger, in the same county, is a low circular enclosure, about three hundred feet in diameter. It has a slight exterior ditch. There is an opening for entrance on the north-west side, near where the east and west road crosses the work. Two small streams of living water pass along the sides of it. The situation is low and flat, with a slight rise on the west, which overlooks the interior of the enclosure. It possesses no natural strength of position, and was doubtless designed for other purposes than defence.

4

FORT NEAR PAINESVILLE.

On the west bank of Grand river, about three miles east of Painesville, is a narrow peninsula of soap stone and flags, which has been fortified by the ancients. A tall growth of hemlock furnishes a refreshing shade, to which the citizens resort for May-day pic-nics, and Fourth of July celebrations. A small creek runs outside the point, which is about 200 feet wide by 600 in length, entering the river at the apex. The elevation is from 40 to 60 feet above water level. At the extremity of the point is a lower bench, across which is a low bank and ditch.

About 400 feet farther back from this are two parallels across the peninsula, which are 86 feet apart. In most places it is nine feet from the bottom of the ditches, to the summit of the walls. All the ditches are on the outside and are well preserved. There are very few places where a party could climb up the soap stone cliffs, without the aid of trees or ropes. The course of this projecting point is east and west, joining the mainland on the west. In this direction there is higher land within 300 feet of the outer parallel.

FORTIFIED HILL NEAR CONNEAUT.

On the south side of the creek above the village of Conneaut, in Ashtabula county, is a detached mound of shale, about seventy feet high, which is crowned with an ancient fortress, or strong-hold, represented in the plan here inserted.

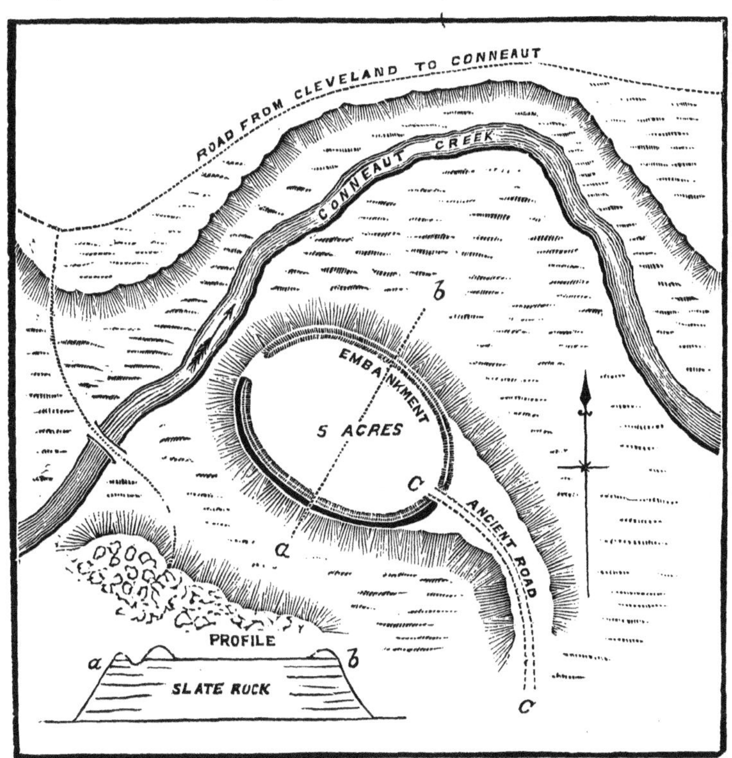

On the north side there is a low bank of earth following the crest of the hill. There is here no berme, or level space, outside of the embankment.

On the south side, where the bluff is not as steep and difficult of ascent as on the north, there is a ditch between the parapet and the crest, as represented in the profile, *a*, *b*. Outside of the ditch is a low bank on the edge of the natural slope. Thus the side having the least natural strength, was made stronger by art. It would be almost impossible, for men to ascend the steep escarpment of soap stone on the north. A narrow ridge of gentle ascent, allows of an easy grade on the south-eastern side, where there was in 1840, the remains of an ancient road.

This leads to the gateway at *c*, where there must have been some obstructions of wood like a "porte cullis," which the inmates could open and close at their pleasure. Why there should have been an opening in the enclosing wall, at the end next the river is not apparent. Within the enclosure, embracing about five acres, the soil is black and rich, while it is clayey and lean without. This is a common feature of the old earth-works on Lake Erie. It indicates a lengthy occupation of the place, by human beings. The ground occupied by Indian villages in the north, is always more fertile than the same soil outside of their towns.

In the valley of the creek, there is much good land which the ancients no doubt cultivated. These strong natural positions, resemble the fortified villages of the Moques, on the waters of the Colorado;

which were visited and described by Prof. J. S. NEWBERRY in 1854.

If the North American Indians, had been found intrenched in earth-works, when the whites first knew them; or possessed traditions concerning them, we should attribute the small forts which are upon the waters of Lake Erie, to them. But I have not seen among descriptions of the early French writers, any thing of the kind more permanent than pickets and stockades.

EVIDENCES OF THE PRESENCE OF WHITE MEN NOT KNOWN IN HISTORY.

In 1840, I was requested to examine the stump of an oak tree, which was then recently cut; and which stood in the north-west part of Canfield, Mahoning County, about fifty miles south-east of Cleveland. The diameter was two feet ten inches when it was felled, and with the exception of a slight rot at the heart, was quite sound. About seven inches from the center were the marks of an ax, perfectly distinct; over which one hundred and sixty layers of annual growth had accumulated. The tree had been dead several years when it was cut down, which was in 1838.

When it was about fourteen inches in diameter, an expert chopper, with an ax in perfect order, had cut into the tree nearly to its heart. As it was not otherwise injured the tree continued to grow; the wound was healed, and no external signs of it remained. When it was felled, the ancient cut was exposed. I procured a portion of the tree extending from the outside to the center, on which the ancient and modern marks of the ax are equally plain; the tools being of about the same breadth and in equally good order.

Soon after this I received from JASON HUBBELL, Esq., of Newburg, in this county, a letter describing some ax marks which he had observed, in a large poplar tree situated in that township. In this case the tree was larger, but Mr. HUBBELL considered the age of the cutting, to be from one hundred and fifty to one hundred and sixty years.

Mr. STEPHEN LAPHAM, formerly of Willoughby, Lake county, now of Janesville, Wisconsin, presented to Prof. J. L. CASSELLS a portion of a hickory tree, the stump of which still remains, a few feet from the railway, a mile and a half west of Willoughby.

In a letter to me, Mr. LAPHAM says, "it was cut in May or June, 1848 or 1849, on the farm I then occupied. I sent a hired man to cut some wood, and directed him to fell this tree, which was about two feet in diameter. I saw the tree fall, and measured the length of the wood he was to cut. As the man cut in near the heart, I noticed ancient ax marks. It had been cut into when a sapling about four inches in diameter. There was the old dry bark on the tree, above and below the old cut. There was eleven inches of growth outside of the cut, and about forty-six rings or layers to the inch. The tree was green and sound when it was cut. I preserved the piece near the heart, with the old marks on it."

I examined this stump in 1859, and now have the piece which Mr. LAPHAM preserved. It was difficult to count the layers of annual growth, but there were more than four hundred. Mr. LAPHAM was of the opinion, that the first chopping was done before Columbus landed on this continent. If so it cannot have been the work of white men. The style of the cut is that of a perfectly sharp ax, in all respects like the work of a good chopper of our times.

Although the rule is, that one layer of growth accumulates each year, there are exceptions, though they are very rare. Four hundred years before 1848 would carry us back to 1448, forty-four years before the island of St. Salvador was discovered.

There are trees which form two terminal buds in a year, and in that case two layers of growth are formed. If it was so in this case, the time elapsed would be two hundred years, instead of four hundred, and the date would be about 1648.

Another instance of the work of old choppers, is furnished in the following letter from H. L. HILL, Esq., of Berlin, Erie Co., O.:

BERLIN HIGHTS, Jan. 23, 1859.

In the summer of 1831, I felled one of the giant oaks of the forest, which was about three feet in diameter. It was cut for the purpose of making wagon hubs. One cut or length, was sawed off, the size of the hubs marked out, leaving six to ten inches around the heart. As we split the bolts, three cuts or strokes, of a sharp narrow bitted ax were plainly visible, the chips standing outward from the tree as distinct as when they were first made.

My brother and myself counted *two hundred and nineteen* rings of annual growth outside of the cuts. It was with the greatest difficulty, we were able to count the fine growths near the butt of the tree, and may have made a mistake of a few years. The tree stood on lot seven, Range seven, Berlin township, on a dry piece of ground, nearly surrounded by wet land; for about twenty rods forming good ground for a camp.

In the spring of 1857, I pulled out the stump of this tree, and in plowing through the ground where it stood; turned up the ax you saw in the Museum. I think it must have been between the roots of the tree, or we should have seen it before.

Yours respectfully,

H. L. HILL.

If the cuts mentioned by Mr. Hill, were made by the Indians with their rude squaw axes, they possess no special meaning. Those upon the Canfield and the Willoughby trees were by a different tool, a well formed ax, with a clear sharp cutting edge. Very soon after the French and the English encountered the Indians 1608–20, they were furnished with squaw axes. These axes were narrow bitted, made of iron or inferior steel, and were never kept in order by the Indians.

Where they have used them upon modern trees, the style of the stroke at once shows it to be this kind of a tool. It is never sharp enough to cut a surface smooth, like a modern choppers ax. The Jesuits were among the Iroquois of Western New York as early as 1656, but we have no historical traces of them as far west as Ohio.

The Canfield tree must be considered a good record as far back as 1660.

Many historians infer that LA SALLE passed through Northern Ohio, from the Illinois river in the winter of 1682–83.

That he made a journey by land from Crevecoeur to Quebec in that winter cannot be doubted, but there is no proof on which side of Lake Erie he traveled. It is far more probable that he avoided the hostile Iroquois, and bearing northward crossed the Detroit river, where the Indians were friendly to the French. A hasty traveller like him, could have left few marks of his ax. There must have been hundreds of trees on the Western Reserve, upon which axes had been used, in order to furnish us, so many examples after a lapse of two centuries.

THE RACE OF RED MEN.

Champlain is the earliest authority, in relation to the savages upon the great lakes. He spent twenty-five years among them, beginning with the year 1603, four years before the settlement of Jamestown, Virginia, and sixteen before the Pilgrim fathers set foot on Plymouth rock. He identified himself with them as hunter, trader, and warrior.

In 1609 he accompanied a war party of Algonquins through Lake Champlain, to attack the Iroquois, whom they fought between Lake George and Crown Point. On both shores of the Ottawa river were the "Algommequins," Ottawas, or Attawawas. The Hurons, or Wyandots, were then seated between Lakes Huron and Ontario. Between Huron and Erie were the "Petuns," or Tobacco nation.

On the south of Lake Ontario were the five confederate nations, whom the French called Hiricois, or Iroquois. By means of their alliance, they were too powerful, for any other nation or confederation.

They were also more intelligent, built better cabins and strong holds; and cultivated more maize. This superiority, enabled them to send large hunting parties, and war-like expeditions, far beyond their admitted bounds. Sometimes their dreaded warriors crossed Lake Ontario and attacked the Algonquins, pursuing them even to Lake Superior.

Then the savage crowd surged southward, into Pennsylvania; overcoming the Lenni-Lenape, or Delawares; and even to Virginia and South Carolina. Where is now the State of Ohio, CHAMPLAIN places the "Neutral nation," whose fate is involved in much obscurity. Farther West he fixes the nation "which has plenty of buffaloes," and North of them, around the "Great Lake," or Lake Michigan, are the "Astistaquenonons," or the "Nation of the Fire," afterwards known as Mascoutens. His ideas about Lake Superior were very imperfect, such as Indians usually give of their country. (See a portion of his map, inserted beyond.) During his explorations, and for nearly half a century afterwards, neither the French or the Algonquins could venture on Lake Erie. The Iroquois were not cleared away, from the East end of that Lake, till after a number of French expeditions against them, assisted by their Indian allies, north of the lakes.

It was not until 1635, the French reached Lake Superior, and did not become well acquainted with it till 1659–'60. It was still later when they reached Lake Erie, in 1679. CHAMPLAIN, when his map was published in 1632, supposed Lake Michigan to be the greatest of the lakes, and that there was a fall between it and his "Mer Douce," or Lake Huron. Lake Superior is there represented as a small body of water, including an island on which there was copper. The "Puant or Skunk Indians," afterwards known as Winnebagoes, he supposed were situated North of this lake. Indian tribes appear in history under so many names, and changes of residence, that it requires special research to follow them from CHAMPLAIN'S time to our own. When the French undertook to secure the friendship of the Iroquois, and detach them from the the English, by means of their missionaries, in 1654, there were two nations inhabiting the eastern end of Lake Erie.

This scheme succeeded only for a short time. In 1656 the Onondagas, or "Onnontaques," murdered most of the Huron christians, whom the Jesuits brought with them, and so threatened the lives of the missionaries and traders, that fifty-three of them withdrew, under cover of night, and after incredible toils, reached Montreal, April 3d, 1657.

Other missionaries were tortured, and burned as martyrs to the cause of Indian civilization. While the Jesuits were among the Iroquois, they discomfitted the nation of the Chat, Cat, or Raccoon, which occupied the shore of Lake Erie on the south-east.

This nation, that of the Erries, Eries, Erigas, or Errieonons, of the east end of the lake, and another on the heads of the Alleghany, known as the Andantes, soon disappeared from history. The irresistible Iroquois warriors, principally Senecas, crossed the straits between Erie and Ontario, and blotted out or dispersed the Neutral nation. In 1655 they assailed the Eries, storming their rude forts, getting over their pickets by means of canoes, planted as scaling ladders, and enslaved or destroyed the nation.

They did not so easily blot out the Andantes, who resisted until the year 1672, but were finally, like the Neutrals, not only exhausted, but obliterated. (PARKMAN, 22–23.)

It was thus the various families of the Five Nations, became possessed of the north-eastern part of Ohio, as far west as the Cuyahoga river, claiming still farther to the west. When the Tuscarawas, or Tuscaroras, were added to the confederacy, they were seated upon the waters of the Beaver and the Muskingum.

The Hurons, having been driven to the west end of the lake, retained possession west of the Cuyahoga, but neither party felt safe in settling to the east of it, in eastern and north-eastern Ohio, which thus became a border country; where the stragglers from both nations, had the courage to hunt for game and for each other. Although LA SALLE had ventured to establish a post at Niagara, in 1678, and in the winter of 1678–9, had built the "Griffin," a small vessel, above the Falls of Niagara; and had successfully sailed in her through Lake Erie to Lake Michigan, we do not know of any French on the south shore of this lake at that time. French traders and missionaries, may have coasted along the north shore, among their friends, the Hurons; but they have left no record of such journeys.

In moving to and from the Mississippi, they had been compelled, for fear of the Iroquois, to make a wide circuit, passing up the Ottawa river, making a portage to Lake Nepissing, descending thence to Lake Huron, and continuing the voyage by way of Mackinaw, and St. Joseph, reached the waters of the Illinois river.

It was not until 1688, they established a trading post at the outlet of Lake Huron, on the ground where Fort Gratiot was afterwards built. LA SALLE before this had performed a journey that compares in endurance, fortitude and courage, with the fabled labors of Hercules. During the months of February and March, 1680, he traveled on foot, from his Fort on the Illinois river, avoiding the Iroquois south of the Lakes, to Quebec; a distance of about twelve hundred miles. Perhaps some of the Jesuit Missionaries, had gone as far west as the Cuyahoga before this time. But I know of no evidence to this effect. On the north shore, the French did not make a permanent lodgment until the year 1701; at which time they erected Fort Pontchartrain, at Detroit. They were still unwilling to trust themselves among the Iroquois, of the south shore. Their progress in the affections of those tribes was very slow. It was about forty years after they located at Detroit, before they built a fort at Erie, Pa., which they called Presque Isle. They reached Sandusky, and built a fort there in 1754, and of course had other establishments on this lake, between Erie and Sandusky. By examining that part of LEWIS EVANS' Map, which is inserted in the notice of the early maps of this region; it will be seen that in 1755, they had a trading station on the west side of the Cuyahoga, opposite the mouth of Tinker's Creek.

But between the years 1700 and 1760, our certain knowledge of the Indian tribes in Ohio, is very meagre. As they were our immediate predecessors on this soil, and have already become nearly extinct, their history possesses a deep interest. I have not, however, space to do more than quote a narration made by BLACKSNAKE, a Seneca chief, to some gentleman of Buffalo, N. Y., in July, 1845, giving the Indian version of the extirpation of the Eries, the nation from whom our lake has received its name, by which their memory will be perpetuated so long as the waters flow.

DESTRUCTION OF THE ERIES.

"The Eries were the most powerful and warlike of all the Indian tribes. They resided at the foot of the Great Lake, (Erie,) where now stands the city of Buffalo, the Indian name for which was '*Tu-shu-way*.'

"When the Eries heard of the confederation which was formed between the Mohawks, who resided in the valley of that name, the Oneidas, the Onondagas, the Cayugas, and the Senecas, who resided, for the most part, upon the shores and the outlets of the lakes bearing their names respectively, (called by the French the Iroquois nation,) they imagined it must be for some mischievous purpose. Although confident of their superiority over any one of the tribes, inhabiting the countries within the bounds of their knowledge, they dreaded the power of such combined forces. In order to satisfy themselves in regard to the character, disposition, and power, of those they considered their natural enemies, the Eries resorted to the following means.

"They sent a friendly message to the Senecas, who were their nearest neighbors, inviting them to select one hundred of their most active, athletic young men, to play a game of ball, against the same number to be selected by the Eries, for a wager which should be considered worthy the occasion, and the character of the great nation, in whose behalf the offer was made.

"The message was received and entertained in the most respectful manner. A council of the "Five Nations" was called, and the proposition fully discussed, and a messenger in due time despatched with the decision of the council, respectfully declining the challenge. This emboldened the Eries, and the next year the offer was renewed, and after being again considered, again formally declined. This was far from satisfying the proud lords of the "Great Lake," and the challenge was renewed the third time. The blood of the young Iroquois could no longer be restrained. They importuned the old men to allow them to accept the challenge. The wise councils which had hitherto prevailed, at last gave way, and the challenge was accepted.

"Nothing could exceed the enthusiasm with which each tribe sent forth its chosen champions for the contest. The only difficulty seemed to be, to make a selection, where *all* were so worthy. After much delay, one hundred of the flower of all the tribes were finally designated, and the day for their departure was fixed. An experienced chief was chosen as the leader of the party, whose orders the young men were strictly enjoined to obey. A grand council was called, and in the presence of the assembled multitude, the party was charged, in the most solemn manner, to observe a pacific course of conduct towards their competitors, and the nation whose guests they were to become, and to allow no provocation, however great, to be resented by any act of aggression on their part, but in all respects to acquit themselves worthy the representatives of a great and powerful people, anxious to cultivate peace and friendship with their neighbors.

"Under these solemn injunctions, the party took up its line of march for Tu-shu-way. When the chosen band had arrived in the vicinity of the point of their destination, a messenger was sent forward to notify the Eries of their arrival, and the next day was set apart for their grand entree.

"The elegant and athletic forms, the tasteful, yet not cumbrous dress, the dignified, noble bearing of their chief, and more than all, the modest demeanor of the young warriors of the Iroquois party, won the admiration of all beholders. They brought no arms. Each one bore a bat, used to throw or strike a ball, tastefully ornamented, being a hickory stick about five feet long, bent over at the end, and a thong netting wove into the bow. After a day of repose and refreshment, all things were arranged for the contest. The chief of the Iroquois brought forward and deposited upon the ground, a large pile of elegantly wrought belts of wampum, costly jewels, silver bands, beautifully ornamented moccasins, and other articles of great value in the eyes of the sons of the forest, as the stake, or wager on the part of his people. These were carefully matched by the Eries with articles of equal value—article by article, tied together and again deposited on the pile.

"The game began, and although contested with desperation and great skill by the Eries, was won by the Iroquois, and they bore off the prize in triumph—thus ended the first day.

"The Iroquois having now accomplished the object of their visit, proposed to take their leave, but the chief of the Eries, addressing himself to their leader, said their young men, though fairly beaten in the game of ball, would not be satisfied unless they could have a foot race, and proposed to match ten of their number, against an equal number of the Iroquois party, which was assented to, and the Iroquois were again victorious. The "Kauk-was," who resided on the Eighteen Mile Creek, being present as friends and allies of the Eries, now invited the Iroquois party to visit them, before they returned home, and thither the whole party repaired. The chief of the Eries, as a last trial of the courage and prowess of his guests, proposed to select ten men, to be matched by an equal number of the Iroquois party, to wrestle, and that the victor should despatch his adversary on the spot, by braining him with a tomahawk, and bearing off his scalp as a trophy.

"This sanguinary proposition was not at all pleasing to the Iroquois; they however concluded to accept the challenge, with a determination, should they be victorious, not to execute the bloody part of the proposition. The champions were accordingly chosen—a Seneca was the first to step into the ring, and threw his adversary, amid the shouts of the multitude. He stepped back, and declined to execute his victim who lay passive at his feet. As quick as thought, the chief of the Eries seized the tomahawk, and at a single blow scattered the brains of his vanquished warrior over the ground. His body was dragged away, and another champion of the Eries presented himself. He was as quickly thrown by his more powerful atagonist of the Iroquois party, and as quickly dispatched by the infuriated chief. A third met the same fate.

"The chief of the Iroquois party, seeing the terrible excitement which agitated the multitude, gave a signal to retreat. Every man obeyed the signal, and in an instant they were out of sight.

"In two hours they arrived in Tu-shu-way, gathered up the trophies of their victories, and were on their way home.

"This visit of the hundred warriors of the Five Nations, and its results, only served to increase the jealousy of the Eries, and to convince them that they had powerful rivals to contend with. It was no part of their policy, to cultivate friendship and strengthen their own power by cultivating peace with other tribes.

"They knew of no mode of securing peace to themselves, but by exterminating all who might oppose them; but the combination of several powerful tribes, any of whom might be almost an equal match for them, and of whose personal prowess they had seen such an exhibition, inspired the Eries with the most anxious forebodings. To cope with them collectively they saw was impossible. Their only hope, therefore, was in being able, by a vigorous and sudden movement, to destroy them in detail. With this view, a powerful war party was immediately organized to attack the Senecas, who resided at the foot of Seneca Lake, (the present site of Geneva,) and along the banks of the Seneca river. It happened that at this period, there resided among the Eries a Seneca woman, who in early life had been taken prisoner, and had married a husband of the Erie tribe. He died and left her a widow without children, a stranger among strangers. Seeing the terrible note of preparation for a bloody onslaught upon her kindred and friends, she formed the resolution of appraising them of their danger. As soon as night set in, taking the course of the Niagara river she traveled all night, and early next morning reached the shore of Lake Ontario. She jumped into a canoe, which she found fastened to a tree, and boldly pushed into the open lake.

"Coasting down the lake, she arrived at the mouth of the Oswego river in the night, where a large settlement of the nation resided.

"She directed her steps to the house of the head chief, and disclosed the object of her journey. She was secreted by the chief, and runners were dispatched to all the tribes, summoning them immediately to meet in council, which was held at Onondaga Hollow.

"When all were convened the chief arose, and in the most solemn manner rehearsed a vision, in which he said a beautiful bird appeared to him, and told him that a great war party of the Eries, was preparing to make a secret and sudden descent upon them, and destroy them; that nothing could save them, but an immediate rally of all the warriors of the Five Nations, to meet the enemy before they should be able to strike the blow. These solemn announcements were heard in breathless silence. When the chief had finished and sat down, there arose one immense yell of menacing madness. The earth shook, when the mighty mass brandished high in the air their war clubs, and stamped the ground like furious beasts.

"No time was to be lost; a body of five thousand warriors was organized, and a corps of reserve consisting of one thousand young men, who had never been in battle. The bravest chiefs from all the tribes were put in command, and spies immediately sent out in search of the enemy; the whole body taking up a line of march, in the direction from whence they expected the attack.

"The advance of the war party was continued for several days, passing through successively the settlements of their friends, the Onondagas, the Cayugas, and the Senecas; but they had scarcely passed the last wigwam, near the foot of Ca-an-du-gua (Canandaigua) Lake, when their scouts brought in intelligence of the advance of the Eries, who had already crossed the Ce-nis-se-u (Genesee) river in great force. The Eries had not the slightest intimation of the approach of their enemies. They relied upon the secresy and celerity of their movements, to surprise and subdue the Senecas almost without resistance.

"The two parties met, at a point about half way between the foot of Canandaigua Lake and the Genesee river; and near the outlet of two small lakes, near the foot of one of which (the Honeoye), the battle was fought. When the two parties came in sight of each other, the outlet of the lake only intervened between them.

"The entire force of the five confederate tribes, was not in view of the Eries. The reserve corps of one thousand young men, had not been allowed to advance in sight of the enemy. Nothing could resist the impetuosity of the Eries, at the first sight of an opposing force on the other side of the stream.

They rushed through it, and fell upon them with tremendous fury. The undaunted courage and determined bravery of the Iroquois, could not avail against such a terrible onslaught, and they were compelled to yield the ground on the bank of the stream. The whole force of the combined tribes, except the corps of reserve, now became engaged. They fought hand to hand and foot to foot. The battle raged horribly. No quarter was asked or given on either side.

"As the fight thickened and became more desperate, the Eries, for the first time, became sensible of their true situation. What they had long anticipated had become a fearful reality. *Their enemies had combined for their destruction*, and they now found themselves engaged, suddenly and unexpectedly, in a struggle involving not only the *glory*, but perhaps the *very existence* of their nation.

"They were proud, and had hitherto been victorious over all their enemies. Their superiority was felt and acknowledged by all the tribes. They knew how to conquer, but not to yield. All these considerations flashed upon the minds of the bold Eries, and nerved every arm with almost superhuman power. On the other hand, the united forces of the weaker tribes, now made strong by union, fired with a spirit of emulation, excited to the highest pitch among the warriors of the different tribes, brought for the first time to act in concert, inspired with zeal and confidence, by the counsels of the wisest chiefs, and led on by the most experienced warriors of all the tribes, the Iroquois were *invincible.*

"Though staggered by the first desperate rush of their opponents, they rallied at once, and stood their ground. And now the din of battle rises higher, the war-club, the tomahawk, the scalping knife, wielded by herculean hands, do terrible deeds of death. During the hottest of the battle, which was fierce and long, the corps of reserve, consisting of one thousand young men, were, by a skillful movement, under their experienced chief, placed in the rear of the Eries, on the opposite side of the stream, in ambush.

"The Eries had been driven seven times across the stream, and had as often regained their ground; but the eighth time, at a given signal from their chief, the corps of young warriors in ambush rushed upon the almost exhausted Eries, with a tremendous yell, and at once decided the fortunes of the day. Hundreds, disdaining to fly, were struck down by the war-clubs of the vigorous young warriors, whose thirst for the blood of the enemy knew no bounds. A few of the vanquished Eries escaped, to carry the news of the terrible overthrow to their wives and children, and their old men, who remained at home. But the victors did not allow them a moment's repose, but pursued them in their flight, killing without discrimination all who fell into their hands. The pursuit was continued for many weeks, and it was five months before the victorious war party of the Five Nations returned to their friends, to join in celebrating the victory over their last and most powerful enemy, the Eries.

"Tradition adds, that many years after, a powerful war party of the descendants of the Eries came from beyond the Mississippi, ascended the Ohio, crossed the country, and attacked the Senecas, who had settled in the seat of their fathers at Tu-shu-way. A great battle was fought near the present site of the Indian Mission House, in which the Eries were again defeated, and *slain to a man*. Their bones lie bleaching in the sun to the present day, a monument at once of the indomitable courage of the 'terrible Eries,' and of their brave conquerors, the Senecas."

The above spirited relation is taken from the *Buffalo Commercial*, of July, 1845, whose editor remarks:

"Its accuracy may be implicitly relied upon, every detail having been taken from the lips of BLACKSNAKE, and other venerable chiefs of the Senecas and Tonawandas, who still cherish the traditions of their fathers. Near the Mission House, on the Reservation adjoining this city, can be seen a small mound, evidently artificial, that is said to contain the remains of the unfortunate Eries, slain in their last great battle. The Indians hereabouts believe that a small remnant of the Eries still exist beyond the Mississippi. The small tribe known as the Quapaws in that region, are also believed to be remains of the Kauk-was, the allies of the Eries."

BLACKSNAKE was living in 1860, and resided upon the Allegheny river, above Warren, in Pennsylvania. He was then more than a century and a quarter old. His form was scarcely human; shrivelled, bent and helpless; but he was able to converse intelligibly, his memory reaching back to the days when the French first descended that river to the Ohio. His narrative possesses that exquisite interest of which history is capable, when it is written fresh from the lips of those who form a part of it.

Even after the English Crown had supplanted the French, the Indians were promised a secure home on the waters of Lake Erie and of the Ohio. By a proclamation of 1763, the same year of the treaty of Paris, all settlers are forbidden to trespass upon the Indian grounds north of the Ohio. It was doubtless the honest intention of the British authorities, to devote the territory of this and of all the north-western States, to Indian occupancy. When the boundaries of the United States were discussed at the close of the Revolution, the British Commissioners insisted upon the Ohio as the line on the west. The reasons they urged were the guarantees they had given their Indian allies. Dr. FRANKLIN was inclined to accede to this boundary, but the other Commissioners would not hear of it. Little did he foresee the progress of events.

CHRONOLOGICAL ORDER

OF

LEADING EVENTS.

1535—JAQUES CARTIER, a Frenchman, ascended the St. Lawrence as far as Hochalega, a Wyandot village near Montreal. An attempt to found a colony on the river, five years afterwards, entirely failed and its history is lost.

1539—The Iroquois Confederacy formed.

1603—Monsieur SAMUEL CHAMPLAIN landed at Quebec, and in 1608 made a permanent settlement there, the same year of the establishment at Jamestown, Virginia.

1615—CHAMPLAIN and LE CARON explore Lake Huron, by them called "Mer Douce."

1635—The Jesuit Missionaries reached the Sault St. Mary.

1647—Monsieur DE LONGUEVILLE reported to have been at the rapids of the Fox river, Wisconsin.

1654—Onondaga Salt Springs discovered by Father SIMON LE MOINE.

1659—Two French traders winter on Lake Superior.

1660—The Abbe MESNARD establishes missions at Kewenaw Bay, (St. Theresa,) and at La Pointe, (Chegoimegon.)

1661—MESNARD perished in the woods near Portage Lake, on Lake Superior.

1668—DABLON and MARQUETTE founded a mission at the Sault St. Mary.

1671—MARQUETTE establishes a mission at St. Ignace, on the main land, west of Mackinaw.

1673—MARQUETTE reaches the Mississippi, by way of the Fox river.

1679—LA SALLE builds the schooner "Griffin" at Cayuga creek, near Tonawanda, and sets sail August 7th, for Green Bay.

1681—LA SALLE and TONTI are at Mackinaw "Old Fort," on the main land, south of the Straits.

1682—LA SALLE discovers the mouth of the Mississippi river, April 7th.

1686—A fort built by the French at the outlet of Lake Huron, now Fort Gratiot.

1690—The French and the Iroquois, after three-quarters of a century of war, conclude a peace, and the French occupy Lake Frie.

1701—Fort Pontchartrain built at Detroit.

1712—The Tuscarowas, or Tuscororas, from North Carolina, became a part of the Iroquois Confederacy, from that time known as the "Six Nations."

1726—The "Six Nations," for the third time, put their lands on the shores of Lake Erie, under the protection of the English. This treaty embraces a tract sixty miles wide from the Cuyahoga to Oswego.

1744—The "Six Nations" at Lancaster, Pennsylvania, deed all their lands within the Colony of Virginia, to the King of England.

1749—The French take formal possession of the country, on the waters of the Ohio.

1753—They erect Forts at Presque Isle, (Erie) Pa., Le Beuf, (Waterford) and Venango (Franklin.)

1755—The French propose to the English to retire east of the Allegheny mountains, and themselves to remain west of the Ohio.

1760—Canada conquered by the English. Their posts on this Lake, taken possession of in the fall by Major ROGERS.

1763—First general conspiracy of the north-western Indians, under PONTIAC, PONTEACK, or PONDEACH.

1764—The expeditions of Cols. BRADSTREET and BOQUET, against the Ohio Indians.

1765—The Ohio country made part of Canada by act of Parliament.

1766—JONATHAN CARVER explores the upper Lakes and upper Mississippi.

1768—Treaty of Fort Stanwix, (Rome, N. Y.) in which the British covenant with the Indians not to pass the Ohio.

1770—Moravian Missions founded on the Big Beaver River, not far below New Castle.

1776—British Traders at Cuyahoga.

1777—The British and Indians hold a conference at Oswego, New York.

1778—Fort Laurens built by Congress on the Tuscarora River, near Bolivar, two miles below where FREDERICK POST established a mission in 1761.

1782—The British establish a Fort at Sandusky, Ohio.

1784—England refuses to deliver up the western posts.

1786—Blankets and other goods obtained at Cuyahoga, from British traders, for our troops at Pittsburgh; and flour delivered here for the British.

The Moravians establish a mission at the mouth of Tinker's Creek, in Cuyahoga County. Soon after, a British vessel is wrecked within the present city of Cleveland.

EARLY MAPS OF THE LAKE COUNTRY.

Upon the geography of the region of the Lakes, there is nothing, based upon personal observation, earlier than CHAMPLAIN's map, a portion of which is given on the next page. He spent his life among the Indian tribes of the valley of the St. Lawrence, either in a friendly or a warlike character. Those on the North of the St. Lawrence, (originally St. Laurent); were secured to the French interest by his personal influence. He always went with them across the river southward, to make war upon their enemies, the Iroquois, who were friendly to the English. In 1634, CHAMPLAIN published his map of New France. The French had not, at this time, dared to venture upon Lake Erie, neither had they the benefit of information from Indians, who lived upon its shores. In his expedition of 1615 against the Onondagoes, on the waters of the Oswego River, and the Senecas at Canandaigua Lake, CHAMPLAIN obtained some knowledge of that

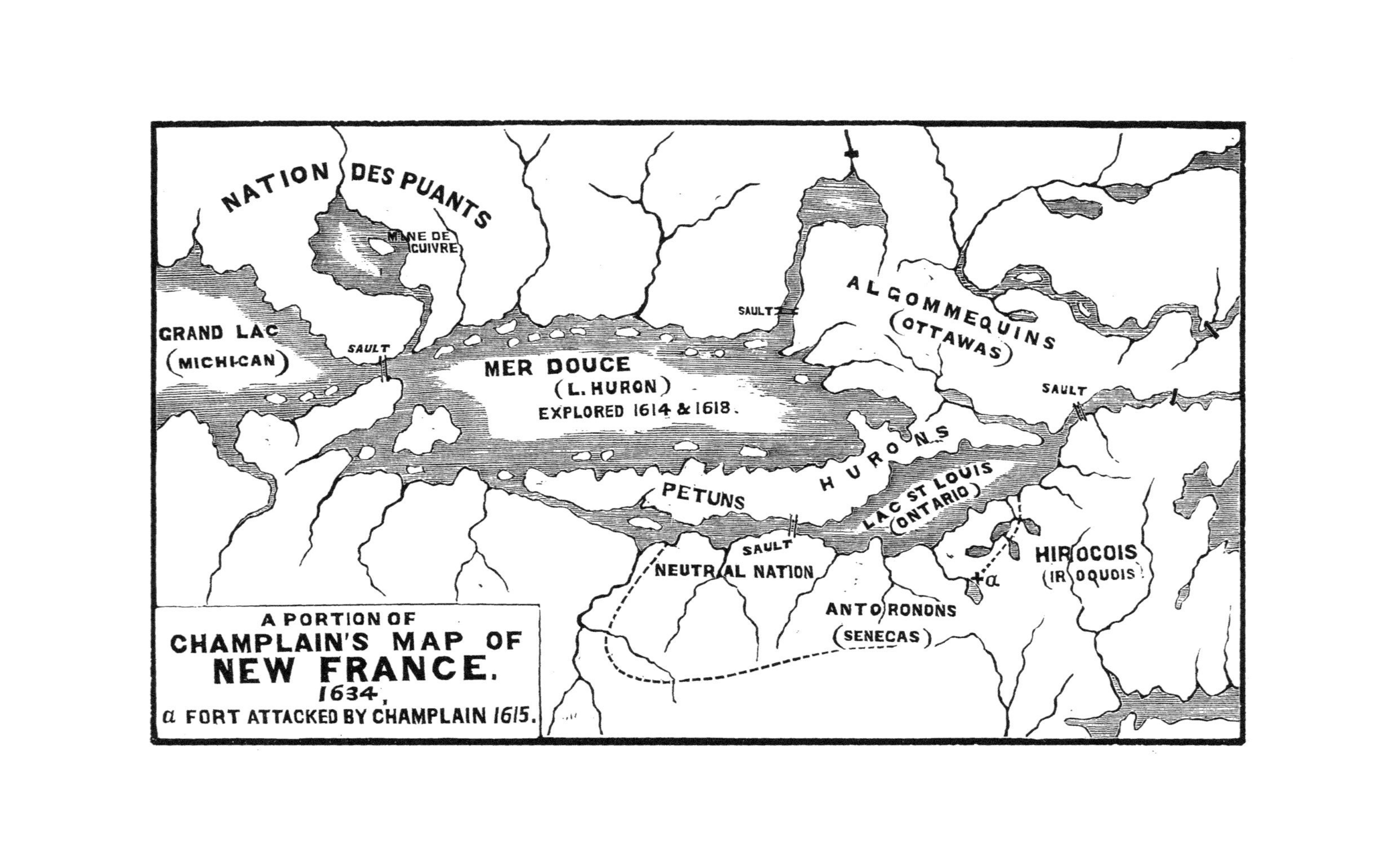

A PORTION OF
CHAMPLAIN'S MAP OF
NEW FRANCE.
1634,
α FORT ATTACKED BY CHAMPLAIN 1615.

country. His route is shown on the map by dotted lines; and the position of the Seneca Fort by the letter *a*. From the country of the "Antoronons" or Senecas, on the head of the Genessee River; and of the "Carantouannais," on the head waters of the Susquehanna, an Indian road or trail, led away to the westward, and the streams running north into Lake Erie. The Falls of Niagara are noticed only as a rapid or sault, like the other rapids of the St. Lawrence. From thence, a grand strait, with Islands, connecting Lake St. Louis, or Ontario with Lake Huron, is all the representation given of Lakes Erie and St. Clair. CHAMPLAIN only knew that his "Mer Douce" had a connection with Lake Ontario, but of the existence of another great lake, between them, he was clearly ignorant. His route to Lake Huron was always through the friendly tribes, by way of the Ottowa River, and "Lac de Biserenis" or Lake Nepissing. Evidently, he had not explored the "Grand Lake" (Michigan) or Lake Superior. The "Puants" or Winnebagoes, who occupied the north-western parts of Lake Michigan, he supposed were north and east of Superior. The Chippeways, Ojibways, or Sauteurs, were at that time, as they have been since, the masters of the shores of that lake. If CHAMPLAIN had been upon the waters of Lake Michigan, he would not have put the sault, at the outlet of that lake, instead of Superior. Neither would he have represented the last named lake, as a diminitive body of water, not larger than Lake Nepissing. The fact of the existence of copper, he derived from the Indians.

But grotesque as his map appears to us, it possesses much interest. It shows where the savage nations were located, when they were first encountered by the whites. The Iroquois held the waters of Lake Champlain, the Hudson River, and the Upper Susquehanna. On the North shore of Lake Ontario were the Hurons, afterwards known as the Wyandots. On the North shore of Lake Erie, the "Petuns," or Tobacco Indians were located.

Not long before the Iroquois achieved their first great victory over the Eries, which occurred about 1655, they expelled the Neutral Nation from the shores of the Niagara river. The Iroquois called the Neutrals, the Nation of the "Cat," meaning the wild cat, an animal of the family of the lynx. By the French, the Eries were also known as Cats, but this name they applied to the raccoon. In this way, the two Nations are confounded. Their fate was alike, but they were not even allies. The Eries, under the name of Erigas, remained a long time in Ohio, having been driven from the Genessee river, past Buffalo, to the heads of the Scioto. They were originally of the Iroquois stock, speaking a dialect of the same language. As usual, when people of the same lineage become enemies, their hatred is more fierce and lasting, than where there is no community of blood.

At the eastern end of Lake Michigan, a great river comes in from the South, whose head waters are as low in latitude as the capes of Virginia. A large river discharges into Lake Huron, near the western portion, opposite an island. On this is located the "Gens de Feu," or nation of the Fire, since called the Mascoutens. Another large river from the south, discharges into what answers to Lake Erie. On the sources of the three last named streams was the nation "which has plenty of Buffaloes." Numerous Indian villages, fields, and graves, are represented on these rivers, and throughout all the country. There are also abundant mountains, in all parts of the western and north-western country, as well as in New England and Virginia.

LEWIS EVANS' MAP—1755.

Neither had the English much reliable knowledge of Lake Erie, until after the year 1700. As soon as peace was secured by the French, with the Iroquois, they hastened to possess the country west of the Allegheny mountains. The English were equally hasty in opposing them. LEWIS EVANS, of Philadelphia, assisted by Governor POWWALL, of New Jersey, between 1740 and 1750, gathered materials for the map of 1755. Captain THOMAS HUTCHINS, who was the Engineer to Colonel

BOQUET'S expedition of 1764, also published a map, embracing a part of Lake Erie, and the Upper Ohio. JOHN FITCH, the great American improver of steam-boats, and who invented more of its useful parts than any other man, published a map of the Ohio country in 1784 or 1785. In March, 1780, he was made prisoner by Indians, at Blennerhasset's Island, near Marietta, on the Ohio, and taken by them through the country to Detroit. He obtained from them what information he could; drew, engraved and printed, the map with his own hands.

EVANS included in a general sketch, all the country westward from the sea coast, to the Mississippi River, which is remarkably accurate. His detailed map extends no farther West than the Great Miami. As early as 1670, the Jesuit Fathers published a map of Lake Superior, which appears to have been corrected by celestial observations. It seems impracticable to construct a chart of so large a tract, with so much geographical accuracy, without such corrections. The positions of important points on EVANS' map, do not appear to have been determined by astronomical instruments; but his sources of local information, must have been very numerous and reliable.

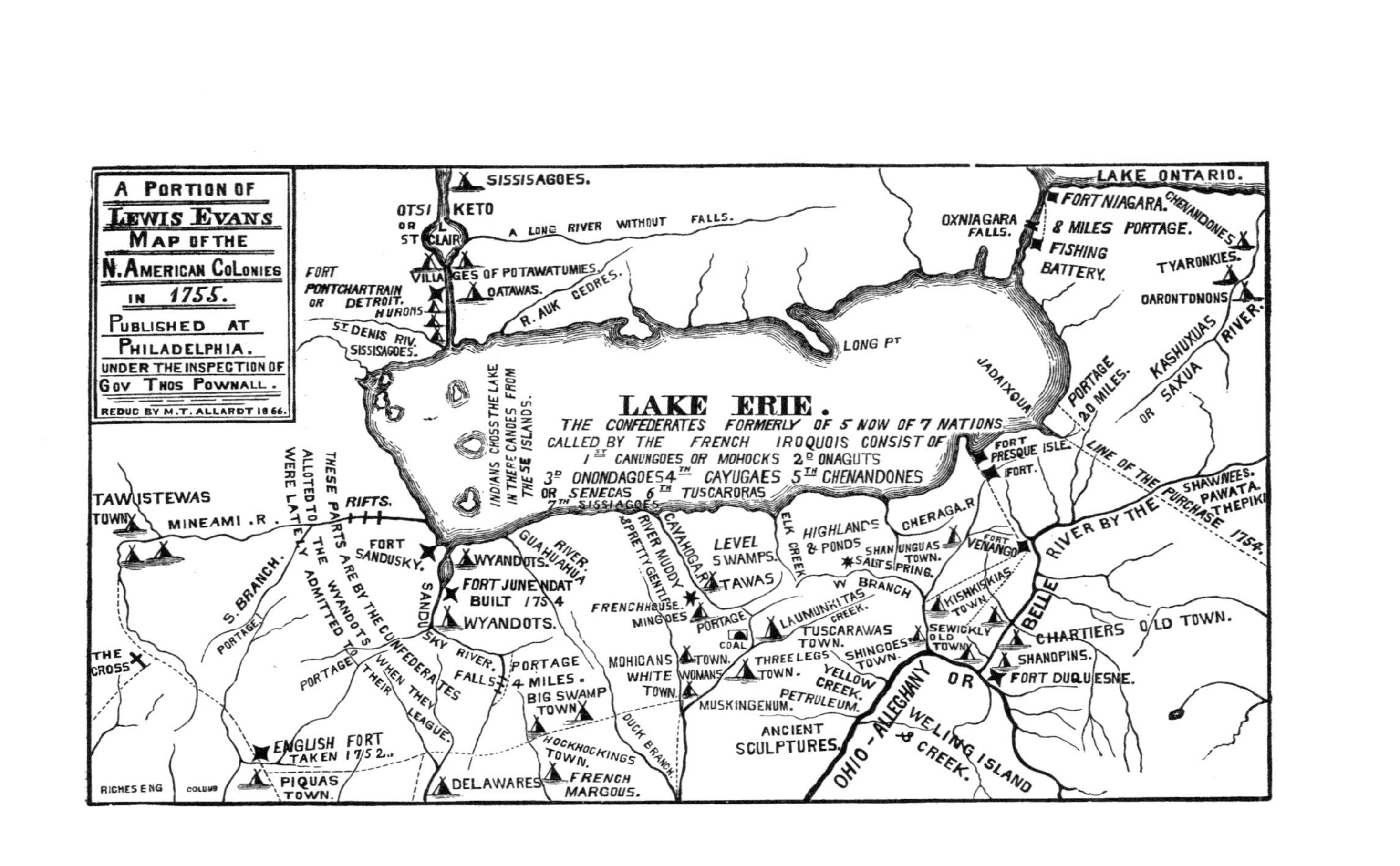
A PORTION OF
LEWIS EVANS
MAP OF THE
N. AMERICAN COLONIES
IN 1755.
PUBLISHED AT
PHILADELPHIA.
UNDER THE INSPECTION OF
GOV THOS POWNALL.
REDUC BY M. T. ALLARDT 1866.
LAKE ERIE.
THE CONFEDERATES FORMERLY OF 5 NOW OF 7 NATIONS
CALLED BY THE FRENCH IROQUOIS CONSIST OF
1ST CANUNGOES OR MOHOCKS 2D ONAGUTS
3D ONONDAGOES 4TH CAYUGAES 5TH CHENANDONES
OR SENECAS 6TH TUSCARORAS
7TH SISSIAGOES
INDIANS CROSS THE LAKE IN THERE CANOES FROM THESE ISLANDS.
LAKE ONTARIO.
SISSISAGOES.
OTSI KETO OR ST CLAIR
A LONG RIVER WITHOUT FALLS.
VILLAGES OF POTAWATUMIES.
OATAWAS.
FORT PONTCHARTRAIN OR DETROIT.
HURONS.
ST DENIS RIV.
SISSISAGOES.
R. AUK CEDRES.
LONG PT
OXNIAGARA FALLS.
FORT NIAGARA.
CHENANDONES.
8 MILES PORTAGE.
FISHING BATTERY.
TYARONKIES.
OARONTONONS.
KASHUXUAS OR SAXUA RIVER.
PORTAGE 20 MILES.
JADAIXOUA
FORT PRESQUE ISLE.
FORT.
LINE OF THE PURCHASE 1754.
SHAWNEES.
PAWATA.
THEPIKI
RIVER BY THE
BELLE
CHERAGA.R
FORT VENANGO
TAWISTEWAS TOWN
MINEAMI .R.
RIFTS.
THESE PARTS ARE BY THE CONFEDERATES ALLOTED TO THE WYANDOTS WERE LATELY ADMITTED TO THEIR LEAGUE.
WHEN THEY
FORT SANDUSKY.
SANDUSKY RIVER.
WYANDOTS.
FORT JUNENDAT BUILT 1754
WYANDOTS.
GUAHUAHUA RIVER.
S. BRANCH.
PORTAGE
PORTAGE
FALLS
PORTAGE 4 MILES.
BIG SWAMP TOWN
THE CROSS
ENGLISH FORT TAKEN 1752.
PIQUAS TOWN.
RICHES ENG
COLUMB
DELAWARES
HOCKHOCKINGS TOWN.
FRENCH MARGOUS.
DUCK BRANCH.
LEVEL SWAMPS.
ELK CREEK
HIGHLANDS & PONDS
SHANUNGUAS TOWN.
SALTS PRING.
CAYAHOGA.R
TAWAS
RIVER MUDDY & PRETTY GENTLE.
FRENCHHOUSE.
MINGOES
PORTAGE
COAL
W BRANCH
LAUMUNKITAS CREEK.
TUSCARAWAS TOWN.
SHINGOES TOWN.
KISHKISKIAS TOWN.
SEWICKLY OLD TOWN
MOHICANS TOWN.
WHITE WOMANS TOWN.
THREE LEGS TOWN.
YELLOW CREEK.
PETRULEUM.
MUSKINGENUM.
ANCIENT SCULPTURES.
OHIO - ALLEGHANY OR
WELING ISLAND & CREEK.
CHARTIERS OLD TOWN.
SHANOPINS.
FORT DUQUESNE.

His title is quite a geographical memoir, and reads thus:

"A GENERAL MAP
OF THE
MIDDLE BRITISH COLONIES IN AMERICA,
VIZ:
VIRGINIA, MARILAND, DELAWARE, PENSILVANIA,
NEW JERSEY, NEW YORK, CONNECTICUT AND RHODE ISLAND;
OF
Aquaishuonigy Country, of the Confederate Indians, comprehending Aquaishuonigy proper, their place of residence; Ohio and Tiiuxsaxrunthe, their deer hunting country, Couxsaxrage and Skaniadarade, their beaver hunting countries of the Lakes Erie, Ontario and Champlain, and a part of New France; wherein is also shown the antient and present seats of the Indian Nations."

NOTE.—"The Confederates, July 19, 1701, at Albany, surrendered their beaver hunting country to the English, to be defended by them for the said Confederates, their heirs and successors forever, and the same was confirmed Sept. 14, 1728, when the Senecas, Cayugaes and Onondagoes, surrendered their habitations from Cayahoga to Oswego, and sixty miles inland to the same for the same use."

A comparison of the early maps, gives the best history of the migrations of Indian tribes. Their rapid extinction, is also made conspicuous by such comparisons. In place of the "Petuns" of Champlain, on the North of Lake Erie, towards the Falls of Niagara, are, according to EVANS, the "Sissisoquies." Between the Oswego and Genessee (Kashuxca) Rivers are the "Cayugaes"; on the heads of the Genessee, the Senecas; and in Ohio, the Erigas, or Eries. No notice is taken of the Neutral Nation. The "Chawanes" (Shawnes and Shawanese,) were then on the Ohio, around the mouths of the Scioto, and the Kenhawa. On the Great "Mineami," (Miami,) were the "Tawixtawis," and the Mineamis. The Hurons, Wyandots, or "Wiandots," had been pushed from the North shore of Lake Ontario, to the western part of Lake Erie, embracing both shores.

For local details, the map of EVANS' is a great advance upon CHAMPLAIN'S. The outlines of Lake Erie are too large every way, but the resemblance to nature is easily traced. Several of the Indian trails and portages are given, showing their principal routes of travel, by land and by water.

A great war path extended southerly from the Tawixtawi towns, at the Forks of the Maumee, to the French post on the Great Miami; afterwards known as Loramies; thence to the mouth of the Scioto, and to the Blue Licks in Kentucky. From Loramies or the Piqua towns, another led eastward to the Delaware towns, on the Scioto; and thence across the Hockhocking, probably at Lancaster, to the White Woman's town, at the forks of Muskingum, near Coshocton. Coal is laid down on the Tuscarawas, near Bolivar; petroleum on the Ohio, near Yellow Creek; and salt water on the Mahoning River, in Trumbull county.

At the issuing of this map, the French were in possession of all parts of Lake Erie, and its waters. No Englishman had traversed this country, unless it was some unknown prisoner among the Indians. The first of these we know of, was here in 1754-5. HUSKE's map prefixed to DOUGLASS' summary; a general history of North America, 1760, has the following title:

"A MAP *wherein the errors of all preceding maps, British, French and Dutch, respecting the rights of Great Britian, France and Spain, and the limits of each of his Majesty's provinces are corrected.*"

CARRYING PLACES BETWEEN THE OHIO AND LAKE ERIE. *From the Topographical Description, &c. By Capt.* THOMAS HUTCHINS, 60*th Regiment, London,* 1788.

"The *Canawagy* Creek, (Chatauque) when raised by freshets, is passable with small batteaux, to a lake, (Chatauque) from whence is a portage of twenty miles, to Lake Erie, at the mouth of the *Jadagque*, but this is seldom used, as the *Canawagy* has scarcely any water in a dry season."

Chatauque is no doubt derived from "Jadagque," or "Jadaixqua," according to EVANS.

"French Creek affords the nearest passage to Lake Erie, being navigable by a very crooked channel, with small boats to *Le Beuf*. The portage thence to *Presque Isle* is fifteen miles."

"Beaver Creek has sufficient water for flat boats. At Kishuskes, about sixteen miles up this creek, it has two branches, which spread opposite ways. One interlocks with French Creek and *Cherage*; the other with *Muskingum* and *Cayahoga*, on which, about thirty-five miles above the forks, are many salt springs. It is practicable for canoes about twenty miles further."

"*From Muskingum* to *Cayahoga*, a creek that leads to Lake Erie, which is muddy and not very swift, and nowhere obstructed with falls or rifts, is the best portage between the Ohio and Lake Erie."

"The mouth is wide and deep enough to receive large sloops from the lake, and will hereafter be of great importance."

"The lands on the southern shore of the lake, and for a considerable distance from it, for several miles East of the Cayahoga, appear quite level, and are extremely fertile."

EXPEDITIONS OF MAJOR ROGERS, MAJOR WILKINS, AND COL. BRADSTREET.

1760, 1763, 1764.

In reference to the English expeditions into the lake country, which followed the French War, I have not space to notice them fully.

Major ROBERT ROGERS, of the Provincial Rangers, which were raised in New Hampshire, left Fort Niagara with his battalion in October, 1760, to take possession of the French Posts. The command sailed in batteaux, capable of carrying fifty men, which coasted along the south shore. When the wind was fair they made good progress; if it was unfavorable, their boats having sails were capable of beating against the wind.

Major ROGERS was a bold, restless, enterprising, intriguing man, who had served with distinction in the French War. He traveled extensively throughout the lake country, and published two volumes in reference to it in 1765. His Journal of the expedition to Detroit is very full. It contains the progress of nearly every day, with the courses and distances made on each stretch by the boats.

Historians have assumed, that the celebrated meeting of PONTIAC, "PONDEACH" or "PONTEACH," with Major ROGERS and his Rangers, haughtily demanding by what authority the English troops entered this country, occurred at the mouth of the Cuyahoga.

"On the 7th of November, 1760, they reached the mouth of the Cuyahoga river, the present site of Cleveland. No body of British troops had ever advanced so far. The day was dull and rainy, and, resolving to rest until the weather should improve, ROGERS ordered his men to prepare their camp in the neighboring forest. The place has seen strange changes since that day."

"Soon after the arrival of the Rangers, a party of Indian chiefs and warriors entered the camp. They proclaimed themselves an embassy from PONTIAC, ruler of all that country, and directed, in his name, that the English should advance no further until they had had an interview with the great chief, who was close at hand.

"He greeted ROGERS with the haughty demand what his business was in that country, and how he dared to enter it without his permission." (PARKMAN'S Conspiracy, pp. 147–148.)

ROGERS himself leaves the place of this meeting in much obscurity. In his Journal he does not speak of PONTIAC, but in his "Concise Account," published in the same year, that warrior, with his lordly bearing, is made conspicuous. The place where the interview was held is not described.

"Nov. 4th, 1760, set out from Presque Isle, (Erie) and made about twenty miles. Nov. 5th, lay by on account of the weather. Nov. 6th, advanced ten or twelve miles. Nov. 7th, set out early and come to the mouth of the Chogage river. Here we met with a party of Attawawa Indians, just arrived from Detroit." (ROGERS' Journal, p. 214.)

After some parley, the Indians held a council, and promised an answer the next morning. Nothing is said of the Chief, or of their assuming a threatening attitude. In the morning, they gave a reply, and said their warriors should go with the party. They were given presents, and charged to prevent annoyance on the way, by sending some sachems with Capt. BREWER, who was driving the cattle along shore.

Major ROGERS was detained at "Chogage" until the 12th. That day, by his reckonings, stearing various courses, he made forty-one miles and reached "Elk river, as the Indians call it." Elk river, or "Elk creek" upon EVANS' map, is east of Cuyahoga. During the 4th, 5th and 6th of November, Major ROGERS had advanced from thirty to thirty-two miles, which did not place him beyond Conneaut creek. How far he moved on the 7th, is not stated.

From Conneaut creek to Grand river, is forty miles; and thence to Cuyahoga, thirty miles. Could he have made seventy miles on the 7th? If so excellent a day's work had been done, would not Major Rogers have made note of it? By his reckoning, it is forty-one miles from "Chogage" to the Elk, a distance which they accomplished on the 12th; but this includes the several courses run by his fleet of boats, standing out and in to keep the wind. He did not advance this distance in a direct line along the shore, probably not more than thirty miles, or from Grand river to Cuyahoga. From his Elk creek to Sandusky bay, is fifty miles, as the boats ran; only two rivers having been observed on the way. His failure to note the distance which they made on the 7th, leaves the record very incomplete. On none of the early maps is Elk river laid down west of the Cuyahoga.

In Kalm's travels, (London, 1771,) it is placed first on the east. Upon Jefferson's map, (Notes on Virginia, 1787,) it is the third river east of this; and on Harris' map, (1803,) the fourth. In Morse's Geography, (London, 1792,) there is neither Cuyahoga or Elk rivers, the Grand river being farther west than the Cuyahoga should be.

It would be a very good day's sail in batteaux, to reach Grand river from Conneaut creek. The computed distances from thence to Sandusky, are approximately correct, which leaves a fair presumption in favor of the mouth of Grand river, at Fairport, as the place where the Ottawas held their first interview with the English troops.

But comparing all of ROGERS' statements in regard to this expedition, which are not entirely consistent, it is by no means clear that PONTIAC was a party in this interview. On the morning of the 20th, the command left a river, about ten miles east of Sandusky bay, (Huron river,) encamping that night at the second stream beyond the bay, which should be the creek next west of the Portage, or "Carrying" river. Here Major ROGERS was met again by an embassy, who demanded his business there, representing that they spoke for four hundred warriors, who were at the mouth of the "great streight," to obstruct his passage. He quieted the sachems by explanations and promises, and on the 21st, they all set forward in good humor. (ROGERS' Journal, p. 218.)

At "Cedar Point," on the night of the 23d and 24th, the same messengers returned, among whom was a sachem of the "Attawawas." The next morning, sixty Indians offered to escort the English to Detroit. PONTIAC is nowhere mentioned. If he was present at a meeting east of the Cuyahoga, he was out of the country of the western Indians, and had no right to question the conduct of the British commander. Until after passing that stream, he was in the Territory of the Six Nations, from which they had driven the Hurons long before, making the Cuyahoga their boundary. All this must have been well known to Pontiac, and to Major Rogers.

Sir William Johnson, while he was Superintendent of Indian affairs, made a journey from his home, on the Mohawk, to Detroit, the next season after the English obtained possession of that place. On his return, by way of the south shore, in the summer of 1761, his Diary has the following sentence:

"Embarked this morning at six of ye clock, and intend to beach near Cayahoga this day."

The "Cayahoga" is a prominent river on Evans' Map, published five years previous. It was well known to Johnson and to Rogers, who describes the country adjacent, in his "Concise Account." If the interview with Pontiac had occurred here, a place already notorious among the Indians and well known to geographers, it would have been properly named. As a misprint, Chogage, is too far from Cayahoga, to warrant the conclusion that the words were meant for the same. Sheauga, the Indian name for Grand River, is much nearer both in sound and orthography.

For the present, therefore, something must be left to conjecture, in reference to the spot where this great Indian warrior and medicine man, asserted his ideas of the supremacy of his people. Finding himself grievously mistaken, he soon concocted a great conspiracy of the north-western tribes, which burst forth simultaneously, upon every English garrison and trading post in the spring of 1763.

The French fort, Junendot, at Sandusky, does not appear to have been garrisoned at this time. Between 1760 and 1763, the British put a schooner afloat on Lake Erie, called the "Gladwyn," which carried supplies to the post at Detroit, and the upper forts. In the last named year, the conspiracy performed its bloody work. The history of that murderous conflict is so familiar, that I confine myself to other events, referring those who would understand this savage tragedy, in all its horrible details, to the fascinating narrations of PARKMAN.

Major ROGERS commanded a detachment, sent to the relief of Detroit during the seige of 1763. His battalion of provincials, assisted in covering the retreat of DALZELL'S command, after their defeat at Bloody Run, on the morning of July 31st.

An important expedition was sent into the Indian country in the fall of 1763, in command of Major WILKINS. On the night of the 7th of November, it was shipwrecked, and so thoroughly disorganized as to be obliged to return.

Prof. J. P. KIRTLAND, of Rockport, resides near the reputed spot where this calamity occurred. He has thoroughly investigated the historical proofs in support of his opinion, and has kindly furnished me his conclusions, with a description of the relics found there. This valuable paper is inserted entire:

DISASTERS

ATTENDING THE EXPEDITIONS OF MAJOR WILKINS, AND COLONEL (AFTERWARDS GENERAL) BRADSTREET, NEAR THE PRESENT CITY OF CLEVELAND.

BY J. P. KIRTLAND, M. D., LL. D.

The lapse of a century casts an oblivious shade over imperfectly recorded events. That two expeditions, engaged in prosecuting the Pontiac War, were wrecked on Lake Erie, the one in the Autumn of the year 1763, the other about the same period in the year following, are well established historic facts. Neither authors nor tradition have, however, attempted to point out the exact locality where those events occurred.

Since the first settlement of the township of Rockport, some fifty years since, the attention of observing individuals has been awakened, by the frequent discoveries of vestiges of military implements, and other articles, not usually scattered at random in a new and uncultivated country.

Those discoveries have been made at two localities:

First.—In the vicinity of the junction of Rocky River with Lake Erie, embracing the sandy beach bordering the Lake, and the right bank of the river; and the high bluff now known as Tisdale's Point, which is an extension of the left bank into the Lake, and which presents a perpendicular rocky face, seventy feet high, on its Lake front.

Second.—McMahon's beach, which borders the Lake, under a high clay bank, fronting the farms of Messrs. BROWN, McMAHON, Col. MERWIN, and the late Gov. WOOD, and, also embracing the ridge extending eastwardly from the last named farm, by the residences of FREDERICK WRIGHT, JOHN WILLIAMS, and Fletcher's Hotel, to the present crossing of Rocky River on the Plank Road bridge.

The first named locality is seven miles, and the second from eight to ten miles west of Cleveland.

A careful examination of the several discoveries, in connection with the historical items furnished by the authorities to which reference is here made, leads to the conclusion that the catastrophe which befel WILKINS' expedition, happened at the first named locality, and that of BRADSTREET'S at the second.

The correctness of this conclusion will be confirmed, by an examination of the peculiar and dangerous character of these localities during a storm, and of the manner in which these vestiges must have been lost; and a more complete comprehension of the terrific scenes attendant on those disasters would thereby be gained. GOV. CASS, in an address before the Historical Society of Michigan, in the year 1834, though laboring under some important errors in regard to the wrecking of Bradstreet's expedition, had a full conception of the horrors of that catastrophe.

Few of the present generation know, that either of these events have occurred; fewer still are aware of the pecuniary loss and human suffering they involved.

WILKINS' EXPEDITION.

PONTIAC, with his hostile tribes of savages, captured most of the British forts in the west, and murdered their garrisons, in the spring of 1763. The posts at Detroit and Fort Pitt, successfully resisted his first attacks. A vigorous seige was carried on against them by the savages, during the summer following. While troops were collecting under Col. BOQUET, (or Bouquet,) for the relief of Fort Pitt, a flotilla of batteaux from Albany ascended the Mohawk river, by portages reached Wood Creek, and ultimately, Fort Schlosser, on Niagara river, above the falls. In the autumn of that year, six hundred British regulars, with arms, military stores, and a train of artillery, embarked under command of Major WILKINS, They attempted to ascend the river, and advance to Detroit.

After some delay and loss, from attacks of the

Seneca Indians, they reached Lake Erie, but on the 7th of November, were driven on shore by a violent storm, lost twenty boats, with fifty barrels of provision, some field pieces, and all of their ammunition. Seventy men and three officers, including their surgeon, were drowned. These officers were Lieut. DAVIDSON, of the train, Lieut. PAYNTER, and Dr. WILLIAMS, of the 80th regiment; also a French pilot. After the storm abated a council of war was held, and decided that the survivors should return to Niagara, where they ultimately arrived.

The exact locality of WILKINS' disaster has hitherto been a matter of uncertainty. Some persons suppose it was on the north shore of the Lake. The evidences to sustain this conclusion are the following:

A published "Diary of the seige of Detroit," kept by a private soldier in the garrison at that place, states as follows:—"Nov. 18, 1763.—This morning two Indians arrived from "Point-aux-Pins," with a letter, one-half wrote in Erse, and the other in English, from Major MONTERIFE, (Moncrieffe,) giving an account of the batteaux being cast away, on the 7th instant, at the highlands, beyond the said point."

Sir WM. JOHNSON, in a letter to the Lords of Trade, locates the disaster at ninety miles from Detroit; and Lieut. Gov. COLDEN, in a letter to the same Board, fixes it at "two-thirds of their way to Detroit."

If "Point-aux-Pins" could be designated, the question would at once be determined; but at the time of the writing of the diary, no locality on the shores of Lake Erie was designated by that name. Such is the inference, from the fact that on LEWIS EVANS' map of the Middle Colonies, published in London, dated June 23d, 1755, eight years before the wrecking of this expedition, no locality is distinguished along the Lake as "Point-aux-Pins."

It is true that a recent map in BELL'S History of Canada, has that name affixed to a headland in Kent District, on the north shore of Lake Erie, but it is evidently of modern application. It is equally true that for ages a similar point, covered with tall pine and spruce trees, has been and is still a prominent object for observation, jutting into the Lake some twenty rods east of the mouth of Rocky River.

Such evergreen headlands are favorite land-marks for the voyageurs of these western waters, who have never been blessed with the knowledge of charts and surveys. They are in the practice of using "the Point of Pines" as a common term, applicable to evergreen headlands indiscriminately, and in the year 1763 were equally likely to use it in reference to either of those two points.

The distance from Detroit specified by Sir WM. JOHNSON and GOV. COLDEN, are in favor of Rocky River; and the fact that the Indians carrying MONCRIEFFE'S dispatch from "Point-aux-Pins" to the commander at Detroit occupied eleven days in its transmission, renders it certain that their route must have been along the south shore of the Lake, among hostile tribes, and could only have been pursued stealthily, at night. The north shore, where the population were not hostile, could have been traveled over by Indian expresses in two days.

The presence here of numerous vestiges of military implements, and their absence from the Canada locality, is almost positive evidence in favor of the former.

A trivial link, sometimes, is found to connect fragments, so as to form a strong chain of circumstantial evidence, and render it as certain as the most positive. Such a link is lying before me. The blade of a surgeon's amputating knife, described in the annexed notes, could have belonged to no other person than the unfortunate Dr. WILLIAMS of the 80th British regulars.

By aid of the facts furnished by historians, an intimate knowledge of the locality, and the character of the autumnal storms, taken in connection with these discoveries, any one can figure to himself the succession of tragic scenes as they occurred, without requiring much play of imagination.

Maj. MONCRIEFFE reported in the Newport, Rhode Island *Mercury* of December 19th, 1763, that "at 11 o'clock at night they were overtaken by a violent storm, which came on suddenly."......"The whole detachment was in danger of being lost, as every batteaux that reached shore was more than half full of water."

When thus threatened they doubtless attempted to gain a safe harbor within the mouth of Rocky River. The channel is narrow, and lies immediately in contact with the high and perpendicular cliff forming the terminus of the left bank. The eastern margin of the channel is bounded by a hidden sand-bar, covered with a few feet of water, extending at right angles into the Lake a number of rods. During a storm the waves sweep over this bar with tremendous force, breaking some sixty to eighty feet in height, against the cliff. A boat, to enter the river at such times, must hug the cliff, amidst the surf, in order to avoid this concealed bar.

An inexperienced pilot would, however, give that surf a wide berth, and, as a consequence, would be stranded on the bar. This, no doubt, was the fate of several of their batteaux; others were probably driven high and dry, on the sandy and marshy beach east of the bar; and others succeeded in reaching a safe harbor within the mouth of the river. Those upon the bar, if they were not at once sunk in the changeable and engulphing quicksands, would soon be dashed in fragments by the force of the waves. The batteaux were built of light materials, to fit them for two extensive portages, over which they passed, between the Hudson river and Lake Erie. The capacity of each was adapted to the carrying of one hundred men, arms, ammunition, stores, and a small cannon, which was placed upon the bow. Such a craft was illy adapted to resist the forces here acting upon it. The crews of the boats which gained the harbor no doubt sought a landing-place. It was not afforded in those days by the eastern or right bank of the river, which then consisted of a marshy tract of bottom land, or of precipitous cliffs; and the left bank was of a similar character, except just within the point, where a gully of lower inclination, running from the margin to the level of the upland, rendered access to the latter comparatively easy. Through this gully the survivors found a refuge from the uncomfortable lowlands, inundated and swept by the surf. Here they formed a camp fire, within a circle of boulders, and around it collected the vestiges from their wrecks. They remained till the storm abated, probably three days, as that is the period usually occupied by autumnal storms on Lake Erie. A period as long as that, is indicated by the accumulation of ashes and charcoal lately disinterred.

Here were probably brought the bodies of their drowned comrades, together with their arms, clothing, etc., among which were the pocket-case instruments of their dead surgeon. The bayonet here found belonged to some of the soldiers, and the eroded case knife to their cuisine. (*Vide* annexed note.**) The dead were probably buried on the adjacent plateau, in the native forest, now occupied as a lawn by Capt. TISDALE.

In due time the men were recruited, their clothing dried, and the surviving boats repaired. The ammunitionless expedition then retired down the Lake, and ultimately arrived in safety at Fort Schlosser, without having afforded any relief to the garrison at Detroit.

Two miles north-westerly from the locality of this disaster, following the Lake shore, we arrive at the long and narrow spit of land known as McMAHON'S beach. Undoubted evidences determine it to have been the seat of a still more destructive catastrophe, which befel

BRADSTREET'S EXPEDITION.

The Indian war continuing into the summer of 1764, Col. BOQUET advanced with his forces from Fort Pitt to the Muskingum river, and Col. BRADSTREET, with a well appointed army of three thousand men, entered Lake Erie in a flotilla of batteaux.

After a campaign of varied success, in which the conduct of the latter compares very unfavorably with the former, who, duped by the duplicity of the savages, and laboring under a heavy censure from his commander in chief, commenced his return down the Lake, with a force of about eleven hundred men.

On the 18th of October, 1764, he precipitately left Sandusky Bay, not even recalling his scouts and hunters. "The boats of the army had scarcely entered Lake Erie when a storm descended on them, destroying several, and throwing the whole into confusion. For three days the tempest raged unceasingly, and when the angry Lake began to resume its tranquility, it was found that the remaining boats were insufficient to convey the troops. A large body of Indians, together with a detachment of provincials, were therefore ordered to make their way to Niagara, along the pathless borders of the Lake. They accordingly set out, and after many days of hardship reached their destination, though such had been their sufferings from fatigue, cold and hunger, from wading swamps, swimming creeks and rivers, and pushing their way through tangled thickets, that many of the provincials perished miserably in the woods. On the 4th of November, seventeen days after their departure from Sandusky, the main body of the army arrived in safety at Niagara, and the whole, embarking on Lake Ontario, proceeded to Oswego. Fortune still seemed adverse to them, for a second tempest arose, and one of the schooners, crowded with troops, foundered in sight of Oswego, though most of the men were saved."—*Parkman, p.* 476–7. Additional facts are furnished in *Stone's Life of Johnson, p.* 230, as follows:

"The sequel of the expedition was singularly unfortunate. When a few days out from Sandusky, and about to encamp for the night, Col. BRADSTREET, instead of landing at the mouth of a neighboring river, [Rocky, or Cuyahoga?] where the boats could have lain in safety, persisted in disembarking at a spot which it was told him was visited by heavy surfs. The result of his obstinacy was, that a heavy storm arising, twenty-five of the batteaux were dashed in pieces, and most of the ammunition and baggage lost, together with the field train of six brass cannon. A hundred and fifty men were therefore compelled to make the journey to Niagara on foot, through a wilderness of four hundred miles, filled with savage men and savage beasts, and crossed by deep rivers and fearful morasses. Many perished on the way, and those who finally reached Niagara were spent with fatigue, cold and hunger. On the 4th of November the main body of the army, weary and shattered, entered the gates of Fort Niagara. Stragglers continued to come in, day after day, nor was it until the last of December, that all the survivors reached their homes."

FRANKLIN B. HOUGH, M. D., of the Bureau of Military Statistics, at Albany, N. Y., has had the goodness to furnish me with copious extracts from unpublished letters of Sir WM. JOHNSON, written in the winter of 1763, and spring of 1864, and now on file in that bureau. They were addressed to Gen. GAGE, CHARLES LEE, Lt. Col. EYRE; also, to the Lords of the Board of Trade, and to some unknown person. They confirm the statements of the foregoing quotations, and furnish other particulars.

In his letter to Gen. GAGE he imputes the wrecking to BRADSTREET'S relying solely upon a Detroit pilot, "a notorious villian,"—a Frenchman, who had been in the confidence of the late Capt. DALYELL or DALZELL, whose death he caused the year before, by betraying him into an ambuscade. This pilot, it seems, refused to run into a large river [Black River] after the storm commenced; and at length persisted, contrary to the sentiment of the army, in drawing up his boats along an open and exposed beach, [McMAHON'S,] though, had he gone a little farther, another large river [either Rocky or Cuyahoga,] afforded a safe harbor. As a consequence, before the following morning one-half of his boats were lost, and he buried his cannon and ammunition "by day, all in the sight of ye French villian," whom he fears, will, on his return, cause them to be taken up, and employed against Detroit.

He also alludes to the overland return of 170 Indians and Rangers, without an ounce of provision at their starting, and speaks of the kindness of the Seneca Indians of Chenusio, [Genesee,] treating famished soldiers with great humanity, feeding them gradually till they recovered, &c. The loss of officers and men by the wreck, was, it is said, made the subject of legislative action, reports and petitions, in the colony of New York. If the records and documents should be examined in relation thereto, more light would no doubt be obtained on the subject.

That the storm must have overtaken the expedition somewhere between Sandusky and Black river, is evident from the fact that off the latter place, the army had already become alarmed, and were anxious to run into that port. That McMahon's beach was the place where the disaster occurred, is equally evident, for no other "open beach," such as the one described, is to be found east of Black river and west of Rocky river, and along this beach vestiges of an extensive wreck have been found.

It appears that the boats were closely drawn up against the shore, without any special precaution, the crews and troops encamped on the then dry beach. A furious north-westerly storm soon raised before it the waters of the Lake, swept the surf over the beach, and broke with terrific force against the abrupt clay banks. This occurred suddenly, during the night. The frail batteaux were either sunk, dashed to fragments, or driven high over the bar, to the base of the cliffs. One-half of their number, it seems, were destroyed before morning. The men, amidst these horrors, in darkness and confusion, could only find safety by reaching the overlooking plateau, through several gullies which are cut through it down to the level of the Lake—and also through the narrow interval skirting McMahon's run. The banks of these gullies, are also nearly as inaccessible at many places as the clay cliffs fronting the Lake; and in wet weather are equally as slippery and impassable. In a bank of a gully on Col. MERWIN's farm, a bayonet was found a few years since, forced to its base into the tenacious clay, some six or seven feet above the bottom of the run, which had evidently been used as a fixture, by which the retreating soldiers drew themselves up to the top of the bank.

In another instance, a company of soldiers, invested with their bayonets, belts and cartridge boxes, gained the upland skirting the right bank of McMAHON's run, probably wet and fatigued, stripped themselves of their cumbersome implements, and piled them systematically and soldierly-like, against the foot of a chesnut tree. After the lapse of more than half a century, the bayonets were found by McMAHON, covered with leaves and herbage. Near by a musket barrel was also discovered by him, enclosed in the fork of a tree by the growth of wood. It had been placed in an inclined position, and had there remained undisturbed until the tree had completely invested it.

The morning ensuing found the survivors in melancholy groups, overlooking an angry and tumultuous lake, the beach strewed with the bodies of their dead comrades, and the remains of their boats, arms and provision. The number of lives here lost is not known.

When the storm abated, BRADSTREET proceeded to launch and repair such of his boats as had escaped destruction, and to collect and bury the cannon and ammunition which could be recovered. The place of their deposit, was probably at the eastern part of a clay cliff, some ten rods west of the mouth of McMahon's run. From time to time the lake has infringed on this cliff. Some years since two six pound cannon balls, and numerous musket balls were washed out. The cannon had either been disinterred and removed in early days by the British, or washed into the Lake by the wearing away of the shore.

One of the batteaux, cast high upon the bottom land near this cliff, and probably rendered unseaworthy, was burned, to prevent its falling into unfriendly hands. The nails, rudder hangings, bow ring, and other irons, as well as the ashes and charcoal remaining after its destruction, were ploughed up by McMahon many years since.

The other vestiges that were discovered in this locality are referred to in the annexed description.

What became of the British regulars belonging to the expedition we know not, but it is inferred that they embarked in the surviving boats, on their way to Niagara, taking with them all the provisions; leaving the Provincials and friendly Indians to make their way provisionless, through an inhospitable wilderness to the same point of destination. These Provincials were under the command of the then Maj. Israel Putnam, subsequently Major General in the service of the United States; and with him was the same Indian Chief, who captured him near Ticonderoga, in the year 1758. After the surrender of Montreal to the British, these two renowned partisans met, became friends, and the latter joined that part of BRADSTREET's expedition, under PUTNAM's command.

This body of Provincials was raised in Connecticut, New York, and New Jersey. Massachusetts refused to participate, in furnishing her quota.

It is remarkable that no minute history of the overland journey which closed this campaign has been preserved. The individuals who went out from those three colonies were intelligent, and in the practice of writing. It is very probable that some neglected garrets contain diaries and correspondence, filed away with forgotten papers, which would furnish details of this expedition. Their track from McMAHON's beach to the crossing of Rocky river, near the present plank road bridge, is made evident by the various articles dropped along the way. The immediate shores of the Lake between these two points, though seventy feet above the water, was wet and swampy. To avoid this they resorted to the dry ridge running through the premises of FREDERICK WRIGHT and JOHN WILLIAMS, and curving parallel to the river through Mr. PATCHEN's grounds, to the place of the present plank road gate. Here they prepared for their tedious march, disencumbered themselves of all useless and perhaps some valuable articles; before attempting to pass the high and precipitous banks of the river. Many of these articles have been discovered in recent times.

Some one entrusted with a sack or box of gun flints, containing several quarts, threw down his charge near the residence of FREDERICK WRIGHT, by whom it was disinterred a few years since. An antique silver teaspoon, was ploughed from the earth at the earliest cultivation of JOHN WILLIAMS' orchard, forty years ago—an utensil that no doubt belonged to some officer's mess. A sword and several bayonets were also ploughed up, a little north and east of that place, according to common report.

In the gardens of Mr. PATCHEN, at the Plank-Road House, coins have been found, bearing date early in the last century; one, a French silver coin, of the year 1714, and an English copper penny, of 1749. These coins were probably thrown down in discarded clothing, or in forsaken knapsacks.

Nothing more is known of their sufferings during their march to Niagara, than is contained in the letters of Sir WM. JOHNSON. On their arrival at Albany the Regulars went into winter quarters; the Provincials proceeded to their homes, and were disbanded.

Gen. BRADSTREET died at New York in 1772.

From the time of these disasters to the war with Great Britain, these localities were not much frequented by the Indians, and only cursorily visited by white hunters; hence these relics escaped observation, until the present population commenced their settlements about the year 1815.

These views are believed to afford a correct solution of the historical problem, involved in the above discoveries. They are left for either confirmation or rejection by future investigations.

Ample room remains for further research at both localities. A number of cannon are doubtless concealed in the sands, fronting McMahon's beach, and the bar extending into the lake from the right bank of Rocky river. Storms and fishermen's nets, are annually revealing other vestiges of these disasters.

DESCRIPTION OF THE RELICS.

1st. An ancient and elaborately finished sword thrown by the surf on the beach fronting the right bank of the river, in the year 1820, which was picked up by Orin Joiner, a member of the family of Datus Kelley. The hilt terminated in a ponderous lions head, which, and the guard, were of pure and solid silver. It was subsequently sold to a Cleveland goldsmith, and the silver was melted down for other uses.

If I am correctly informed, the lion's head was, in the last century, the insignia, to designate the naval from the land service of Great Britain—hence it is inferred that this sword belonged to a naval officer attached to the flotilla—probably the commander.

2d. In the spring of 1842, a heavy storm broke up and rearranged the hidden sand bar, extending at right angles with the beach, from the east bank far into the lake. Evidences were abundant at that time that one of the sunken barges, which had been engulphed in the quicksands, for more than three-fourths of a century was also broken up. Gun-flints, brass guards of muskets, eroded bayonets and fragments of musket barrels, were cast on the shore or were found among the sands in shoal water. Many of these articles were observed by JOHN WILLIAMS, Capt. BURLINGHAME, and FREDERICK WRIGHT; who are among the few survivors of our early settlers that recollect the circumstances.

In one night, the last named individual, hauled in six bayonets, while sweeping this bar with his seine, soon after that storm occurred.

The surf also threw high upon the beach, the bow-stem of a large boat or batteau. The wood was much chafed, and water-soaked, a heavy iron ring-bolt, perforating it, secured by a nut, was deeply incrusted with rust. A thick coating of aquatic moss or algæ, invested a portion of the wood, while other portions had evidently been buried in the sand. It remained on the shore for a year or two, when it was burned by fishermen, and I secured the ring-bolt.

At that time, it attracted the attention of common observers, and was in their minds, indefinitely associated with the other relics, but no one in the vicinity, was then in possession of the historical facts connected with those two disasters.

Since the year 1850, no further discoveries have been made on that beach.

3d. In the year 1859, a bayonet was thrown out by a plow on the margin of the plateau, overlooking the left bank of the river, between TISDALE's point, and the highway, running from the plank-road to the residence of Col. MERWIN. In the year 1863, Capt. TISDALE, while constructing a private road to his residence on the point, uncovered with a plow, the circle of boulders inclosing a quantity of ashes and charcoal—the remains of a camp-fire, to which allusion has already been made, and which is near where the bayonet was discovered.

On the outer margin of the circle were, dug out of the earth, the remains of a case-knife, nearly consumed by rust, and the blade of a surgeon's amputating knife. The bayonet and the amputating knife I have among my collection of relics.

4th. The ring-bolt, rudder irons, nails, and other remnants of a consumed batteau, were exposed by clearing of the bottom at the mouth of McMahon's run, soon after the first settling of the township.

5th. A stack of bayonets, covered with accumulated soil, rubbish and rank vegetation, and the remains of a musket, resting in the crotch of a tree, encased in the growth of wood; were discovered about the same period of time, as were the relics of the batteau.

6th. Several years later, two six-pound cannon balls and a number of leaden musket balls, were exposed to view, by undermining, by the Lake of the clay-cliff, which rises from the western margin of the bottom lands. These, no doubt, were among the articles, buried by Bradstreet, with his cannon and ammunition, as described by Sir Wm. Johnson.

All of the aforenamed relics were discovered by Mr. McMahon, and most of them were preserved by his family for a considerable time. All seem now to be lost, except the two six-pound cannon balls, which the family retain, and one of the musket balls, that is in my possession.

7th. About the year 1831, a young daughter of Datus Kelly, now Mrs. Charles Carpenter, of Kelly's Island, found an antique silver spoon on the beach, opposite the present residence of Col. Merwin. She dug it out of the sand while at play. It is thick and heavy for its size, the workmanship, which is coarse, is evidently old, and is of the model of those that were common, in the more wealthy families in New England during the last century.

On the under side of the tip of the handle, the initials I. C. are engraved, and on the same side near its junction with the bowl, are stamped the initials of the maker, A. S. Mrs. CARPENTER has had the care and good taste to retain it in her possession as an interesting relic.

8th. On the 4th of July, 1851, OSCAR TAYLOR, in company with several young men, while bathing in the lake at McMAHON'S cove, some forty rods west of the run, discovered in the water a teaspoon similar in all respects, except the engraved initials are S. T. He now resides at New London, Wisconsin, and retains the spoon. On the same occasion STEPHEN M. TAYLOR found an old bayonet near that locality, but neglected to preserve it.

9th. Still farther to the west, on the beach opposite the farm of Mr. BROWN, the proprietor discovered many years since, an iron or steel tomahawk, constructed to answer also the purpose of a pipe for smoking. It is lost.

10th. In the year 1859 an extensive slide from the high land, overlooking the lake and the right bank of McMAHON'S run, took place. While examining it, EDWIN BIDWELL noticed the end of a bayonet, still bearing the metallic tip of the sheath, projecting from the undisturbed margin of the bank, about twelve inches below the surface, the depth of the soil that seems to have accumulated over many of these relics, dropped on the land, a hundred years since. This bayonet was invested in the fine grained blue clay, formed from the breaking down of the adjacent shales, in which condition it is thrown upon the margin of the high banks of the lake, by the surf during storms. So perfectly did this investing material, protect the bayonet against the action of erosive agents, that it now retains much of its original polish, and is entire in all its parts. Through the kindness of Mr. B. I have it in my collection.

11th. In the same collection are also a number of bayonets, less perfect, collected by the families of Gov. Wood and Col. Merwin. These, at different times, were thrown up by the surf, or were drawn out of the water by fishermen's seines. One thus obtained was still attached to a large fragment of a musket barrel.

Two years since, a very entire and perfect musket barrel was obtained in the same manner, and presented to me by the fishermen. It belonged to an English Queen's arm of the last century. It exactly receives the bayonet found by Mr. Bidwell, and the lead ball, washed from the clay bank at McMahon's run.

The locality, along the beach at Col. Merwin's, where many of these relics have been found, is a favorite fishing ground, but the fishermen, after a few trials, are annually compelled to abandon it, as their seines are certain to become entangled by hidden and fixed objects some rods from the land. Often they are cut and injured, and they draw in various relics. The remains of some of BRADSTREET's engulphed batteaux are doubtless the obstructions against which they become arrested.

12th. Pursuing the survivors' track from the beach, where they were overwhelmed by the storm, we first arrive at the ridge, near the house of FREDERICK WRIGHT. There he some years since disinterred the collection of gun flints above referred to. In quantity they are said to have amounted to a peck or more. They were adapted to the heavy musket, but had never been used. I have not succeeded in obtaining a specimen; though the authority upon which the above statement is made, is good.

13th. Still further east along the ridge is the orchard of JOHN WILLIAMS, where, at the first breaking up of the ground, a silver teaspoon was exposed, some thirty or more years since. It was retained by him until recently, when it was lost. From report it seems to have been similar to those previously described, and doubtless belonged to some of the officers of the expedition.

A vague report also states that a number of relics, including a sword and several bayonets, were in early times discovered in the next lot east, lately owned by WM. ALLEN. No satisfactory confirmation of it can be obtained.

14th. A few rods still farther to the east, in the garden of the Patchen Inn, Mr. SILVERTHORN, in 1862, while excavating to put out a fruit tree, discovered some three or four dollars in silver, in small pieces of change, of French and English coinage, one bearing date in 1717, and all of them earlier than 1764. It is to be regretted that he soon passed them off at their nominal value.

15th. Mr. P. A. DELFORD, residing at the plank-road gate, discovered, in 1863, while digging in his garden a few rods from the last named locality, two copper pennies of 1749, bearing the effigies of GEORGE II. of Great Britain.

I have perhaps been tediously minute in these details, but my object was to facilitate the labors of any future investigator, who may attempt to divest this subject of any remaining doubts and obscurities.

A theory, to account for the manner in which these relics were scattered and deposited, at these several points has been already given.

A tumulus or grave of unknown dead, long since observed, on the right bank of the Rocky river, I have not noticed; yet I have little doubt, it has an intimate connection with one or the other of these disasters.

It is situated one hundred and fifty feet east of

the plank road bridge, at the head of a gully, that formerly cut, from the high ground down to the bottom land, near the present bridge. This gully has been partially obliterated, by the construction of the road. In its pristine condition, it was the only accessible way, from the river to the uplands, except a similar gully nearer the lake, and at the head of which that ancient camp-firé was established, on the left bank of the river.

This tumulus was observed at the time of the clearing of the land, forty years since, but as it was ascertained that it abounded with human bones, the early cultivators were careful to shun it. It then rose from two to three feet, above the level of the adjacent ground, and was about one rod square. The covering of earth was so thin that a spade easily reached the bones; and the surface was strewed with their fragments.

The common belief was, that it was an Indian grave. Mr. WORDEN, plowing the field with two yoke of oxen, seventeen years since, attempted to level it down by running his plow deeply through it. His furrows seemed to consist mostly of human bones, skulls in large proportion; and all in a very perfect state of preservation. He again interred them, and avoided any further disturbance of the locality. He informed me, that his sons, then small lads, picked up, from the rubbish of bones many small articles, such as metallic buttons and pieces of iron. The former were entire, the latter were nearly destroyed with rust. It was a mystery with him and his family, how the early Indians should possess so many of these articles. One of those sons, now an adult, confirms fully the statement of his father.

In 1861 Mr. EATON again plowed into it, and threw up bones in like manner. Of the large ones, he brought me at least two bushels, including a dozen craniums, and I subsequently made additional collections.

On examining them, they evidently were middle aged or younger adults, and all males. I pronounced them to be either Greeks or Anglo-Saxons, and not then knowing, that a Greek colony had ever settled within the Union, I concluded, of course, they must have belonged to the latter race — which was confirmed by the decision of one of the most perfect of craniologists in our country. My further conclusion was, that they were the remains of those who perished in one of the shipwrecks, on the adjacent coast.

The following year, Mr. KIRKPATRICK and myself, made a thorough exploration to the bottom of the tumulus. This we reached at the depth of two or three feet, after digging through a rich compost of bones and decayed animal matter. The bottom tier of skeletons at that place, had not been disturbed since their interment. We examined two—one large and middle aged, the other somewhat smaller and younger, judging from the teeth and length of the bones. Both were lying on their sides, thrown there in a careless manner. By the front of the large one, and near its middle, lay in close contact, the following articles, to wit: two small fragments of ancient Indian pottery, of the days of the race of mound building; one valve of the unio siliquoides of the western rivers; a knife, or spatula formed from bone, and the peculiar bone of one of the sexes of the raccoon. They occupied a small place only, and could have been embraced as charms, or amulets in an Indian's pouch, or the pocket of a soldier as objects of curiosity.

This discovery led to the conclusion that they all were Indian skeletons, but on re-examining such of the craniums as have not been lost, I am led to believe that the one of large size, found at the bottom of the grave, was that of an Indian, while the others were Anglo-Saxon.

The grave was evidently shallow, not over three feet deep. The bodies were thrown in one on another without much care, and were covered superficially, raising the tumulus two or three feet above the surface of the adjacent ground, in the manner soldiers are many times buried on recent battle-fields.

That these individuals perished in one or the other of those wreckings, can be hardly doubted. That BRADSTREET had with him many Indians is certain, but nothing is known as to the number of men he lost; though that number was considerable is inferred from the fact that "the losses of officers and men by the wreck, was made the subject of legislative action." That WILKINS lost a specified number, is well established; seventy men and three officers, but whether he was accompanied by Indians is not recorded. Such was probably the fact, for they were wont to take part in all military movements in those days, and he would need them as scouts and guides to his expedition. One or more were probably lost, and were thrown into the bottom of this grave. Its dimensions adapted it for the reception of about the number of his dead.

Another view may be taken. I may err in the conclusion, that one was an Indian's skull. All may be Anglo-Saxon. The Indian amulets, may have been collected by a sailor while among the Indians, retained as curiosities in a pocket of his clothing and with his person buried in this grave, after he perished.

J. P. K.

We have the example of HERODOTUS for introducing discussions and opposing statements, in cases where the evidence is not historically conclusive. He gives in this way an interesting variety, and an air of candor to his narrations.

Prof. KIRTLAND's investigations leave reasonable doubts, in reference to the locality of Major WIL-

KINS' disaster. The additional testimony which I now introduce, favors the impression that it occurred on the north shore, nearly opposite Cleveland, but does not entirely relieve the obscurity of the subject.

A letter in the Newport *Mercury*, (R. I.,) of December 26th, 1763, states the shipwreck to have happened at "Point-aux-Pins," or Pine Point, already referred to by Prof. KIRTLAND. Pine Point is the only recognized name, for a short spit which projects into the Lake at the "Rond-eau," Rondout, or round water, on the Canada shore. This point is visible on EVANS' map, but is there without a name. It projects in a southerly and westerly direction into the water, the bearing of which upon the question of locality, will appear upon reading the following extract, to which reference has already been made.

Extract from the "Newport Mercury," December 26*th*, 1763, *from a New York letter dated December* 19*th*.

"The same day Major MONCRIEFFE arrived here from Niagara. He belonged to the detachment under the command of Major WILKINS, destined from Niagara for Detroit, by whom we learn that on the 7th, ultimo, at 11 o'clock at night, eighteen of their boats foundered on Lake Erie, in a violent storm at south-east, which came on suddenly, by which seventy brave men were drowned.

"Among the number was Lieut. DAVIDSON of the train, and nineteen of his men, also Lieut. PAYNTER and Doctor WILLIAMS of the 80th, and a French pilot. The whole detachment was in danger of being lost, as every batteaux that reached the shore was more than half full of water, by which means sixty odd barrels of provisions, all the ammunition but two rounds to the man, which the officers saved in their hands, and two small brass field pieces were lost; and that after holding a council of war it was thought most prudent to return to Niagara."

A wind at south-east, or in a southerly direction, could not have been the occasion of a dangerous sea on a straight southerly coast. In turning any projecting land on the north shore, a storm at any point of compass, south of an east and west line, would be dangerous, if it was severe.

Among the manuscripts of the Maryland Historical Society, at Baltimore, is the unpublished journal of Lieut. JAMES GORELL, who was in the expedition. The Rev. E. A. DALRYMPLE, secretary of the society, has transcribed for my use, what relates directly to the shipwreck.

From allusions to attacks from the Indians in other parts of the journal, he supposes the party to have followed the southern shore of the Lake. This extract, however, states that they were delayed by contrary winds at "Long Point" ten days. On EVANS' map this is the name given to the slender promontory opposite Erie, which it has retained ever since. No other point of that name or character exists in any part of Lake Erie.

Extract from the Journal of Lieut. JAMES GORELL *concerning the shipwreck of Major* WILKINS' *command, November 7th,* 1763.

"At 10 o'clock at night we set sail and continued all night and next day, until we came to the long point. There we were obliged to stay for ten days. The day we left we got a good wind until we came to a place called Fish Creek, where we were obliged to lay nine days more; on the ninth day the wind favored us, and the Major ordered us all up, with instructions to keep well out from the land and to continue all night. About two hours after dark there arose a storm, and we lost nineteen batteaux, the most of them the largest and best. Lieut. DAVIDSON and all the powder boats were lost in this storm. (*Not legible.*) Was drowned, of the artillery, Lieut. PAINTER, late of the Independent, Doctor WILLIAMS, of the 80th regiment, with four sergeants, sixty-three privates and one Canadian. The next day we attempted to gather the wreck, but found little or none, except Lieut. DAVIDSON and about six men, which we buried. As soon as the Indians were gone out of sight (they were sent by land to Detroit), we set sail and arrived at Niagara the latter end of November."

The distance from the "Rond-eau" in a direct line to Detroit is sixty miles; by way of the Lake shore between ninety and one hundred. From Rocky river by land to the same place, is one hundred and fifty to one hundred and sixty miles. No mention is made by MONCRIEF or GORELL, of the post at Presque Isle on the south shore, where they would have called, and received supplies had they passed that way. The south shore route is nearly one hundred miles longer than the north, a distance which it was of great consequence to save, at this season of fall storms on the Lake.

ROGERS took the southern route because he was required to visit Fort Pitt, and to procure cattle from that region. The object of BRADSTREET'S expedition was to strike the Ohio Indians living on the south shore.

All the relics procured at Rockport may have belonged to BRADSTREET'S party, whose boats were no doubt scattered by the storm and came ashore at different points. One of the contemporary accounts states, that they stood boldly out on the Lake, hoping to weather the rocky portion of the coast, before they were beached. Between Long Point and Rondout, on the Canada shore, is Catfish creek, which may have had that name at that time. The number of bodies recovered was only six, while those buried at Rocky river, were from sixty to seventy. This is the extent of our present knowledge upon this subject.

FRENCH AND ENGLISH TRADERS.

The mouth of the Cuyahoga, was a point of too much consequence among the Indians, not to bring traders here at a very early day. Between 1700 and 1750, the French extended their forts and trading posts, to all points on the waters of the lakes and of the Ohio river. In the last named year they had a fort at Sandusky, and in 1755 a trading house on the Cuyahoga, opposite the mouth of Tinker's creek.

James Smith, of Pennsylvania, spent the winter of 1755—6 on the "Cayahoga," not as a trader, but as a prisoner among the Delawares. He left a narrative of his captivity, in which the country watered by the Cuyahoga, the Black, and the Kilbuck rivers, is fully described. From 1760 to 1764, Mary Campbell, a young girl captured in Pennsylvania, lived on this river, most of the time near the foot of the falls, at the forks below Akron.

After the British took possession in 1760, French and English traders continued together, to traffic with the Indians on the waters of lake Erie. No doubt a post was kept up, at some point or points on the river during a large part of the eighteenth century, but such establishments are so slight and temporary, that they are seldom noticed in history. A trading house is a very transient affair. A small log cabin covered with bark, constituted all of what is designated as an establishment. If the Indian customers remove, the trader follows them; abandons his cabin, and constructs another at a more convenient place. Within a year the deserted hut is burned to the ground, and all that remains is a vacancy of an acre or two in the forest, covered with grass, weeds, briers and bushes.

In 1786 a lively trade in furs is known to have been carried on here. Of the energetic half civilized men, who for so many generations carried on this business, we know personally nothing; except in regard to JOSEPH DU SHATTAR and some of his companions. Mr. EBENEZER MERRY, of Milan, Huron County, Ohio, in 1842 had a conversation with Judge S. A. ABBEY, in which he stated that he had known DU SHATTAR. He had from a youth been in the employ of the North-West Fur Company, along this lake. The mouth of the Cuyahoga and Sandusky, were principal points. About 1790 he married MARY PORNAY, at Detroit, and commenced trading on his own account. He had a post nine miles up the river, which is probably the one whose remains have been observed in Brooklyn, opposite Newburg.

Here his second child was born in 1794. JOHN BAPTISTE FLEMMING and JOSEPH BURRALL were with him a part of the time. While he was at Sandusky one of his voyageurs, by the name of BEAULIEAU, appropriated the wife of an Indian. This proceeding, and the continued presence of fire-water gave rise to frequent quarrels. Their establishment at Sandusky was attacked by the Indians, in order to rescue BEAULIEAU'S squaw, and many goods were seized. The remainder were saved by a compromise effected with rum.

On the Cuyahoga, a fight occurred with the Indians in reference to a rifle. The Indians attacked them at another time, intending to capture their spirits, to obtain which they will risk whatever they possess. Some of the savages were killed and the remainder retreated. A trader was killed on the lake shore about ten miles below Grand river. DU SHATTAR was living in 1812, and assisted in capturing JOHN O'MIC and SEMO, on Locust Point, the murderers of MICHAEL GIBBS and DANIEL BUELL at Pipe creek, near Sandusky.

THE MORAVIANS IN CUYAHOGA COUNTY.

1786-1787.

Those who escaped alive from the slaughter of the Pennsylvanians, under Col. WILLIAMSON, located themselves around Sandusky. But although they were here among their kindred, the Delawares, they were not in a place of safety. The Indians threatened and annoyed them, until at last they appealed to Col. DEPUYSTER, the British commandant at Detroit. He treated the missionaries and their converts with humanity. This gentleman made great efforts to soften the ill will of their savage enemies. The praying Indians remained near Detroit during four years. They built a village on the Huron river of Michigan, which was called New Gnadenhutten. In May, 1786, they determined to plant a "settlement" on the Cuyahoga river, within the limits of this county. The officer in command at Detroit procured two small vessels, the Beaver and the Mackinaw, to bring them, their provisions and other luggage to this place. They left New Gnadenhutten because the Chippewas were dissatisfied at seeing them on the Huron. With their usual bad luck, after they were near enough to have a view of the mouth of the Cuyahoga, a violent storm drove them back to the islands opposite Sandusky. It was now one month since they had embarked at Detroit, and they were not more than half way to their destination. Two of the missionaries, YOUNGMAN and SENSEMAN, had left New Gnadenhutten in May, 1785, so that the responsibility of directing their affairs remained with ZEISBERGER and HECKEWELDER.

The North-Western Fur Company, to whom the vessels belonged, could spare them no longer, and sent orders for the Beaver to return. It was barely possible to crowd the weak, the sick and the young, with the heavy luggage into the Mackinaw. The others were landed in the woods on the shore opposite Sandusky bay. From thence they straggled along, crossing the bay in a very destitute condition. Those who were healthy and strong, whether men or women, took the great trail along the Lake shore on foot, led on by their brother ZEISBERGER. For those who could not travel by land, canoes were built, and Brother HECKEWELDER embarked with them on the 7th of June. Both parties reached the Cuyahoga on the same day. The schooner Mackinaw had also been here, and had landed their blankets, mats and other property, including some provisions. Congress had ordered five hundred bushels of corn for their support, but it never came. A firm by the name of Duncan, Wilson & Co., of Pittsburgh, were engaged in furnishing supplies to the Indians of Lake Erie. They had flour in store on the west side of the river, and had the liberality to relieve the immediate wants of this distressed company. They immediately proceeded up the river. The site of their mission was on the east bank of the Cuyahoga, a short distance below the mouth of Tinker's creek, to which they gave the name of Pilgerruh, or the "Pilgrim's Rest." Near it there had been a village of Ottawas, where some ground had been cleared. This they planted with corn. On the 13th of August they celebrated the Lord's supper. In the month of October their village was so far completed, as to furnish comfortable lodging for the coming winter. Mr. HECKEWELDER then left the community, whose numbers at this time I cannot ascertain, and started for the old station at Bethlehem, Pa. A brother by the name of WM. EDWARDS, had arrived at the Pilgrim's Rest, who remained with ZEISBERGER during the winter.

Their chapel was completed and consecrated on the 10th of November. It was never their design to remain permanently at Pilgerruh.

Their rich lands in the more genial valley of the Muskingum, were ever present to their minds as their future home. But they were not destined to see those pleasant fields, to drink the sweet waters of the spring at Schoenbrunn, or to weep over the bones of their slaughtered companions; until after more trials, and after painful and distant wanderings.

The majority of the Delawares were still their enemies. At Sandusky they had friends enough, however, to keep them advised of the designs of their pagan brethren. A Delaware chief sent them word, privately, that they would be wise not to go to the Muskingum.

General BUTLER, who was the Indian agent at Pittsburgh, also advised them to remain at Pilgerruh. Captain PIPE, a noted chief of the Delawares, desired them to come and settle at the mouth of the Huron river, a place which was known by the name of "Petquotting."

One of the Moravian writers and missionaries, by the name of LOSKIEL, speaking of the dilemma they were now in, remarks that the "missionaries were not concerned as to their own safety. If that alone had been the point in question, they would not have hesitated a moment to return to the Muskingum. But they dare not bring the congregation committed to their care, into so dreadful and dangerous a situation."

They resolved to abandon the project of a return, and after celebrating Lent and Easter at Pilgerruh in the spring of 1787, they prepared to remove to the mouth of Black river. Their last service on the banks of the Cuyahoga, is said to have been an occasion of deep religious interest. Their hearts were full of devotion and of gratitude, notwithstanding the dangers by which they were surrounded.

On the 19th of April, the last prayer was heard in their chapel at the "Pilgrim's Rest," which was no sooner concluded than they set forward.

One part descended the river in canoes, and coasting westward, reached the mouth of Black river. Another party proceeded on foot to the same place, with which they were well pleased, and had hopes that the unconverted Indians would suffer them to remain in peace.

They had enjoyed this expectation only three days, when a peremptory message came to them from the principal chiefs of the Delawares, to proceed forthwith to Sandusky.

This band of simple, patient and harrassed children of the woods, decided at once to obey, looking with confidence to heaven for protection.

The praying Indians of Ohio, whom the United brethren of Moravia had induced to separate from their savage neighbors, had the misfortune to be suspected by all parties. Those Americans who constituted the frontier men of the West, living at the verge of the settlements in Kentucky, Virginia and Pennsylvania, regarded the Moravians as secretly leagued with the French, and after the Revolution, with the English. This was the cause of the massacre on the Muskingum, in March 1782. On the other side, the north-western tribes of Indians, including those of Ohio, who were in league with the British, regarded the praying Indians as no better than Whites. It was this feeling that led the Delawares, a tribe to whom many of ZEISBERGER'S band belonged, to keep a strict watch over them. They stood in constant dread of the chiefs of their own tribe. They were afraid to return to the Muskingum, because it displeased the Delawares and other nations, and thus lived in daily expectation of persecutions. It was not an unexpected event, therefore, when they were ordered away from Black river, after they had left the Cuyahoga. Only three days were they permitted to remain there, supplying themselves with fish, which they speared in the river, by torch light. They then felt compelled to enter their canoes and remove to Petquotting, at the mouth of the Huron river. As they passed along near the shore, vegetation began to show the influence of spring. The buds upon the trees of this dense forest, were expanding into miniature leaves; grass, flowers and rank herbage were springing up under the shade of their branches. But the mind of these wanderers, was in sad contrast with the peace and beauty of the scene. They were full of apprehension. The message of the Delawares was couched in dominant and angry terms. There were with them two young men, by the name of MICHAEL YOUNG and JOHN WEYGAND, vainly endeavoring to support their timid souls, as they entered the Huron river, and tied their canoes to the shore at Petquotting. This must have been about the first of May, 1787, the message of the Delawares having been delivered on the 27th of April. By the 11th of May, they had erected huts, giving to their new residence the name of New Salem. On the first of June, they had built a chapel, and celebrated the Lord's supper in it. In the winter of 1789–90, a powerful league was formed among the north-western Indians against the United States. The Moravians were required to join it, and as they were suspected by their Pagan brethren, it was determined at their council fire, that they should be removed to the interior, near Fort Wayne, which was then called Keyequash. In their distress they again applied to the commandant at Detroit, who being touched by their demeanor and their helplessness, again gave them relief. He sent a vessel to the mouth of the Huron river, in April, 1790, and selecting a place on the river Thames in Canada, transported them thither.

To this settlement they gave the name of Fairfield, where they remained in safety during the Indian wars under HARMAR, ST. CLAIR and WAYNE. In the year 1797, when their reverend father, ZEISBERGER, had attained the age of seventy-seven years, their lands on the Muskingum were surveyed, and patented to them by the United States. It seemed that all obstacles were now removed, to their return to their desired home in Ohio. A part of the band returned there in the spring of 1798. They found, after an absence of sixteen years, nothing but the ruins of their houses, weedy and deserted fields, and the graves of their kindred. Some remained at Fairfield, in Canada. In 1804, a part of them returned to New Salem, on the Huron river. On the Muskingum, they rebuilt the villages of Gnadenhutten, Salem and Schoenbrunn, and established a new settlement, under the name of Goshen. The faithful old ZEISBERGER died in the year 1808, but at this time his grave cannot be identified. As the country adjacent became more populous with whites, the converted Indians, and probably their white neighbors, thought it best for them to abandon their settlements. The United States purchased their lands and improvements on the 4th of August, 1823, and they returned to Canada, where some of them still survive. The grave yard at Goshen was reserved from sale, also ten acres around the church at Beersheba, together with the parsonage, church lot and grave yard, at Gnadenhutten. Thus terminated the Moravian settlements in Ohio, after a precarious and painful existence of sixty years.

In the month of April, 1788, while ZEISBERGER and his congregation were at Petquotting, the first settlement of whites was founded in Ohio, at the mouth of the Muskingum. As these emigrants were from the land of churches, they considered religious services to be an essential part of the new colony. They brought with them the Rev. DAVID BRECK, and afterwards the Rev. DANIEL STORY, who, under the Rev. MANASSEH CUTLER, formed a church at Marietta. In the fall of the same year, a settlement was made at Columbia, near Cincinnati, and a Baptist church was established there in 1790, under the charge of the Rev. DANIEL GANO. These congregations worshiped God, as the Pilgrims had done before them, with arms in their hands, surrounded by savages, whose minds were filled with wonder and revenge. During the second year of the settlement at Cleveland, (1797,) the Rev. SETH HART held the position of General Agent and Chaplain, for the Connecticut Land Company on the Reserve. He has left no evidence of his spiritual efforts, and according to tradition, he was not a very zealous laborer in the vineyard of Christ. In this part of Ohio, the first regular dispensation of gospel truth occurred in Youngstown, in September, 1799, under the Rev. WILLIAM WICK, of the Presbyterian persuasion. A church was organized there the next year, during the last months of which the Rev. Jos. BADGER arrived as a missionary from Connecticut, to the settlements on the Western Reserve. From this period, being the commencement of the present century, the history of WICK, BADGER, ROBBINS, and the other pioneer ministers who planted Christianity throughout the Reserve, is within the reach of all.

As the labors, privations, and even names of these early teachers are forgotten, I append a list of them here:

Date of arrival.	*Name.*	*First station.*	*Persuasion.*
1761.	FREDERICK POST,	near Bolivar,	Moravian.
1761.	JOHN HECKEWELDER,	do.	do.
1768.	DAVID ZEISBERGER,	Venango Co., Pa.	do.
1768.	JOHN ETWEIN,	Forks of Beaver River,	do.
1772.	HECKEWELDER and ZEISBERGER,	on the Muskingum,	do.
1773.	DAVID JONES,	on the Scioto,	Baptist.
1775.	JOHN JACOB YOUNGMAN,	on the Muskingum,	Moravian.
1775.	—— ROTHE,	do.	do.
	Number of members, 369.		
1777.	WM. EDWARDS,	on the Muskingum,	Moravian.
1777.	JOHN JACOB SCHMICK,	do.	do.
1780.	SARAH OHNEBURG, afterwards Mrs. HECKEWELDER,	on the Muskingum,	Moravian.
1780.	MICHAEL YOUNG,	do.	do.
1780.	—— SHEBOSH,	do.	do.
1780.	—— SENSEMANN,	do.	do.
1782.	JOHN MARTIN,	do.	do.
1787.	JOHN WEYGAND,	on the Cuyahoga.	do.
1788.	DANIEL BRECK,	Marietta,	Congregational.
1788.	DANIEL STORY,	do.	do.
1788.	DANIEL GANO,	near Cincinnati,	Baptist.
1799.	WILLIAM WICK,	Youngstown,	Presbyterian.
1800.	JOSEPH BADGER,	Western Reserve,	Congregational.
1801.	E. F. CHAPIN,	do.	do.
1803.	THOMAS ROBBINS,	do.	do.

ORIGIN OF TITLE.

To those outside of the legal profession, nothing is more uninteresting than discussions upon titles. But the subject is too important to be omitted. In regard to the permanent prosperity of a country, a good system of land titles, is of no less consequence than a good government.

On the Western Reserve, although the system is simple, the history of its origin is somewhat complicated. A thorough exposition would of itself occupy a small volume. I can only present the outlines.

England claimed the North American continent by discovery, in virtue of the voyages of John and Sebastian Cabot, along its eastern coast. The Pope assumed to grant to Spain, a large part of America, but the other powers, paid very little attention to the title of his Holiness; as it was wholly without foundation. By the practice of civilized nations, which constitutes the law of nations; discovery and possession, make up the title to unoccupied countries. In determining the limits of possession under the law of nations, constructive occupation was allowed, whereby the party who held the mouth of a river took the country which is drained by it.

Thus Spain, by the explorations of DE NARVAEZ, and DE SOTO, on the Gulf of Mexico; became possessed of the country of the Apalachicola, Mobile, Pearl, and Mississippi rivers, early in the 16th century.

She soon lost a large part of this territory, by the failure of continuous possession, and the French taking advantage of her neglect, extended their occupation over it. Coming in by way of the St. Lawrence in 1535, and fixing themselves there in 1603, they pushed forward in every direction.

In 1660 they reached the west end of Lake Superior; in 1673 they were on the upper Mississippi, and on the 7th of April, 1682, LA SALLE arrived at its mouth.

The English had frequently tried to dislodge them, by negotiation and by force, but without success. By the year 1749, French military posts had entirely surrounded the English colonies. They were continually contracting the inner cordon of their forts, until they were brought in immediate contact, with the frontier positions of the British Crown. The French then held the Bay of Funday, Fort Cohasset on the Connecticut, and Crown Point on Lake Champlain.

They held Oswego, Niagara, Fort Erie, opposite

Buffalo, Presque Isle (Erie, Pa.), the Allegheny and Ohio rivers. This dangerous proximity brought on the old French war of 1754. Before appealing to arms, the French offered a boundary, commencing on the Gulf of Mexico, at the mouth of the Apalachicola, thence up the same to its source. From its head waters the dividing line between the English and French colonies, was to follow the crest of the Allegheny mountains; to the sources of the Susquehanna; and thence to Crown Point, and the Bay of Funday.

As a counter proposition, the English offered to accept the line of the Allegheny mountains, as far as the eastern branches of the Ohio; diverging thence to their junction at Pittsburg; up the Allegheny river, and French creek to Presque Isle, on lake Erie; and thence along the shore, through lake Ontario, the outlet of lake Champlain, and the sources of the Atlantic rivers. This being refused, the war was begun; which in 1760, ended in the conquest by the English, of all the French possessions, east of the Mississippi, except the island of Orleans.

With the Indians, the French policy was quite different from that of the English, and the Americans. The French did not ask for territory, except as tenants of so much as might be necessary for temporary cultivation, around their forts. Their treaties were made to secure peace and traffic.

The French have little taste for colonizing new

countries, for the purpose of permanent cultivation. But whatever rights the French had in the Indian country, became English; by conquest, secured by the treaty of February 13, 1763; and as the Indians were their allies, they stood in the position of a conquered people.

Between the colonies and the crown, there arose at once the question of title, to the lands beyond the Alleghenies; included in all the colonial charters.

The Sovereigns of England not only made grants in this country of immense extent, for very trifling considerations, covering many times over the same territory; but they claimed the power to amend, alter, and annul previous patents, a power which was frequently exercised.

Virginia at first included a large part of North America: from latitude thirty-four to latitude forty-eight north, thence west and north-west to the Great South Sea; which was at that time a geographical myth. While the Pilgrim fathers were on the sea, in search of a new home; where they could be exempt from religious persecution; James the First, king of England, on the 3d of November, 1630, divided Old Virginia; constituting a northern and a southern colony; under the names of the "London" and "Plymouth" companies. The charter of the Plymouth company, is tediously verbose, granting to forty favorites of the crown, mostly nobles; the country between latitude 40 and 48° north, stretching indefinitely, to the mythical South Sea, on the west. This territory was forever to be called "New England." It covered the Dutch settlement on Hudson river, and subsequent grants to the Duke of York, now constituting the State of New York; most of Pennsylvania, Ohio, Canada and the north-western States.

The "Council of Plymouth" was made a corporation, with most extensive political and personal privileges; on condition of rendering to the king, one-fourth part of all the gold and silver that might be discovered. They had exclusive rights of trade, free of duty, except as to imports to England. It was made a heinous crime to speak evil of "New England" or the corporators. The object of the grants are set forth in these words: "The principal effect which we can desire or expect of this action is the conversion or reduction of the people in those parts to the true worship of God and christian religion."

In 1630, the Council of Plymouth, sitting in the county of Devon, England, granted to Robert, Earl of Warwick, its President; "All that part of New England, in America, which lies and extends itself from a river there called Narragansett river, the space of forty leagues upon a straight line near the sea shore, towards south-west, west and by south, or west, as the coast lieth, towards Virginia, accounting three English miles to the league, all and singular, the lands and hereditaments whatsoever, lying and being within the bounds aforesaid, north and south in latitude and breadth, and in length and longitude, and within all the breadth aforesaid throughout all the main lands there, from the western ocean to the South Seas." What lands were meant by this description, or what were not included in it, constituted the legal puzzle of a century and a half.

On the 19th of March, 1631, Earl ROBERT conveyed the same premises "more or less," to Viscount SAY AND SEAL BROOK, and his associates, which is called the "Patent of Connecticut." It is under this patent she claimed a large part of Pennsylvania and Ohio, and from which her claim to the Western Reserve is derived. The limits of Connecticut north and south were finally determined to be the forty-first parallel, and the parallel of forty-two degrees and two minutes north. As doubts were entertained of the validity of Warwick's patent, to found a political government; and the colony of Massachusetts encroached upon that of Connecticut, recourse was had to King CHARLES the Second, who granted a most ample charter on the 23d of April, 1662, which also fixed the northern boundary.

Lord SAY AND SEAL was still living, and a fast friend of the Puritans. He was also in power at court, and in favor with CHARLES Second. JOHN WINTHROP the Governor, who was sent to England to procure this charter, had in his possession a ring; which once belonged to CHARLES the First. This was presented to the King, delighting his royal heart exceedingly. Whatever they desired was put into the charter, which served as a constitution, until after the United States became independent of Great Britain.—[*Trumbull's History of Connecticut.*]

The charter of the "London Company," covering a large part of North America, had been annulled by judicial process in 1624. The subsequent grant to the Duke of York, extended across the St. Lawrence indefinitely to the north-west. Connecticut and Massachusetts, under the charter of the Plymouth Company, reached to the Great South Sea.

After the Peace of Paris, and before the revolution, the Indians made grants of territory to Great Britain, embracing parts of New York, Connecticut, Pennsylvania and Virginia, as these colonies were then described. They had much reason to claim, that having borne much of the expense, and furnished a large part of the soldiers, to carry on the war with the French and Indians, the lands thus wrested from their enemies, should be confirmed to them. Whether under the law of nations, the King had a right to grant them territory, which lay beyond the rivers emptying into the Atlantic, he now held this disputed country by a good title, and they insisted that he was bound to make good his ancient promises. The Crown took a different view

In the fall of 1763, all the colonists were excluded from lands beyond the mountains, by royal proclamation.

Before the French war, the "Ohio Land Company" had been formed, with extensive grants in Ohio and West Virginia. The colony of Virginia had issued bounty land warrants, to her soldiers who fought against the French. As she claimed, under the almost limitless charter of the London Company, the holders of these warrants had a roving commission, to plant themselves at will in the western country. These bold soldiers paid little heed to the King's proclamation, or to the savages, who protested fiercely against their intrusions. Even WASHINGTON came to the Great Kenhawa and located his warrants. Projects for land companies and settlements, in the valley of the Ohio, were being vigorously prosecuted, when the war of the revolution broke out. When it closed, all the rights which the English government possessed, either from French or Indian conquest, were transferred by the same right of the conqueror, and by treaty, to the United States.

Immediately after the peace of 1783, the American Congress took measures to obtain cessions of Indian lands. Their commissioners, beginning at Fort Stanwix in 1784, afterwards at Fort McIntosh, Fort Harmar, and other points on the Ohio, in 1785–6, concluded what are called treaties, with the Six Nations and many western tribes.

In these negotiations, although matters had the appearance of bargain and sale, a certain amount of goods and money, for a given quantity of land, the terms were those of a conqueror, dictating to the vanquished. The Indians had fought with the British, against us, as they had with the French, against the English. Victory placed them again in the position of a conquered people. These treaties were not those of parties, equal under the law of nations, but were articles of settlement at the conclusion of a war. The Indians always regarded them as stipulations made under duress, to be kept no longer than they were obliged to do so by force.

They had learned under British rule, that the government would permit no sales by them to other parties. They had been guarantied by the British crown, a permanent home, west of the Alleghenies; into which the white men had been forbidden to enter. This was done in good faith by the British authorities, but the issue of war had abrogated her authority; a war to which the Indians were parties.

The possession of the soil is evidently due to those who will cultivate it. The earth was not intended as a mere hunting ground for the savage. By his mode of life, he requires about six miles square to support a family. He draws his subsistence from the spontaneous production of nature, always exhausting and never adding any thing to her resources.

Of course the earth cannot in this way fulfil its destiny, and support the increasing millions that are incessantly appearing upon it. In 1736 all the savages, with which the Jesuit Missionaries were acquainted, on the waters of the lakes and of the Mississippi, did not exceed 80,000. Within the limits of Ohio, there were probably more Indians about the time of the Revolution, than ever before. By Capt. HUTCHINS' estimate, made in 1787, there were not of them to exceed 7,000 souls. The whole number, would not have made a city of the second class, as fixed by our statutes.

The old difficulty between the colonies and the crown, revived immediately after the revolution, between the same parties as States, and the confederation of the United States of America. All the old questions of boundary, came up anew. New York, at an early day, consented to a liberal curtailment of her claims. The pressure of the war, the wisdom, forbearance and patriotism of those times, and the financial difficulties which oppressed the nation, all conspired to make the discussion temperate, and finally secured a happy result. Congress held the Indian grants. Some States had no indefinite western boundary, on which to found a claim. These had, like the others, sent their citizens into the field, and supported them there. Like the colonies in the French war, they had acquired a moral right to a portion of the proceeds of the conquest. The discussion continued from the formation of the confederation, until the year 1800, before everything connected with the western lands was adjusted.

Connecticut, having been ousted of her pretensions in Pennsylvania, was tenacious of her claims to the west of that State. By her deed of September 14, 1786, she limited herself to a tract, about as large as Old Connecticut, in the north-eastern part of Ohio, commonly called the "Western Reserve." To this as to all other western lands, the title was eventually made sure by compromise; the United States refusing to consider the comparative value of the conflicting claims of the States.

In addition to the relinquishment of 1786, a farther compact was made between the State and the Government, by which Connecticut, in 1800, relinquished to the United States, all claim of political jurisdiction, and the latter confirmed to her the title to the soil.

That personal enterprise which is engendered by wars, expends itself in the United States, upon the new territories. The provincial soldiers of the old French war, and of the campaign under Col. Bouquet, 1764, were the men who became the pioneers on the waters of the Ohio. Very soon after the Revolution, our immediate ancestors began to look westward. Their courage did not allow them to fear their red enemies. Wars are not wholly without compensation. It required precisely such characters, as the impoverished soldiers of the Revolution, to conquer the western wilds. Men who had never been toughened by the exposures and dangers of the camp, would not relish such undertakings. Perhaps many of these, would not have sought after fortune in such remote regions, had not the war left them with nothing but their physical strength, ambition and courage. The rich wilderness which they had seen, had been conquered by their exertions. It was therefore in accordance with a fearless spirit, coupled with necessity; that they entered upon the dangerous task of subduing the western wilderness.

In 1788 the settlement of Ohio was commenced, by an association of New England soldiers. During the next year a purchase of three millions of acres, was made in western New York, through the agency of BENJAMIN GORHAM and OLIVER PHELPS; embracing the rich lands which border upon Seneca and Canandaigua lakes.

In Ohio the most accessible portion lies adjacent to the Ohio river, where the first lodgments were made, at Marietta and Cincinnati.

For thirty years, rude highways had been in existence over the ridges of the Allegheny mountains, made by BRADDOCK and FORBES, to the forks of the Ohio, at Pittsburg. From thence, in boats, they could float onward with the stream. The settlements, following the impulse of the old French war, had passed the crests of those mountains, and already occupied some of the valleys of the streams.

The northern route to Ohio was more difficult. The entire breadth of the State of New York must be penetrated, mostly by a land route, through a country not broken by mountains, but by marshes, lakes and streams, more impracticable than mountains. It required a few years more time, for them to reach the northern borders of this State.

Settlers had forced their way as far west as Canandaigua. A horse trail had been opened along the old Indian trail to lake Erie, at Buffalo, when the project of occupying this portion of the State was set on foot. OLIVER PHELPS, of Connecticut, the partner of GORHAM, of Massachusetts, in the New York purchase, was disposed to strike still deeper into the western country.

On the 14th of September, 1786, the State of Connecticut made a deed of cession, whereby she released to the United States; all right, title, interest jurisdiction and claim, which she had north of the forty-first parallel, and west of a meridian to be run at a distance of one hundred and twenty miles, west of the west line of the State of Pennsylvania; extending north to the parallel of forty-two degrees and two minutes.

The State of Connecticut, made no disposition of the territory, between the Pennsylvania line and the meridian referred to, lying between forty-two degrees two minutes, and forty-one degrees. It was thus reserved to herself, from which it received the title of the "Connecticut Western Reserve." All the States, having claims to the territory north-west of the Ohio; having relinquished their claims, except to the Reserve; the United States proceeded to establish a government over it, and passed the famous "Ordinance of 1787."

As the State of Connecticut, had never relinquished her claim to the Western Reserve, she considered such an extension of jurisdiction, to be in violation of her rights. She very soon after, provided for the sale of her reserved lands in this region.

As the claims of the several States, to western lands under their conflicting grants, and the mode of settlement are fully set forth in the Land Laws of the United States; I notice them only incidentally here.

In October, 1786, that State had passed a resolution, authorizing a committee of three persons, to sell that part, which lies east of the Cuyahoga river and the old portage path; by townships of six miles square. The price was limited to three shillings currency per acre, which is equal to fifty cents in Federal money. Six ranges of townships were to be surveyed, lying next to the Pennsylvania line; to be numbered from lake Erie southward, and not less than twenty-seven dollars in specie, was to be paid per township to defray the expenses of survey. Five hundred acres of land in each township, was reserved for the support of the gospel ministry; and five hundred acres for the support of schools.

The first minister who settled in a township, was entitled to two hundred and forty acres. Until a republican government should be established, the general Assembly, undertook to provide for the preservation of peace and good order among the settlers.

At their session in May 1787, some alterations were made, in the manner of surveying and numbering the townships, and the mode of making conveyances.

No attempt was made to execute the surveys. A sale was made however, to General SAMUEL H. PARSONS, of Middletown, of a tract embracing twenty-four thousand acres, afterwards known as the "Salt Spring Tract," in Trumbull county. This patent was executed by the Governor and Secretary, February 10, 1788. [Hon. T. D. WEBB.] It is described by ranges and townships, as though the lines had been run and marked upon the ground. General PARSONS had explored the country, and found the location of the well known Salt Spring, near the Mahoning river, which was considered very valuable. This spring is laid down by EVANS, on his map of 1755. The Pennsylvanians had recourse to it during the revolution, and cabins had been erected there. In 1785, Col. BRODHEAD, commanding the troops at Fort Pitt, had orders to dispossess them, and did so. The Indians soon burned the cabins they had erected. General PARSONS, was appointed one of the Judges in the north-western Territory, but was drowned in the fall of 1788, at the falls of Beaver river. Considerable quantities of salt had been made by Indians and traders before the settlement, and for a number of years after, its manufacture was continued by the pioneers.

General PARSONS was the only purchaser from the State, until the Connecticut Land Company was organized, giving him the choice of lands east of the Cuyahoga. The description in his patent is as follows: "Beginning at the north-east corner of the *first* township in the *third* range; thence northerly, on the west line of the second range, to forty-one degrees and twelve minutes of north latitude; thence west, three miles; thence southerly, parallel to the west line of Pennsylvania, two miles and one half; thence west, three miles, to the west line of said third range; thence southerly, parallel to the west line of Pennsylvania, to the north line of the first township in the third range; thence east to the first bound." [LEONARD CASE.]

Although no surveys were made, General PARSONS proceeded to make sales and deeds, of undivided portions, to various parties. His patent was recorded in the office of the Secretary of State, at Hartford, but the United States having organized the county of Washington, embracing this tract, it was again recorded at Marietta, as were many of the deeds made by him. Afterwards, when the conflicting claims of the State and the federal government were harmonized, as doubts remained in regard to the validity of Washington county, north of the 41st parallel, they were recorded again at Warren, in the county of Trumbull. No taxes were effectually imposed upon the inhabitants of the Reserve, until after the organization of Trumbull county. Before that time, the settlers were left in a state of nature, so far as civil government was concerned. They were once disturbed by the authority of the United States, at the time when they were supposed to be included in Jefferson County.

ZENAS KIMBERLY made his appearance in this region, to enquire into the matter of taxation. As they did not acknowledge the jurisdiction of the United States, he was beset by ridicule and laughter, until he concluded to leave them.

[T. D. WEBB.]

In May, 1792, the Legislature of Connecticut granted to those of her citizens, who had suffered by depredations of the British, during the revolution, *half a million of acres*, to be taken off the west end of the Reserve, exclusive of the Islands. As no one except PARSONS had purchased lands under the resolutions of 1786–7, a new mode of disposing of her western lands was adopted, in May, 1795.

Numerous parties entered the field as purchasers. Under the last resolution, a committee of eight citizens, representing each county in the State; was empowered to sell, three millions of acres; next west of the Pennsylvania line, at a price not less than one million of dollars being a third of a dollar per acre. The names of the committee were

JOHN TREADWELL,	JAMES WADSWORTH,
MARVIN WAIT,	WILLIAM EDMOND,
THOMAS GROSVENOR,	AARON AUSTIN,
ELIJAH HUBBARD,	SYLVESTER GILBERT.

Speculation in wild lands had already become epidemic in New England. BENJAMIN GORHAM and OLIVER PHELPS had sold their New York purchase to ROBERT LIVINGSTON, of Philadelphia, who transferred it to a company in Holland, by which the tract was afterwards known as the "Holland Purchase."

The committee, and the several adventurers, spent the summer of 1795 in negotiations. General WAYNE's successful movements, through the Indian country from the Ohio, to lake Erie, during the previous year; had convinced the British and Indians that the United States intended to occupy Ohio, whoever might oppose. The purchasers, were, notwithstanding; required to take all risks of title and of possession. Another condition was imposed upon the committee; which required them to dispose of the entire three million of acres, before concluding a sale of any part of it.

John Livingston and others were in the field as competitors of the Connecticut men, but were induced to accept for their share, the supposed surplus, a million or more of acres.

On the 2d of September, 1795, the bargain was concluded. A sufficient number of individuals had presented themselves, willing to take the entire tract at the sum of one million two hundred thousand dollars; whose names, and their respective proportions are here given:

Joseph Howland and Daniel L. Coit,	$30,461
Elias Morgan,	51,402
Caleb Atwater,	22,846
Daniel Holbrook,	8,750
Joseph Williams,	15,231
William Love,	10,500
William Judd,	16,256
Elisha Hyde and Uriah Tracey,	57,400
James Johnston,	30,000
Samuel Mather, Jr.,	18,461
Ephraim Kirby, Elijah Boardman and Uriel Holmes, Jr.,	60,000
Solomon Griswold,	10,000
Oliver Phelps and Gideon Granger, Jr.,	80,000
William Hart,	30,462
Henry Champion, 2d,	85,675
Asher Miller,	34,000
Robert C. Johnson,	60,000

Ephraim Root,	42,000
Nehemiah Hubbard, Jr.,	19,039
Solomon Cowles,	10,000
Oliver Phelps	168,185
Asahel Hathaway,	12,000
John Caldwell and Peleg Sanford,	15,000
Timothy Burr,	15,231
Luther Loomis and Ebenezer King, Jr.,	44,318
William Lyman, John Stoddard and David King,	24,730
Moses Cleaveland,	32,600
Samuel P. Lord,	14,092
Roger Newberry, Enoch Perkins and Jonathan Brace,	38,000
Ephraim Starr,	17,415
Sylvanus Griswold,	1,683
Joseb Stocking and Joshua Stow,	11,423
Titus Street,	22,846
James Bull, Aaron Olmsted and John Wyles,	30,000
Pierpoint Edwards,	60,000
	$1,200,000

The committee of eight, immediately made deeds to these purchasers, of as many twelve hundred thousandths in common, of the entire tract, as they had subscribed dollars on the above list. These deeds and the subsequent drafts were recorded in the office of the Secretary of State, at Hartford; and afterwards transferred to the Recorders office at Warren. They are very lengthy, reciting the substance of the resolution, and the mode of sale to the grantees. It does not appear that any part of the consideration was paid in hand. [T. D. Webb.]

CONNECTICUT LAND COMPANY.

According to this record, the number of original parties was thirty-five, although it is generally represented as thirty-six. There were this number of bonds given to the State by them, for the above stated sums; which were secured by personal security at first, and afterwards mortgages upon the land. The first purchasers, however, represented other persons who were also constituted members of the company, fifty seven in number.

The different grantees in the deeds from Connecticut, gave the Trustees a list of the persons whom they represented, and the Trustees issued a stock certificate to each, in accordance with the articles of the association. Some of those who had given their bonds failed; and others persuaded the State to accept bonds and mortgages from them individually. They gave a bond to the Treasurer of State, and a mortgage of the lands which were aparted to them in severalty under the draft of 1798, east of the Cuyahoga.

They gave also another style of security, called

the "Trust and benefit mortgages," covering their interests in common then undrawn. These were so worded, that the Trustees of the Land Company, after draft, made another mortgage to the State, in which the original purchasers had the right of redemption. [LEONARD CASE.]

A partnership, or association, was immediately formed by the purchasers; who called themselves the "Connecticut Land Company"; all of whom joined in a deed of trust, to JOHN CALDWELL, JONATHAN BRACE, and JOHN MORGAN, covering the entire purchase. As special corporate powers were not given them by the Legislature, and doubts existed as to the validity of their political franchises; this course was necessary for the convenient management of their business. The trust deed bears date September 5, 1795, and with few exceptions, the deeds of the Trustees are the source of title, to lands on the Western Reserve. As late as 1836, all of the original Trustees were living, and joined in deeds of lands within this city.

OLIVER PHELPS, JOHN LIVINGSTON, and others, proposed to take the remainder, being the "excess," lying between the three million, and the five hundred thousand acre tracts. This scheme finally took the form of what is called the "Excess Company," of whom Gen. HULL, afterwards conspicuous at Detroit, was the principal owner. Shares in this company were sought after with as much eagerness as those in JOHN LAWS company of the Indies, having about the same basis of value.

The State guaranteed nothing either as to title or quantity. She only transferred all the rights she possessed, as well political as those of property under the patent of Earl WARWICK, and the charter of CHARLES the Second. So little was known at this time, of the respective powers of the States and the United States, under the Constitution of 1787, that many of the parties thought the Land Company had received political authority, and could found here a new State. They imagined themselves like WILLIAM PENN, to be proprietors, coupled with the rights of self government.

Articles of association, fourteen in number, were signed by the proprietors, on the same day with the trust deed. These articles are very elaborate, providing for the government of the company, giving extensive powers to the directors, pointing out in detail the mode of survey, partition and sale; authorizing transferable certificates of stock, and determining the manner of proceeding at meetings of the company. These articles of agreement were so full and particular that, no changes were found necessary, in order to carry on and complete the business of the company.

For the purpose of voting and assessments, the concern was divided into four hundred shares. Provision was made, in case one-third of the interest should demand it, to set off to the applicants one-third of the property in a body, but no such demand was made.

The affairs of the company were entrusted to the management of seven directors, and the gentlemen below named were elected to form the first board:

OLIVER PHELPS, of Suffield.
HENRY CHAMPION, 2nd, of Colchester.
MOSES CLEAVELAND, of Canterbury.
SAMUEL W. JOHNSON.
EPHRAIM KIRBY.
SAMUEL MATHER, Junior, of Lynn.
ROGER NEWBERRY, of West Windsor.

The annual meetings of the company were to be held in Hartford, in October, from whence New Connecticut was to be governed, as New England had been by the "Council of Plymouth" in England. It would be exceedingly interesting to reproduce the official transactions of the company, while it held the soil of the Western Reserve, from 1795 to 1809, if the limits of this book would admit. I can only touch upon their most prominent acts and proceedings.

They determined to extinguish the Indian claims, and survey their possessions into townships, of *five miles* square, bounded by lines crossing each other at right angles, to be run north and south, east and west. The proprietors were required to club together and draw by townships, as in a lottery; after which the owners received a deed, and made their own sub-divisions into lots. Twelve thousand nine hundred and three dollars and twenty-three cents of purchase money, represented a township in the first draft. To equalize the townships, a committee was appointed to explore them.

Moses Cleaveland, one of the directors, was made general agent, to conduct the surveys. Augustus Porter, of Salisbury, who had been engaged in surveys for Gorham and Phelps, in the Holland purchase since 1789, was made principal surveyor. Seth Pease, of Suffield, was given the place of mathematician and surveyor. He went to Philadelphia for instructions and instruments, to be procured of the astronomer, David Rittenhouse. The other surveyors were John Milton Holley, Richard M. Stoddard and Moses Warren, Jr. Their journey from Old Connecticut to New, with their boatmen, chainmen and axemen, is fully described in the extracts which I give from the journals of Cleaveland, Holley and Pease.

It has not been practicable to procure their diaries in full, or to insert them entire where they have been obtained.

The mode of dividing the property among its owners, was cumbrous; but was made so by a jealous regard to justice in the distribution. Six townships east of the Cuyahoga, were to be subdivided for sale, for the general benefit of the Company. Four more townships of the next best quality, were to be surveyed into four hundred lots, of one hundred and sixty acres each: equal to the number of shares, to be drawn by lot; three thousand dollars purchase money representing a share.

What remained on the east of the Cuyahoga, was to be divided into as many portions, to be called a draft, as there were townships of equal value. To come at this much coveted equality, the committee on partition, were required to select the best full township, as a draft; and add fractional townships, tracts, and lots, to all the others, until the less desirable ones, were made in all respects equal to the best.

The avails of the six townships, sold for the general benefit, after the general expenses were paid, were distributed in subsequent drafts.

In the first draft the committee on partition made *ninety-two* parcels, each equal in value to the best township, which parcels covered all the territory to be drawn east of the Cuyahoga.

By foreclosure or by arrangement, the State of Connecticut became the private owner of some lands on the Western Reserve, which were sold by her agents. The late LEONARD CASE, of Cleveland, transacted a large part of this business. Thus through forms and proceedings that are complicated, a simple and safe system of titles has been secured

SURVEYS OF 1796.

We owe many thanks to the surveyors, for their intelligence and industry in making note of events. Other members of the expedition of 1796–'97, kept memoranda of their travels, some of which will appear in their proper places. It is due to the general system of New England education, that her sons are able, wherever they go in unexplored countries, to record intelligibly, what passes under their observation.

JOHN MILTON HOLLEY'S JOURNAL.

This day, *April 28th*, 1796, started from Dover for Lake Erie, lodged first night at Jas. Dakins', second day at Col. Porter's; left there about 1 o'clock with friend Porter, lodged second night at Johnson's in Spencertown, third night at Wendell's Hotel, Albany.

Sunday dined at Shenectady, and lodged at Esquire Miles' in New Amsterdam, thence through

Ballantine and Germanflats, and lodged at TALCOTT's, next night at DEAN's in Westmoreland, and thence to MOREHOUSE's, thence to (torn off), thence to SANBORN's in Canandaiqua. (A portion lost.)

The 6th of May.—Lodged at Mons. SANBORN's in Canandaiqua, was gone to the Eutrantiquet (Ironduquoit) from Tuesday morning till Wednesday evening.

Tuesday, May 19th, '96.—Left Canandaiqua for Eutrantiquet bay, lodged at RICHARDSON's in Stonestown.

May 31st.—In the afternoon left Canandaiqua for Gerundicut (Ironduquoit) a second time.

STOW and STODDARD came from Sodus, on lake Ontario, with information that three boats were cast away, but no lives or property lost; in consequence of which we left Canandaiqua the 31st of May, for Gerundicut, slept the first night at HOWE's in Boughtontown.

June 1st.—went to the landing to see our boat, but as it had not arrived, PORTER, STOW and myself embarked on DUNBAR's boat, to go to the great lake to meet our boat, but as luck would have it we went in the boat about half a mile to the landing, unloaded, and PORTER with four hands returned to Little Sodus, to give relief to those who were cast away, and STOW and myself with our hands encamped on the Gerundicut. Built a bark hut, and the men lodged in it the first night. STOW and myself lodged on the floor at DUNBAR'S. Go to SMITH'S mill and see if there is any flour or wheat, and if so, if there are barrels, if not, call upon STEEL, get four barrels of pork at CHAPIN'S and two barrels of flour at CHAPMAN'S.

June 3d.—Gen. CLEAVELAND at evening arrived at Canandaiqua and gave us information that the boats had gone from Whitestown to Fort Stanwix, and Mr. STOW got a letter from the British minister, or charge des' affaires, to the commanding officer at Fort Oswego, requesting permission for our boats to pass unmolested. This information, together with the favorable prospect of wind and weather at that time, gave us great hopes that the stores would get on safely and rapidly, but on Saturday morning there sprang up in the north-west a storm, and blew most violently on the shore of the Lake. This proved fatal to one of the boats, and damaged another very much, though we went a little forward to a safe harbor, and built several fires on the bank of the Lake as a beacon to those coming on. After the disaster had happened, the boat that was safe went on to the Gerundicut with a load, and left the other three, including the one that was stove, at Little Sodus, encamped near the Lake. Among the passengers were two families, one of the women with a little child. The water at Gerundicut is about two rods wide and twelve to fourteen feet deep, very crooked and great obstruction for boats. Started for Canandaiqua and arrived on the morning of the 4th.

All these misfortunes happened in consequence of not having liberty to pass the fort at Oswego. Such are the effects of allowing the British government to exist on the continent of America.

June 5th.—The boats left Gerundicut for Niagara.

June 7th.—PARISH returned from Buffalo Creek, with information how the Indians would meet us. At this time the court was sitting at Canandáiqua. I heard my ftiend SALSTONSTALL make a plea in the case of Williamston *vs* Berry. SALSTONSTALL in favor of Berry.

June 14th.—Left Canandaiqua Tuesday for Buffalo creek, lodged first night at THAYERS', in the Gore, was very sick with the headache, second night at BERRY'S, on the bank of the Genesee river; and rode about two miles across the flat to the Indian settlement, six miles from here to Big Spring.

Thence about ten miles to Allen's creek, a stream about two rods wide, and not very deep, the bed is a solid rock, thence nine miles to the bend in Tonawanto creek, thence about sixteen miles to where we cross the creek—this stream is about twice as large as Allen's creek—that is, twice as much water, thence through long openings and swamps, or rather low lands, to Big Fall creek, here is almost a perpendicular fall of about forty feet. Thence to Buffalo creek. This stream runs nearly north, and empties into lake Erie about three miles from the outlet opposite to Fort Erie, it is about ten rods wide at its mouth, and very deep.

June 17th.—At evening we got to SKINNER's tavern, at Buffalo creek.

On the 18th, PORTER and myself went on the creek in a bark canoe, a fishing, and caught only three little ones.

Sunday, 19th June.—Left Buffalo in WINNEY's boat, for Chippewa, had a fair wind down, and arrived about one o'clock at Chippewa, dined at FANNING's, found our goods were not at the Gore, in Chippewa, and was obliged to go to Queenstown after them, and as I could not get a horse was obliged to walk. I got to Queenstown before night and lodged at Col. INGERSOLL's, next morning set out for Buffalo. On the way I stopped to take a view of Niagara Falls. That river, a little above Fort Slusher, is two and one half miles wide. Soon after this the water is very rapid, and continuing on, is hurried with amazing impetuosity down the most stupenduous precipice perhaps in nature. There is a fog continually arising, occasioned by the tumbling of the water, which, in a clear morning, is seen from lake Erie, at the distance of thirty or forty miles, as is the noise also heard. As the hands were very dilatory in leaving Chippewa, we were obliged to encamp on the great island in the river. We struck a fire and cooked some squirrels and pigeons, and a young partridge; two I eat for supper. I slept very sound all night, between a large log and the bank of the river. The next day arrived at Buffalo. About two o'clock this afternoon, the council fire with the Six Nations was uncovered, and at evening was again covered until morning, when it was opened again, and after some considerable delay, Captain BRANT gave General CLEAVELAND a speech in writing.

The chiefs, after this, were determined to get drunk. No more business was done this day. In the evening, the Indians had one of their old ceremonial dances, where one gets up and walks up and down between them, singing something, and those who sit around keep tune, by grunting.

Next morning, which was the 23d, after several speeches back and forth, from RED JACKET to General CLEAVELAND, Captain CHAPIN, BRANT, &c., &c.

General CLEAVELAND answered Captain BRANT'S speech. In short, the business was concluded in this way. General CLEAVELAND offered BRANT one thousand dollars as a present. BRANT, in answer, told General CLEAVELAND that their minds were easily satisfied, but that they thought his offer was not enough, and added this to it, that if he would use his influence with the United States, to procure an annuity of five hundred dollars par, and if this should fail, that the Connecticut Land Company should, in a reasonable time, make an additional present of one thousand five hundred dollars, which was agreed to. The Mohawks are to give one hundred dollars to the Senecas, and CLEAVELAND gave two beef cattle and whisky, to make a feast for them.

Thursday, June 23d.—FARMERS BROTHER, RED JACKET, and LITTLE BILLY, and GREEN GRASS HOPPER dined with the Commissioners. In the course of conversation RED JACKET gave his sentiments upon religion, which were to this purpose. You white people make a great parade about religion, you say you have a book of laws and rules which was given you by the Great Spirit, but is this true? Was it written by his own hand and given to you? No, says he, it was written by your own people. They do it to deceive you. Their whole wishes center here, (pointing to his pocket,) all they want is the money. (It happened there was a priest in the room at the same time who heard him.) He says white people tell them, they wish to come and live among them as brothers, and learn them agriculture. So they bring on implements of husbandry and presents, tell them good stories, and all appears honest. But when they are gone all appears as a dream. Our land is taken from us, and still we don't know how to farm it.

Monday, June 27th.—At five minutes after eleven o'clock we left Buffalo creek. Wind fair when we started, but soon came ahead. We went forward to

Cataragus creek, which is thirty-six miles by land, but not more than twenty-eight by water, where we encamped on the beach for the night. Early in the morning of the 28th we left Cataragus with a fair wind, but had not sailed one hundred rods before it came plump ahead, and we returned into the creek again, and pitched our tents for the day. The wind continued to blow very hard from the north-west, so long that we were obliged to remain there till the first of July. On Friday morning we left Cataragus creek with a fair wind, which lasted till about ten o'clock, when it came more ahead, but we continued rowing, and encamped the next night past the Pennsylvania line, and about sixteen miles from Presque Isle. Next morning run into Presque Isle harbor, by a quarter after ten in the morning—viewed the fort building there by the United States, and the old French fort which was built before the French war. It is now entirely demolished, and a town laid out upon the place. The wind sprang up and we could not land at the landing place, so we run over the bay about one mile to the peninsula and encamped. Here we lay till the next day at evening when we went up the bay to [*wanting.*]

FROM THE JOURNAL OF SETH PEASE.

June 21st.—I set out from Niagara fort, or Newark, went on foot to the landing above the falls, visited the cataract of Niagara; it takes a stone three seconds to fall from the top of the rock to the bottom.

June 22d.—We went on as far as Buffalo creek. The council began 21st, and ended Friday following. The present made the Indians was £500, New York currency, in goods. This the western Indians received.

To the eastern Indians they gave two beef cattle and one hundred gallons of whisky. The western also had provisions to help them home. The Indians had their keeping during the council.

Saturday, June 25th, 1796,—Sun's meridian:

Alt. Lower Limb, ○,	70°	15'	30"
Dip. Sub.,	0	1	25
Parallax +,	0	0	2
Refraction,	0	0	18
○, ½ Diam. +,	0	15	47
○ Declination,	23°	22	49
Sun,	47°	6'	30"
Latitude,	42°	53'	30"

of Buffalo Creek about thirty-five rods north of the mouth.

Monday, June 27th.—We started from Buffalo creek at 11 o'clock, A. M., to cross lake Erie. Steered south, 34° west. Our latitude at noon, forty-two, twenty minutes North. Got to Cataraugus, a convenient harbor.

Tuesday, June 28th.—We got under way about a

mile, the wind sprang up ahead; we tacked about and made the harbor; high wind and some rain.

Friday, July 1st.—We started from Cataraugus. Camped on the lake shore; our latitude forty-two degrees, fourteen minutes. Night calm and clear.

Saturday, we got to Presque Isle about 10 o'clock, A. M. In the afternoon we crossed the bay and camped on the beach. *Sunday*, wind a-head.

Sunday, July 3d.—On examination of the quadrant, we found that one hundred and eighty degrees measured one hundred and eighty degrees and four minutes, by the octant. We went on as far as the portage, got our boats and loading over and camped.

Monday, July 4th, Independence Day.—I traveled by land; good walking on the shore and bank; high springs and streams very plenty and good. We discovered Pennsylvania north line about 3 o'clock, P. M., a stone marked on the north side, and on the south, Pennsylvania forty-two degrees north latitude, variation, seven minutes thirty seconds west, &c.

Monday, July 4th, 1796.—We that came by land arrived at the confines of New Connecticut and gave three cheers precisely at 5 o'clock, P. M., we then proceeded to Conneaut at 5 hours 30 minutes; our boats got on an hour after; we pitched our tents on the east side.

Tuesday, 5th.—At camp. *6th.*—Traversed the Lake shore from the stone at forty-two degrees north latitude, to the stone at the north end of Pennsylvania line.

Thursday, 7th.—In the afternoon we began to measure the east line of New Connecticut. We run about two miles south and encamped by a pond in a swamp. Plenty of gnats and mosquitoes; poor water.

Friday, 8th.—We run about five miles. We crossed creek Independence. Land about middling. Went back one mile to camp; poor water.

EXTRACT FROM THE JOURNAL OF GENERAL MOSES CLEAVELAND.

On this creek ("Conneaught") in New Connecticut land, July 4th, 1796, under General Moses Cleaveland, the surveyors, and men sent by the Connecticut Land Company to survey and settle the Connecticut Reserve, and were the first English people who took possession of it. The day, memorable as the birthday of American Independence, and freedom from British tyranny, and commemorated by all good freeborn sons of America, and memorable as the day on which the settlement of this new country was commenced, and in time may raise her head amongst the most enlightened and improved States. And after many difficulties perplexities and hardships were surmounted, and we were on the good and promised land, felt that a just tribute of respect to the day ought to be paid. There were in all, including men, women and children, fifty in number. The men, under Captain TINKER ranged themselves on the beach, and fired a Federal salute of fifteen rounds, and then the sixteenth in honor of New Connecticut. We gave three cheers and christened the place Port Independence. Drank several toasts, viz:

1st. The President of the United States.

2d. The State of New Connecticut.

3d. The Connecticut Land Company.

4th. May the Port of Independence and the fifty sons and daughters who have entered it this day be successful and prosperous.

5th. May these sons and daughters multiply in sixteen years sixteen times fifty.

6th. May every person have his bowsprit trimmed and ready to enter every port that opens.

Closed with three cheers. Drank several pails of grog, supped and retired in remarkable good order.

July 5th.—Wrote letters to the directors and my wife. Two boats were dispatched under the direction of TINKER to Fort Erie, to bring the remainder of stores left there. The Conneaut is now choked with sand. The stream is capable of admitting boats the greater part of the year, up beyond the Pennsylvania line, which in a straight line cannot be more than four miles.

July 7th.—Received a message from the Paqua

Chief of the Massasagoes, residing in Conneaut, that they wished a council held that day. I prepared to meet them, and after they were all seated, took my seat in the middle. CATO, son of PAQUA, was the orator, PAQUA dictated. They opened the council by smoking the pipe of peace and friendship. The orator then rose and addressed me in the language of Indian flattery, "Thank the Great Spirit for preserving and bringing me there, thank the Great Spirit for giving a pleasant day," and then requested to know our claim to the land, as they had friends who resided on the land, and others at a distance who would come there. They wanted to know what I would do with them. I replied, informing them of our title, and what I had said to the Six Nations, and also assured them that they should not be disturbed in their possessions, we would treat them and their friends as brothers. They then presented me with the pipe of friendship and peace, a curious one, indeed. I returned a chain of wampum, silver trinkets, and other presents, and whisky, to the amount of about twenty-five dollars. They also said they were poor; and as I had expressed, hoped we should be friendly and continue to be liberal. I told them I acted for others as well as for myself, and to be liberal of others property was no evidence of true friendship; those people I represented lived by industry, and to give away their property lavishly, to those who live in indolence and by begging, would be no deed of charity. As long as they were industrious and conducted themselves well, I would do such benevolent acts to them as would be judged right, and would do them the most good, cautioned them against indolence and drunkeness. This not only closed the business, but checked their begging for more whisky.

July 10*th*.—Went with Capt. BUCKLAND about eight miles up the beach; wind ahead. Stopped at Jay creek, then went about three miles farther; part of the way slate rock, and trees had tumbled in; the surf high, making very hard walking on my return; lost one stocking; dined on the beach; went two miles farther and turned in, took a berth with great-coat under a hemlock.

July 11*th*.—Returned to Port Independence; a storm of rain coming on made it uncomfortable, and wet us very decently.

July 12*th*.—Dispatched STODDARD with four men to join PORTER, &c.

LETTER OF AMZI ATWATER.

MANTUA, Jan. 25th, 1846.

JOHN BARR, ESQ.,—*Dear Sir:*—I received your letter of the 10th inst., requesting some information respecting the landing at Conneaut, of the first surveying company on the Reserve, and the appearance of the harbor, &c. I have no means of informing you except from frail memory. But it appears to me the view was so stamped in my mind, that if I was a painter or engraver, I could give a good view of it as it then appeared. I think the following is as good a representation as I can now give:

PLAN OF THE MOUTH 1796.

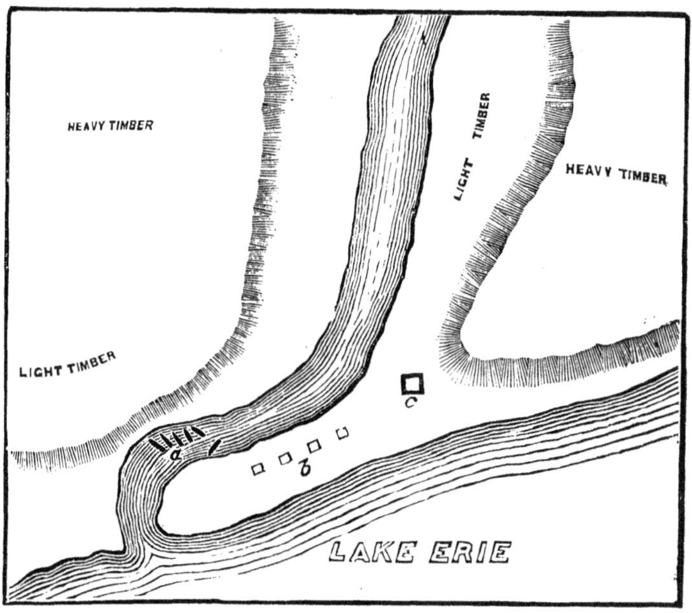

a,—Boats. *b*,—Tents. *c*,—Store House.

The lake at that time was very low, the beach was wide, and the lake calm. There was a wide space between the shore and the high bank, to the east of the mouth, which had resisted the force of the current and the waves, until there was considerable of a grove of midling sized timber grown on it. The south west wind had so long prevailed, that it had driven the creek back, and formed a wide sand bar down to the grove of timber, where it turned short into the lake. There was a considerable space left, between the creek and the high bank, which was covered with small timber and bushes. On this space the tents were pitched and the encampment established, until the store house was built. The store house was built at the end of the grove, near the short bend in the creek.

The boats were taken into the mouth of the creek, and lay along the south bank near the bend. The timber above the high bank, was in appearance like that of the lake shore generally, not very large, but tolerable straight and handsome. It was of a great variety, consisting of almost all the trees common in our country, except evergreens, which were very scarce on our lake shore. If an engraving should be made I wish there might be two. One to represent the appearance of the creek and surrounding shore, with three boats in the creek on the south side, and one entering the creek near the bend, with a group of men driving pack horses and cattle up the beach, near the creek. On the other the boats side by side, on the south side of the creek, near the bend, and further back, and a little up stream, the tents, and in front of them, the agent and surveyors holding the council with the Indians. But I am not a painter or an engraver, and can't direct.

I am well satisfied that the view which I herewith send is correct, except it may be not in a proper proportion, as to the length and breadth of the sand bar and beach. But I know they were then very wide.

Yours,

A. ATWATER.

INSTRUCTIONS OF THE DIRECTORS TO THEIR AGENT.

To MOSES CLEAVELAND, *Esq., of the county of Windham, and State of Connecticut, one of the Directors of the Connecticut Land Company, Greeting:*

We, the Board of Directors of said Connecticut Land Company, having appointed you to go on to said land, as Superintendent over the agents and men, sent on to survey and make locations on said land, to make, and enter into friendly negotiations with the natives who are on said land, or contiguous thereto, and may have any pretended claim to the same, and secure such friendly intercourse amongst them as will establish peace, quiet, and safety to the survey and settlement of said lands, not ceded by the natives under the authority of the United States. You are hereby, for the foregoing purposes, fully authorized and empowered to act, and transact all the above business, in as full and ample a manner as we ourselves could do, to make contracts in the foregoing matters in our behalf and stead; and make such drafts on our Treasury, as may be necessary to accomplish the foregoing object of your appointment. And all agents and men by us employed, and sent on to survey and settle said land, to be obedient to your orders and directions. And you are to be accountable for all monies by you received, conforming your conduct to such orders and directions as we may, from time to time, give you, and to do and act in all matters, according to your best skill and judgment, which may tend to the best interest, prosperity, and success of said Connecticut Land Company. Having more particularly for your guide the Articles of Association entered into and signed by the individuals of said Company.

Oliver Phelps,
Henry Champion,
Roger Newberry,
Samuel Mather, Jun.
} *Directors.*

SURVEYING PARTY OF 1796.

General Moses Cleaveland, *Superintendent.*

Augustus Porter, *Principal Surveyor and Deputy Superintendent.*

Seth Pease, *Astronomer and Surveyor.*

Amos Spafford, John Milton Holley, Richard M. Stoddard and Moses Warren, *Surveyors.*

Joshua Stow, *Commissary.*

Theodore Shepard, *Physician.*

EMPLOYEES OF THE COMPANY.

Joseph Tinker, *Boatman.*	Joseph M'Intyre,
George Proudfoot,	Francis Gray,
Samuel Forbes,	Amos Sawtel,
Stephen Benton,	Amos Barber,
Samuel Hungerford,	William B. Hall,
Samuel Davenport,	Asa Mason,
Amzi Atwater,	Michael Coffin,
Elisha Ayres,	Thomas Harris,
Norman Wilcox,	Timothy Dunham,
George Gooding,	Shadrach Benham,
Samuel Agnew,	Wareham Shepard,
David Beard,	John Briant.
Titus V. Munson,	Joseph Landon,
Charles Parker,	Ezekiel Morly,
Nathaniel Doan,	Luke Hanchet,
James Halket,	James Hamilton,
Olney F. Rice,	John Lock,
Samuel Barnes,	Stephen Burbank.
Daniel Shulay,	No. of Employees, 37

Elijah Gun, and Anna, his wife, came with the surveyors and took charge of Stow's castle at Conneaut.

Job P. Stiles, and Tabitha Cumi, his wife, were left in charge of the company's stores at Cleveland.

Nathan Chapman and Nathan Perry furnished the surveyors with fresh beef, and traded with the Indians.

There were thirteen horses and some cattle; which completes the party of 1796.

MODE OF EXECUTING THE SURVEYS.

Soon after the celebration of the 4th of July, 1796, had been completed, the surveyors with their parties entered upon their duties. A plan of survey determined upon by the company, was first to lay out upon the ground, the forty-first parallel of latitude, as a base line. From thence they were to run lines of longitude five miles apart, due north to lake Erie.

These were to be crossed by east and west lines, also five miles apart, all of which constituted the boundaries of townships, five miles square.

The townships were to be numbered as Ranges, counting from the Pennsylvania line as a meridian, westward, to the number of twenty-four; making one hundred and twenty miles. From the base line they are numbered northward, as Towns; to the shore of lake Erie. Thus Cleveland before it had a name as a township, was designated as No. 7, in the twelfth Range, being twelve townships west of the Pennsylvania line; and seven townships north of the forty-first parallel of latitude.

Port Independence at the mouth of the Conneaut river, is only a couple of miles within the State of Ohio.

In a few hours they found the west line of Pennsylvania, which had been run and cleared only a few years previous. A stone was set up where this line came to the lake, on which was marked the latitude; and which was barely within the limits of the State of Connecticut on the north, according to her grants and charter. Her claims under these instruments, were limited to the parallel of forty-two degrees and two minutes north; on which the lines of Connecticut and Pennsylvania are now fixed. The parties proceeded down the Pennsylvania line, measuring as they went; in order to assist them in finding the forty-first parallel, and also to determine the variation of their compasses. Mr. Holley's journal is so complete a narrative, that I insert it almost without abbreviation.

HOLLEY'S JOURNAL—CONNEAUT TO THE SOUTH EAST CORNER OF THE RESERVE.

Thursday, July 7th, 1796.—Left Conneaut creek in company with Augustus Porter, Seth Pease, and five other men for the south east corner of New Connecticut. We came to the north corner of Pennsylvania, and ran down about five or six rods west of the line. At four miles and sixty-six chains, crossed the Conneaut creek. The banks here are steep. To the end of the eighth mile the land is very similar to the first four or five, not well watered at all. To the end of the thirteenth mile, the land has every appearance of being over flowed in the wet seasons. On the fourteenth mile the land rises and falls, and of course is better. At sixty chains we stop and encamp on high ground for the night. Here, by a very good observation of the Polar star at its greatest eastern elongation, we took the variation of the needle, (which was one degree, thirty-five minutes east elongation of the star.) By a second observation, next morning with the ranges it appeared to be one degree, thirty minutes, (the stars elongation.) The needle varied fifty-three minutes east. PORTER'S compass and mine varied alike. Major SPAFFORD'S ten minutes less. The land to the end of the nineteenth mile is ridgy and better watered, covered with almost all kinds of timber. On the twentieth mile an open Tamarach swamp, twenty-eight chains wide. To the end of the twenty-third mile the land is indifferent, swampy.

Monday, July 11th.—We were stopped by the rain, and encamped near an excellent brook, which we considered a very favorable circumstance. The next morning we left this place and went on to the end of the twenty-fifth mile, through the most abominable swamp in the world. The twenty-sixth mile is part of good bottom land, if it can be kept from over flowing in summer, which I doubt some. On the twenty-seventh mile is a creek (Pymatuning) about sixty links wide. The water before this had all ran north, but when we first came upon this stream the course was north east, then a little way and it was south west, then crooked again and ran south east, and continued on pretty much this course. It is a smooth stream five or six feet deep, and navigable for batteaux. The land on each side is rich, but to all appearance is covered with water the greater part of the year; where we came upon the creek the second time we crossed upon a beaver dam, which was quite a curiosity. The dam consisted of some large sticks or trees thrown across the stream, and filled in with thousands of willows and other small wood; which was so compact as to make considerable of a pond above, from which, through a rich soil was cut several canals and arms, where they live now, as is evident from fresh tracks and newly cut chips and brush. * * *

Tuesday, July 12th.—In the morning we breakfasted in our camp by the little brook, and left the pack horse men to come on after us, but when we had proceeded about a mile, we sent back a hand to tell the men to go round the swamp with the horses, but the swamp continued, and we ran on till night. Here being a hemlock ridge, we were in hopes the horses would be able to find us, but alas! we were obliged to make a little camp of boughs, strike up a fire, and go to bed supperless. In the day time I had eat raspberries, gooseberries, wintergreen berries and wintergreens, and in the night I began to grow sick at my stomach, and soon after vomited up every thing that was in me. Mr. PEASE too had a turn of the cramp, in consequence of traveling all day in the water. We all arose early in the morning, with meagre looks and somewhat faint for want of eating and drinking, for where we camped there was no water, though we had a little rum.

On the morning of the 13th we continued our course down the Pennsylvania line two hundred and sixty rods, through an alder swamp, till we came to a ridge of oak, beach, pine, &c., where we determined to stop and wait the coming of provisions. Mr. PORTER and Mr. HALL took the compass, and were to travel east twenty minutes, to try and find the horses' tracks if they had passed. Mr. PEASE and Mr. SPAFFORD took my compass, and were to do the same to the west, while I stayed on the line. I made up a fire, and was clearing a spot to lie down, when to my joy and surprise I heard a voice back of us, which I quickly answered, and found to be JOSEPH LANDON, one of the pack horsemen (and a good fellow too,) coming with a back load of provisions. We called PORTER and PEASE back as soon as possible, and all partook of a most cheerful and much needed breakfast. After this was over, Mr. PORTER, HALL and LANDON went to help the horses on, as they had found the swamp so large that it was impossible to go round it, and they were obliged to come through, and were about three and a half miles behind. Mr. PEASE, SPAFFORD and myself staid to take care of the packs, &c. After a little time, Mr. SPAFFORD and myself went about half a mile east to the large creek to fish, but were unsuccessful. We returned to PEASE, and enjoyed the day as well as possible. It is now twenty minutes after seven, and we have just heard the voices of our friends returning. The land to the end of the twenty-eighth mile is low, but the soil is rich. There are two runs of water on this mile. The thirtieth mile is fine intervale land; a creek thirty links wide. On the thirty-first mile is a fine creek twenty-five links wide; bottom stony; brisk current; another creek twenty links wide, north-east; land more ridgy, soil good. On thirty-second mile is fine land for wheat; timber chestnut, white oak and maple rises and descends. On the thirty-third mile is a good run of water, good land and ridgy. On the thirty-fourth mile is a fine spring. To the end of the thirty-seventh mile the land is good, level and timbered with maple, beach, oak and white wood, with herbage. The land to the end of the forty-first mile is gentle, rises and descends, good, and timbered with white and black oak, chestnut, pepperage, cucumber and white wood. At the end of the forty-second mile we encamped about 3 o'clock, and waited till morning. From the Pennsylvania line here, we had a most pleasing prospect, a hill at the distance of four or five miles, with the valley that lay between, covered with stately trees and herbage, which indicated an excellent soil, altogether exhibited a delightful landscape, the beauty of which, I suppose, was enhanced from its being the first time we could overlook the woods.

July 16*th*.—On Saturday morning a party of five, ordered by Mr. PORTER, came up. The woods being wet, in consequence of the rain the evening before, we delayed starting till after noon. From this place two men with one pack horse, returned to creek Independence, for provision. We proceeded on our way with five horses. Land to the end of the forty-third mile is composed of rises and descends, the whole generally descends to the south west. The soil rich, timbered with black and white oak, chestnut and black walnut, undergrowth of the same hung together with grape vines. There are three fine springs on this mile. At the last end of the forty-fourth mile we crossed a large smooth stream (Shenango) one chain and twenty-five links wide, course east, stony bottom, banks tolerably high, as far as we could see it was good boating; we waded the stream, it was about two and a half feet deep, but an uncommon dry time. Forty-fifth mile, land rises and descends. Timber, oak and hickory; soil good for grain. On the forty-sixth mile near a run, course east, we encamped for the night.

Sunday, July 17th.—Continued on; the land is level, and good timber, maple, black oak, beech and ironwood. Forty-seventh mile, the first part level, the last part very steep ridges; timbered with oak, the soil poor. The forty-eighth mile more gentle rises, land better, pretty well watered. Forty-ninth mile is very abrupt ridges, stony and poor land, oak timber, and whintleberries. To the end of the fifty-second mile land very much as last described. On the fifty-second mile the land descends to the east, and we overlook several large ridges; on this also, there are large stones which appear like grindstones. On the fifty-third mile we crossed a large creek or river abont two chains and fifty links wide; bottom gravelly, current brisk, abounds with fish, course south west. We waded this and found the depth at this dry season to be more than waist high. We supposed this to be the same stream we crossed on the forty-fourth mile, with the addition of all others that we passed. On this creek is good bottom land timbered with red elm, cherry, crab apple trees, plumb and thorn bush. This has been a wet uncomfortable day. In the morning when we started from our encampment three of our men were looking for the horses that had strayed.

Monday, July 18th.—In the morning. Our horses

have not yet came. It is beginning to rain and we have concluded not to leave our encampment.

Tuesday, July 19th.—We continued our line south. At about one hundred rods from the camp we crossed the river again, where it appears navigable for boats. About twelve rods from the river we crossed a creek four rods wide, gravel bottom. Mr. PORTER went about one half mile up this and found course to be east and west running east. We soon rose on the high land, timbered to the end of the fifty-sixth mile, the land is very similar—rises and descends; timber oak, some maple and beech, well watered, soil in many places good. On the fifty-seventh mile is some interval on a creek twenty-five links wide. Rest of land ridgy and stony. To the end of the sixtieth mile land is ridgy. Land on the sixty-first mile descends to the south; soil a fine light red loam, which is excellent. On the sixty-second mile land continued to descend south, gradually. Encamped on this mile. From the rain yesterday and a shower this morning we have been wet and uncomfortable all day.

Wednesday, July 20th.—Land on sixty-second mile, low and moist. Land on sixty-third mile is excellent and handsome, rises and descends. Sixty-fourth mile, land flat and wet. On the sixty-fifth mile, for seventy chains, descends gently to the south, thinly timbered with white and black oak, undergrowth same kind, and grapevines; at seventy-two chains, to an *Indian path east and west*, we descend on a good intervale. On the sixty-sixth mile we encamped, at five chains, on the north side of a river. This we find to be Big Beaver river (Mahoning.) The course is east, current gentle but brisk, gravel bottom and low banks. It is about four feet deep; we measured across by trigonometry and found it to be about fifteen rods wide. After we came away, LANDON told us he saw two men in a canoe on the opposite shore, and called them to him. They told him they had been at work there (about fifty rods down the river, on the Pennsylvania side,) three years; that the salt springs were about eighteen miles up the river, and they were then going there to make salt; they had not got their families on yet, but should ere long; that about twelve miles below the line, on Big Beaver river, there was an excellent set of mills, and about twenty-five miles below the line, there was a town building rapidly, where provisions of every kind could be procured, and from thence carried by water up the Big Beaver into the heart of the Connecticut Reserve. There are no falls to the source; and it is but sixty miles from the line down to Pittsburgh. Below the town, and above Pittsburgh, there are falls, and a carrying place of two miles. The Big Beaver falls into the Allegheny twenty-five miles below Pennsylvania line. The stream we crossed before is the Little Beaver, and joins with the others. This information we did not get till we had got three miles south of the river, else we should have sent down to the mills. On the forty-second mile, where we encamped, we heard an ox bell and a smaller one off to our right hand, and several of our men went in search of it, supposing there might be inhabitants, but as they descended the hill they lost the sound, and returned without discovering anything, but our conjectures proved true, the men told LANDON that there was a family living there on the Little Beaver. Thursday afternoon we arrived at the corner, and prepared to make an observation of the polar star for the variation of compass. The next day Mr. PORTER and PEASE fixed the quadrant for an observation of the sun at noon. The day was fair and their observation was good. In the evening we again took the variation by the star, and Mr. PEASE observed several of the stars for the latitude. After comparing observations they make the latitude to be forty-one degrees twenty seconds north. We set a large square oak post, on which is July 23d, 1796, north side.

Saturday July 23d.—Mr. WARREN, with a party of thirteen, arrived last evening. Saturday after-noon Mr. PORTER went down to the corner, and set a chestnut post, sixteen inches by twelve, on the south side is latitude forty-one degrees north, variation one minute twenty-one seconds east, west side is south-east corner New Connecticut.—July 23d 1796,

14

on north side, sixty-eight miles Lake Erie; east side, Pennsylvania.

Sunday morning, July 24th, 1796.—I took nine days' provisions and five hands, and am to start as soon as possible with a line for the Lake shore.

This morning Mr. PORTER, STODDARD and LANDON, set out to go down the Big Beaver in search of provisions; took with them two days' allowance for three hands."

Thus after they had distributed themselves along the base line, HOLLEY ran up the first range line, SPAFFORD the second, WARREN the third, and PEASE and PORTER the fourth. The compasses did not work together. Some of their meridian lines converged, while others diverged, causing a variation of half a mile before reaching the Lake. When the cross lines were run, these differences were found to be very material.

The early surveys of the Government of the United States were conducted in the same manner, but it was soon found necessary, in using an instrument subject to so many fluctuations as the ordinary compass, to make a correction of each township line before proceeding to the next. This is done by running a random line across the north end of each township and correcting back. By the system employed on the Western Reserve, the townships were not equal in quantity.

FRESH POWERS GIVEN TO THE AGENT AND SURVEYORS.

HARTFORD, August 26, 1796.

MOSES CLEAVELAND, ESQ.—*Sir*:—The Board of Directors think it advisable, expecting the measure will be approved by the Company at their meeting in October, to request that you, Mr. STOW, Mr. PORTER and the other four surveyors, will consider yourselves a committee to divide the lands in the Western Reserve, according to the mode of partition determined upon by the Company in April. And to effect this you will perhaps judge it expedient, to postpone surveying any of the lots in the six townships for the present, however, this must be left for you to decide upon.

In case the surveys can be completed so far this summer, as that partition can be made according to the mode pointed out, it is the particular wish of the Directors, that this be done in preference to anything else. If partition can be made in the course of the ensuing winter, it will essentially forward the settlement of the lands, and be of very considerable advantage to the proprietors.

If you are of opinion that this object can be accomplished, it will be necessary to obtain information in regard to the quality of the lands in the different townships. The mode of partition agreed to by the Company in April, will determine you what steps are necessary to be taken in this business.

The mode of partition and the articles of agreement entered into with Gen. HULL, so far as they relate to the excess, must be particularly attended to. And unless the lines of the whole territory can be run, so as to ascertain the quantity of the excess, no partition at present can be made. This we conceive may be done, by running a line *from* the north-east boundary upon lake Erie, to the river Cuyahoga, and from thence taking a *traverse*, and continuing the line upon the lake to the north-west boundary, making one hundred and twenty miles.

In respect to the five townships, which the Directors were authorized to sell by the constitution, so many of them as remain unsold, we believe would be well for you to dispose of to best advantage, having particular regard to actual settlement being made; and the greater number of actual settlers the *more* for the interests of the company. And in respect to the township in which by the constitution the first settlements are to be made, and which was to be surveyed into small lots, and those lots sold and disposed of to actual settlers only, we are of the opinion that the sales made to any one settler, ought not to exceed one hundred and fifty or two hundred acres; and that not more than one half of the township be disposed of at present. And in case of your making sales of any of said lots, to sell only to actual settlers. These communications are not intended to interfere with any engagements which you or Mr. PORTER may have made prior to the reception of this letter.

The knowledge which you, and the surveyors have obtained of the Western Reserve, will enable you much more readily to equalize the townships, than any other person. If a committee were to go on to the territory next spring, it would take the whole summer for them, to obtain the information you are possessed of in respect to the land, and would, at the same time, occasion one year's delay in the settlement, use and sale of them.

Should the capital town, viz: the town ordered by the constitution to be surveyed into small lots, not be surveyed this season, it can be done early next spring. The principal object of attention at present seems to be, to make partition of the Reserve as soon as possible.

If equalizing the townships cannot be done this season, it will take most of next summer to effect it, and at very considerable expense. Of course, none of the lands will be sold, and those persons, who are now so engaged to purchase and settle in the Reserve, will look out for settlements elsewhere, which will probably depreciate the value of the lands.

In the mode of partition it is ordered that four of the best townships, be surveyed into lots of one hundred to a township, &c. This can be dispensed with this year, and a division of the rest be made. These four townships can be surveyed into lots next spring, and a division then take place consistent with the mode of division.

Please to write us on the subject of this letter, as soon as you can with convenience.

We are, sir, with sentiments of esteem,

Yours,

OLIVER PHELPS,
HENRY CHAMPION, 2D.
ROGER NEWBERRY.

HOLLEY'S experience in running one of the meridians will serve as a description of the others, which cannot be given in a more interesting form, than in the language of his own field books, omitting the immaterial portions.

"*Monday, July 23d*, 1796.—Left the south line of New Connecticut with PARKER, HAMILTON, GRAY and DAVENPORT, from the first five mile post, north on variation one degree forty seconds east.

Friday, 24th. — Nineteenth mile: encamped in consequence of rain. M'INTYRE came up and brought some bear's meat, which he dried; dry venison and flour.

Monday, Aug. 1st.—Rainy and cloudy. Sent off M'INTYRE for provisions to Conneaut.

Aug. 2d.—Thirty-fourth mile. Took variation, (night of 2d and 3d.) Cloudy; observation bad; my eyes sore; variation two degrees twenty-three seconds. Was obliged to trust to PARKER to see the star and line; dare not run on it; ran on one degree thirty-seven seconds, being that of the Pennsylvania line opposite.

Aug. 5th.—Forty-sixth mile; encamped; cloudy; could not get the variation. M'INTYRE came to us with provisions, and was most joyfully received, as we were then eating our last dinner but one.

Aug. 8th.—Sixtieth mile; at night took variation, one degree fifty-three seconds east.

Aug. 10th.—Sixty-sixth mile; came to the bank of the Lake at forty-eight chains 50 links. Set a chestnut post twelve inches square, marked south side, sixty-five miles, forty-eight chains fifty links, &c. * * *

Just as we were starting for Conneaut, we saw a large party coming along the beach, and supposing them to be Indians, and having only a gill of rum left in our bottle, we were hurrying to a spring to drink it before they could come up, and tease us for it. But to our astonishment, we found them to be two of the parties of surveyors coming in together.

PORTER and PEASE had run their line through to the Lake with all speed, and came to where SPAFFORD and STODDARD struck the Lake, just as they were cutting the last tree. We had a most joyful meeting, and had not proceeded far before we met Esquire WARREN and his party, returning to bring up their line, which they had left seventeen miles from where they started out. Altogether they had what was supposed to be *thirteen* days' provisions.

This meeting was not so cordial as the other had been.

We arrived at Conneaut two hours before sundown, and stayed until we had eaten the fatted calf."

While the four parties were engaged in running up the first four meridians, CLEAVELAND, after conciliating the Indians, made an excursion to the site of the future city, which should bear his name. He reached here on the 22d of July. All of the party must have felt unusually interested, as they approached the spot. Not one of them had seen the place.

As they coasted close along the shore, overhung by a dense green forest, mirrored in the waters over which they were passing, the mouth of the river disclosed itself, as a small opening, between low banks of sand. The man who controls the party, is seated in the stern, steering his own craft; which is gracefully headed into the stream.

His complexion was so swarthy, his figure so square and stout, and his dress so rude; that the Indians supposed some of the blood of their race had crept into his veins.

JOSHUA STOW was probably at this time in this pioneer boat. As they passed into the channel, and the broad river unfolded itself to their view; bordered by marshes, reeds, and coarse grass; their anticipations must have been somewhat moderated.

The flats on the west side, and the densely wooded bluffs on the east, did not present a cheerful prospect for a city. They were confined to the eastern shore, by their agreement with the Indians at Buffalo, and at Conneaut.

It was necessary to proceed some distance along this shore, before there was solid ground enough to effect a landing. As the Indians had, from generation to generation, kept open a trail along the margin of the lake, it is probable that CLEAVELAND'S party, scanning with sharp eyes every object as they rowed along the river, saw where the aboriginal highway descended the hill, along what is now Union lane. Here they came to the bank, and scrambling out, trod for the first time the soil of the new city. While the boat was being unloaded, the agent had an opportunity to mount the bluff, and scan the surrounding land. This view must have revived his enthusiasm, more than the swamps along the river had depressed it. A young growth of oaks, with low bushy tops, covered the ground. Beneath them were thrifty bushes, rooted in a lean, but dry and pleasant soil, highly favorable to the object in view. A smooth and even field sloped gently towards the lake, whose blue waters could be seen extending to the horizon. His imagination doubtless took a pardonable flight into the future, when a great commercial town, should take the place of the stinted forest growth, which the northen tempests had nearly destroyed. But whatever may have been his anticipations, the reality has outstripped them all. Such a combination of natural beauty, with natural advantages of business, is rarely witnessed; to which have been added, what the surveyors could not have foreseen, artificial aids to commerce then unknown.

It is not certainly known, but probably Stiles, and perhaps his wife, were of this party. Enough men were left to put up a store house for the supplies, and a cabin for the accommodation of the surveyors. These rude structures were located a short distance south of St. Clair street, west of Union lane, at a spring on the side hill, in rear of Scott's warehouse. During the season, a cabin was put up for Stiles, on Lot 53, east side of Bank street, north of the Herald Building, where Morgan & Root's Block is now being erected. Thus was the settlement of the city commenced.

By authorities, which will be given hereafter, it will be seen, that houses had before this been built by white people, near the mouth of the river; but not for the purpose of permanent settlement. Col. James Hillman avers, that he put up a small cabin on the east side of the river in 1786, near the foot of Superior street, of which, however, nothing further is known. Sometime previous to 1787, a party who were wrecked, upon a British vessel, between one and two miles east of the river, built an hut, large enough to shelter themselves, through one winter. On the west side of the river, a log store house was erected, prior to 1786, to protect the flour which was brought here from Pittsburg, on the way to Detroit. This building, in a dilapidated state, was standing in 1797, when it was occupied awhile by JAMES KINGSBURY and his family.

Some cabins were erected during the summer near the shore, beyond Euclid creek, which are noticed in the journals of HOLLEY and PEASE. The design and origin of this embryo settlement, is not yet well understood. No one is known to have remained there during the winter of 1796–7.

A Frenchman is reported to have been at Sandusky, not as a settler but a trader. At that time proceeding west of Buffalo; the first white inhabitants on the south shore of lake Erie were located at Erie, Pa.; the next, the families of GUN and KINGSBURY, at Conneaut; and the last and only other settlers, on this bleak wilderness coast were STILES and his wife, at Cleveland, with whom EDWARD PAINE was domiciled as a boarder.

The "Excess Company" must have based their hopes of territory upon the map of EVANS, which represented the south shore of the lake as bearing too much westerly. If it had proved to be true, that from the north-east corner of the Reserve; the coast line was nearly west, their expected surplus might have been realized. Had the English military expeditions, carried instruments for astronomical observations, this great error would have been avoided.

The surveyors were directed to fix this coast line in 1796, not by observations but by a traverse of the shore, made by chain and compass. This work was entrusted to Mr. PORTER, under the supervision of General CLEAVELAND. West of the Cuyahoga, it was to be executed without the consent of the Indians, which rendered the undertaking somewhat hazardous.

They now immediately commenced the traverse of the lake shore. PORTER acting as surveyor, measuring westward along the coast; in order to find where the west line of the Reserve would intersect lake Erie. WARREN, PEASE, SPAFFORD, and HOLLEY again took to the woods, in order to run some parallels westward, from the Pennsylvania line to the Cuyahoga river. WARREN had the town line between Nos. six and seven, Range one. (Vernon and Kinsman.) PEASE between towns seven and eight; SPAFFORD and STODDARD between towns eight and nine, and HOLLEY, between towns nine and ten, or the townships of Hanover and Richmond, Ashtabula county. The extracts which I shall give, from the memoranda of HOLLEY and ATWATER; detail the movements of the surveyors so fully, during the season, that it will not be necessary to notice them particularly. The parallels they were now running should bring them out near the mouth of the Cuyahoga, the line between seven and eight passing through the city of Cleveland. In order to keep strict faith with the Indians, they were directed not to cross the Cuyahoga river, to cut any trees, or make any marks, on the west side. All of the parties when they reached the Chagrin river, supposed they were at the Cuyahoga. The best maps they could procure had no river upon them, between the Grand river and the Cuyahoga. The surveyors were sorely perplexed on encountering this stream, and proceeded down it to the lake.

Much discussion has taken place upon the origin of the name of the Chagrin river. THOMAS HUTCHINS in his "Topographical Description of Virginia, Pennsylvania, &c.," in 1778, notices a stream by the name of "Shaguin," which is said to mean in some Indian language, the "clear water." On HUTCHINS' map of 1764, no important streams are given between the "Cyahoga" and Presque Isle. It is thus not easy to determine what river is meant by the Shaguin. The surveyors all speak of it as then known, as the Chagrin. Grand river is a name evidently of French origin, its Indian name being "Sheauga," from whence the term Geauga is derived, by a very natural corruption. It is highly probable that Chagrin is a title given by the French traders, to this stream from some accident or suffering, such as occurred at Misery river, of lake Superior.

SURVEY OF THE PARALLELS,

AND

SOME OF THE TOWNSHIPS.

FROM HOLLEY'S JOURNAL, 1796.

Conneaut, Saturday Morning, Aug. 13th.— PEASE'S, SPAFFORD'S and my own company, left and went to my line, and down it, to our several places, to start lines for the Cuyahoga. PEASE, SPAFFORD and myself stayed a little longer at Conneaut, and not meeting soon enough, we were obliged to go without dinner. Before night, they came up with us, and we encamped that night and the next together. Early in the morning of the 15th, which was Monday, I left my forty-five mile post, for the Pennsylvania line.

Ran east to the Pennsylvania line with PARKER, SHEPARD, HAMILTON, HACKET, FORBES, and DAVENPORT, Pennsylvania line, at five miles, nineteen chains, fifty links; four chains eighty-eight links north of the twenty-third mile post (from the lake).

Tuesday, Aug. 16th.—Ran west from forty-fifth mile post, first meridian.

Aug. 23d.—Forty-sixth mile at forty chains, eighty links, a river, supposed to be the Cuyahoga, sun two hours high, PARKER and myself set off down the river, to find some marks where PORTER had been along; went three miles in the rain; no marks were to be found; I supposed they had not been up the river, but from every circumstance thought it must be the Cuyahoga, and determined to begin the traverse in the morning.

Wednesday, Aug. 24th.—Began the traverse of the Cuyahoga, as we supposed. We had completed about five miles, when we were overtaken by HALL and MUNSON, who had been in search of us, supposing we might mistake the river, who told us that it was not the Cuyahoga, but the Chagrin, and that friend PORTER was in the mouth of it, waiting to supply us with provisions.

As soon as I heard this I left the traverse, and traveled about three-quarters of a mile, when we came to the lake, a little east of PORTER's encampment. We met with glad hearts. The same night a fair wind sprung up, and PORTER, with his party, left us for Cuyahoga, to supply PEASE with provisions.

Thursday, Aug. 25th.—Left the mouth of Chagrin river. At twelve o'clock, traveled up to where I hit the river first, then followed my line back to the fortieth mile stake.

Aug. 26th.—Ran north on a magnetic course for the lake.

Aug. 27th.—Seven miles, sixty-two chains, fifty links, came to the lake. Returned to the five mile post.

Sunday, Aug. 28th.—Started a line (east) from a five mile post, between ranges eight and nine, and fifty miles from the south line, variation one degree, fifty-six minutes east.

Aug. 30th.—Thirteenth mile. No musquitoes or gnats to plague us.

Monday, Sept. 5th, 1796.—Pennsylvania line at thirty-nine miles sixty chains and eighty-nine links. From thence traveled to Conneaut, and arrived sun about two hours high. We found that Monsieur TINKER had not returned with the boat from "Gerundicut," and Mr. STOW had taken all provisions and stores of every kind, except some few articles of little consequence, packed them up and carried them to the beach to go on board the boat for Cuyahoga.

He had tried in vain twice to load the boat, in consequence of which I saw him, and found he had left about seventy-five pounds pork, and other provisions in proportion. I learned from him that after more serious consideration, Mr. PORTER had determined to alter his first plan of doing the surveying, which was, for me to finish the lines north of the one I had run west, which would continue to grow shorter, the other surveyors to complete the long lines to the south. But as the season is so far advanced, they could not possibly do this and lot the towns on the Cuyahoga, that was necessary. It was concluded that PEASE, SPAFFORD, and STODDARD should run short lines till PORTER could complete the traverse of the lake, west of the Cuyahoga, and I bring up my line. Then we are all to begin upon the towns that are to be settled, some upon the city lots, and others upon that for farms to be sold this fall.

Tuesday, Sept. 6th.—The wind is so favorable this morning that Mr. STOW, loaded his boat, and started for Cuyahoga. Just as he was loading Mr. HUMPHREY, from the New Town settlement, in the Genesee purchase came up with a boat and several men, all proceeding to Cuyahoga, and if proper encouragement was held out, were determined to become settlers. Some persons were with him from Susquehannah, west branch.

One of them who was rather unwell, stayed at Conneaut, and informed me that about two weeks before, he saw JAMES CAMPBELL, and that he was hearty, and in profitable business, surveying about the head waters of the west branch of Susquehannah, and on the Allgheny mountains. Also WEST and SCHOFIELD.

Thursday, Sept. 8th.—Left "Conneaut," to run a line to the lake, and then through to Cuyahoga.

Sept. 9th.—Traveled south to the fifty-fifth mile post and ran east to the Pennsylvania line, five miles, twenty-nine chains, and fifty links.

Sept. 10th.—Ran west from my fifty-fifth mile post.

Sept. 11th.—Thirteenth mile (from Pennsylvania line) variation one degree, thirty minutes.

Sept. 12th.—Came to WARREN's line, twenty chains and thirty-eight links south of his fifty-fifth mile post.

Sept. 14th.—Thirtieth mile complete, ranges six and seven, ran north to lake, (magnetic) two miles, fourteen chains, eighty-three links.

Sept. 16th.—Traveled on the beach towards Cuyahoga. Ate dinner at Grand river. Encamped a little east of the Chagrin river; HAMILTON, the cook, was very cross and lazy—was on the point of not cooking any supper because the bark would not peal, and he knew of nothing to make bread upon, DAVENPORT wet some in the bag.

Encamped Sept. 16th, about three miles east of Cuyahoga—rained and blew very hard towards day.

Saturday, Sept. 17th.—Traveled to the mouth of the river, and after searching considerable time found our friends encamped a little way up the river. Stormy in the afternoon and evening. Variations, PORTER's compass varied one degree, thirty-seven minutes, seven miles up on the fourth meridian, one degree, forty-two minutes at commencement of the thirty-ninth mile, same meridian at the nineteenth mile. Down the Pennsylvania line Mr. PORTER'S compass and mine varied alike fifty-three minutes east, SPAFFORD'S ten minutes less.

42d mile down Penn. line,	HOLLEY'S	compass was	1° 40′ E.
"	PORTER'S	" "	1° 35′ E.
"	SPAFFORD'S	" "	1° 35′ E.
At the S. E. cor. or Reserve	PORTER'S	" "	1° 21′ E.
"	HOLLEY'S	" "	1° 40′ E.
At 33½ miles up 1st merid.	"	" "	2° 23′
" " "	"	ran at	1° 37′
" 35 ms. 51 chs. " "	"	compass was	2° 15′
" " "	"	ran at	2° 00′
" 60 miles 1st merid.	"	compass was	1° 53′
Nine miles up his merid. (2d)	SPAFFORD'S "	"	1° 27′
29½ "	" "	" "	1° 23′
50 ms. 60 chs. "	" "	" "	1° 20′

Ran from SPAFFORD'S line at 1° 30′ E. from PORTER'S 4th meridian and to Cuyahoga at .... 1° 50′

Wednesday, Sept. 21*st.*—At twelve o'clock, M., we packed up everything, and embarked on board the boat for Conneaut, in consequence of not having provisions to stay any longer. We had not a mouthful of meat when we went away, part of a barrel of flour, a bag of flour and two cheeses, and some chocolate, constituted our provisions, (about 30 in number). The two boats and the bark canoe carried us. We had a fair wind, and had sailed about eight miles, when we discovered HALL & Co., on the beach with the cattle. We then went ashore, and found by them that TINKER had arrived at Conneaut with provisions. Esquire WARREN also was there. He sent on two of his men with two horses loaded with flour. Himself and other hands waited to come with TINKER, when the wind should be favorable. This news cheered us up exceedingly, and we returned to Cuyahoga with much lighter hearts than we left it. It was dark when we came to the mouth of the river, and we discovered a fire lighted on the opposite shore.

Just as we entered, PARKER fired a gun. As we passed we saluted the people, and found that they were Indians, from Grand River, who had been west, hunting. We eat a mouthful of supper, and went to bed.

Began to lot the east part of Cuyahoga town, at two and a half miles from the east line, at a corner, on the line that STODDARD ran west into said town.

Thursday, Sept. 22d.—Left Cuyahoga, to lot the east part of the township with SHEPHERD and SPAFFORD. The day before we started from Cuyahoga, we discoved a bear swimming across the river. PORTER and myself jumped into a canoe, and paddled after him, while another man went with a gun up the shore. But there was such a noise and hallooing, that the bear swam back and escaped. MUNSON caught a rattle snake, which we broiled and ate.

Sunday, Sept. 25th.—This day have been troubled with a dysentery, on account of living upon fresh beef.

Sept. 26*th.*—Lots 492, 443, 450, 451. DAVENPORT went in after provisions, and came back just as I was seated to copy my minutes, and to my great satisfaction brought me a letter from my father, and one from MYRON. This I put down as a circumstance affording me as much pleasure as anything that has taken place since I began surveying.

Wednesday, Sept. 28*th.*—I carved upon a beech tree in Cuyahoga town, "MYRON HOLLEY, Jr.," and on a birch, "MILTON HOLLEY, 1796,—Sept. 26th, 1796. Friendship."

Saturday, Oct. 1*st.*—I left Cuyahoga in the boat, to run out several tracts of land in No. 10 range, nine for Capt. PERRY and Mr. MARVIN, Mr. HICKOCK, Mr. ROSE, and PHELPS & Co. Encamped at Chagrin river. Gen. CLEAVELAND, STOW, and fifteen others came to us in another boat.

Sunday, Oct. 2*d.*—Went east to the east line of the township, run south, &c. After running out the company lands, HOLLEY took his old line at the Chagrin river and ran it west between towns nine and ten to the lake, at forty-nine miles thirty-seven chains five links.

Oct. 8*th.*—Started down the beach to mouth of Chagrin river, and found our boat and provisions. Had a fair wind about half way to the Cuyahoga, and rowed the remainder. Arrived at the river about eight o'clock in the evening; found all well.

Monday, Oct. 10*th*, 1, P. M.—Left Cleveland at the mouth of the Cuyahoga to finish lotting the eastern part of said township. SHEPHED and ATWATER, chainmen, LANDON, axman, PARKER, flagman, and HANCHET, cook.

Thursday, Oct. 13*th.*—Encamped for the night; had root water.

Saturday, Oct. 15*th.*—Lay still in consequence of rain.

Oct. 16*th.*—Lots three hundred and eighty-five, three hundred and eighty-seven, three hundred and ninety-four, and three hundred and ninety-five. Came to camp in consequence of hard rain; found no fire; were all wet and cold, but after pushing about the bottle and getting a good fire and supper, we were as merry as grigs.

Monday, Oct. 17*th.*—Lots three hundred and ninety-one and three hundred and ninety-nine. Capt. PERRY took about four pounds of beef, and ate with us four days.

BIOGRAPHICAL NOTICE OF AMZI ATWATER.

BY L. V. BIERCE, ESQ., OF AKRON.

"Died, at Mantua, Portage county, on the 22d day of June, 1851, AMZI ATWATER, aged seventy-six years and one month."

Such is the brief notice that announces to the world the death of the last survivor of the first exploring expedition on the Reserve.

Judge ATWATER was born at New Haven, Connecticut, on the 23d of May, 1776. His parents were poor, and unable to give him anything more than an ordinary education. Ushered into life in the early part of the Revolutionary war, and in that part of the colonies most exposed to the incursions of the enemy, his lulaby was the booming of artillery, or the rattling of musketry. On the defeat of the Americans on Long Island, in 1776, when AMZI was but three months old, his father was called out with the militia for the defense of New

York, from which he returned sick, and with a constitution broken. When old enough, young Atwater was sent to school, where he obtained a little knowledge of reading, writing and arithmetic. So straightened were his parents' circumstances, that he was hired out to work by the day, week or month, as opportunities offered, till he was a man. At the age of eighteen his father hired him out to work for an uncle, for sixty dollars a year, who transfered him over to a man by the name of Watson. "At the end of the year," says Judge Atwater in a letter now before me, "my parents gave me my time with their good advice and blessing." He then hired to Watson for seven months, at eight dollars a month, but he died before that term expired. Being out of employment young Atwater went to Westfield, in Massachusetts, to visit his uncle Rev. Noah Atwater, who was in the habit of teaching mathematics to a class of young men. He invited young Atwater to come and study with him the ensuing winter, which he did. Here he learned the art of surveying, in company with Warham Shepherd, who was one of the first exploring party on the Reserve. In the minutes of that expedition, Warham Shepherd and Amzi Atwater are called "Explorers' Assistants." At this school a friendship was formed between them that lasted till the death of Shepherd.

In April, 1796, being then nineteen years of age, young ATWATER left Connecticut, on foot and alone, with a heavy knapsack on his back, to meet his friend SHEPHERD at Ontario county, New York, with whom he remained until the agents of the Connecticut land company, were ready to commence their survey, when he left for the then unknown west. He joined them at Canandaigua, June 13, 1796.

His business was to collect cattle, and pack horses, with which he went all the way by land.

Having served as chainman, drover, and assistant surveyor faithfully through the year 1796, he returned in the spring of 1797 as one of the assistant surveyors.

The last of the surveyors left the Reserve the fore part of November, 1797, for the most part a sorry, sickly looking set of beings, the very reverse of what they were in the spring.

In 1798–99, Judge ATWATER was in the employ of the Holland Land Company, in the western part of New York, and assisted in running nearly all the township lines. In the fall of 1799 he returned to Connecticut, and spent the winter with his uncle, in study.

In 1800, in company with his brother JOTHAM, he came to Mantua, and made a permanent settlement on the farm where he died.

In 1808, on the organization of Portage county, he was elected one of the Associate Judges, and subsequently held many public trusts, such as his neighbors urged upon him, but which he did not covet. He chose retirement, and in the language of his old friend, ABRAM TAPPAN, of Ashtabula, "his disposition was mild, and he was honest to a proverb."

In a letter to Mr. TAPPAN, written March 24th, 1851, Judge ATWATER says—

"I need not say much how I have run *the line of life.* I have run through some of the swamps of adversity, and over many of the plains of prosperity. My assistants have generally been cheerful, and I may say faithful. My provisions hold out well, and perhaps I have enough to carry me through to the end of my line, which I have good reason to believe will soon be completed."

EXTRACTS FROM THE DIARY OF AMZI ATWATER, 1796.

Arrived at Stow Castle at the mouth of Conneaut river September 14th, there we heard that the other companies were a part of them at the Cuyahoga, and that the Cuyahoga river, was fifteen miles west of the one we had followed to the lake, supposing it to be the Cuyahoga. A boat was at Conneaut going to carry provisions to the other companies at Cuyahoga. We prepared to go on the same, but before we could get the boat out of the creek, it was so near night that we concluded to stay until morning. The wind was so high for several days that we could not go. On the 18th of September four of us were sent to Cuyahoga by land, two leading the pack horses loaded with flour, and the other two driving the cattle. When we were within six or seven miles of Cuyahoga, we saw boats coming from there with the other company in them. They had spent so much of their provisions that they thought it best not to stay there any longer, but when they met us they returned to Cuyahoga. The next day after we got there, I was sent with Mr. Stoddard to survey the south-east part of the township of Cleveland, No. 7, in the twelfth range, in one hundred acre lots, which will be found to vary very much in size. There were two other parties in the east part of the township, under Major Spafford and Mr. Holley. We stayed in the township about two weeks, and then returned to the house at the mouth of the Cuyahoga river. When we arrived at the house, I was sent with Mr. Pease to run out a part of the city plat. We were two or three days in finishing this, when about one-half of the company was dismissed.

MEMORANDA OF ORRIN HARMON'S CONVERSATION WITH AMZI ATWATER.

Amzi Atwater always styled the proprietors of Euclid as mutineers. He has minutely narrated to me the circumstances of the mutiny. They mutinied on their first arrival at Conneaut. The sale of the township of Euclid, was a part of the compromise made then by CLEAVELAND and PORTER. The organization of the company of surveyors and men was of the military order, and they were enlisted the same as in the army, for two years, providing it took so long.

PROCEEDINGS AT CLEAVELAND, SEPT. 30, 1796.

Substance of a contract made at Cleaveland, Sept. 30th, 1796, between MOSES CLEAVELAND, *agent of the Connecticut Land Company, and the employees of the Company, in reference to the sale and settlement of the township of Euclid, No.* 8, *in the eleventh Range.*—(*From memoranda of* ORRIN HARMON, *Esq.*)

On the part of the surveyors forty-one persons signed the agreement. Each party to have an equal share in the township, at the price of one dollar per acre, with interest from Sept. 1st, 1797, to remain in the service of the company faithfully to the end of the year, and to perform certain acts of settlement, as follows:

To settle, in the year 1797, eleven families, build eleven houses, and sow two acres of wheat around each house—to be on different lots. In the year 1798 to settle eighteen more families, build eighteen more houses on different lots, and to clear and sow five acres of wheat on each. There must be also fifty acres in grass in the township.

In the year 1799, there must be twelve more families occupying twelve more lots, (in all forty-one,) with eight acres in wheat. On all the other lots three acres additional in wheat for this year, and in all seventy acres to be in grass.

There must be, in the year 1800, forty-one families resident in the township. In case of failure to perform any of the conditions, whatever had been done or paid was to be forfeited to the company. But the failure of other parties not to affect those who perform. If salt springs are discovered on a lot it is to be excepted from the agreement, and other lands given instead

To this contract are appended as witnesses, the names of Jeffries Marvin, and Nathan Perry, the latter of whom became a resident in 1806, and died at Black river, October 28, 1813.

Persons in the employ of the company who were not parties to this agreement:

Amos Sawtel,	Daniel Shulay,
Nathan Chapman,	Stephen Burbank,
Samuel Barnes,	Joshua Stow,
Robert Hamilton,	

PROCEEDINGS AT A GENERAL MEETING OF THE EMPLOYEES OF THE LAND COMPANY HELD AT CLEAVELAND, SEPTEMBER 30, 1796.

At a meeting of the proprietors of No. 8, in the eleventh range of towns in new Connecticut, held at the city of Cleaveland, on the 30th day of September,

1796, being the surveyors and assistants employed in surveying the summer past the country of New Connecticut.

SETH PEASE chosen Moderator.

MOSES WARREN chosen Clerk.

In said meeting it was agreed, that a majority of votes shall govern in any question before the meeting, without contradiction.

Voted that it be determined by a lottery which of the said proprietors shall do the first, second and third years settling duties, as required by our patent this day executed by MOSES CLEAVELAND, Esq., director of said New Connecticut Land Company, without contradiction.

The lots being drawn, it is as follows:

	No.		No.
SETH PEASE,	1	MICHAEL COFFIN,	2
MOSES WARREN,	2	NATHANIEL DOAN,	3
MILTON HOLLEY,	2	SAMUEL DAVENPORT,	3
AMOS SPAFFORD,	3	TIMOTHY DUNHAM,	1
JOSEPH TINKER,	2	SAMUEL FORBES,	1
THEODORE SHEPHERD,	1	ELIJAH GUN,	3
RICHARD M. STODDARD,	3	FRANCIS GRAY,	2
ELISHA AYER,	1	GEORGE GOODWIN,	2
AMZI ATWATER,	1	LUKE HANCHET,	3
SAMUEL AGNEW,	1	JAMES HACKET,	2
SHADRACH BENHAM,	2	JAMES HAMILTON,	2
STEPHEN BENTON,	3	SAMUEL HUNGERFORD,	1
DAVID BEARD,	3	THOMAS HARRIS,	2
AMOS BARBER,	3	WILLIAM B. HALL,	2
JOHN BRIANT,	3	JOSEPH LANDON,	3

	No.		No.
John Locke,	2	Charles Parker,	2
Asa Mason,	2	Olney F. Rice,	3
Joseph M'Intire,	2	Wareham Shepherd,	1
Ezekiel Morley,	2	Job P. Stiles,	2
Titus V. Munson,	1	Norman Wilcox,	2
George Proudfoot,	1	Total,	41.

The names marked No. 1 are to do said settling duties in the year 1797, and the names marked No. 2 are to do said duties in the year 1798, and the names marked No. 3 are to do said settling duties in the year 1799, agreeable to said lottery.

A true copy of part of the proceedings of the proprietors' meeting.

Examined by Moses Warren, Jr., Clerk.

This copy is in the hand writing of Seth Pease. Mr. Atwater who was one of the parties to this compact, always spoke of the transaction as a mutiny. There is no such mention made of it, so far as I know, in the papers of General Cleaveland, or of the Land Company. If they had regarded the conduct of Messrs. Pease, Spafford and Warren in that light, the proprietors would not have employed them again in the year 1797. After a trial of three months, wherein they had undergone the hardships of forest life, they were no doubt inclined to obtain some additional advantages for their services. The Company, on their part, required an early settlement of their lands.

MR. PORTER'S PLAN OF DISPOSING OF THE LOTS IN CLEVELAND.

"Terms proposed by AUGUSTUS PORTER, for the sale of the one-fourth part of the township of Cleveland after, making the following reservations, to wit: City lots No. 58, 59, 60, 61, 62, 63, 81, 82, 83, 84, 85, 86, 87 and the point of land west of the town, and also some reservations of flats on the river if it should be advisable, after surveying. The aforesaid quarter to be selected in the following manner, to wit: to begin with lot No. 1, and to take every fourth number in succession through the town, which should be offered for sale on the following terms:

"1st. To sell to each person who would engage to become an actual settler in the year 1797, one town or city lot, one ten or twenty acre lot, and one one hundred acre lot, or two one hundred acre lots, or as much less as they may choose, but in all cases to make settlement as aforesaid.

"2d. The price of town lots, fifty dollars, cash in hand.

10	acre	lots,	at	$3.00	per	acre,
20	"	"	"	2.00	"	"
100	"	"	"	1.50	"	"

"Payable 20 per centum in hand, the remainder in three annual payments, with annual interest from date.

SEPT. 28th, 1796.

The above is in the hand writing of AMOS SPAFFORD.

FALL OF 1796 AND WINTER OF 1797.

What was accomplished in 1796 fell short of the expectations of all parties, particularly of the stockholders of the company. About fourteen thousand dollars had been expended upon the expedition. The field books of the surveyors show rapid work, frequently making eight, ten, and sometimes twelve miles in a day. WARREN appears to have been less energetic than the others, however, as he was continued in service the next year, the company must have been satisfied with him. When the season closed, there was a large tract in which no lines had been run. This was all that territory east of the Cuyahoga, west of the fourth meridian and south of the sixth parallel. The southern boundary of the Reserve, had not been continued west of the fourth Range, that is, only to the south-west corner of Berlin. PEASE had run southerly, between ranges eight and nine, one township below the sixth parallel, to the north-west corner of Town five, Range eight, (Mantua,) and thence west to the Cuyahoga, on the north line of Northfield, which he reached on the 6th of September.

None of the six townships intended for sale were allotted, except fractions number seven and eight in the twelfth Range, afterwards Cleveland and Newburg. None of the ten acre out-lots in Cleveland were surveyed. Around these are the one hundred acre lots, numbering from 268 to 486, which, with the in and out lots of the city, cover fractional Towns seven and eight. Why the numbers of the one hundred acre lots were not commenced at number one, I have no means of explaining. The four townships making four hundred lots, intended for distribution, one to each share in the company, were not yet sub-divided. It is probable that all, or nearly all, of the township lines north of the sixth parallel were finished this season.

One cause of delay in the surveys, was the time lost by all the parties when they arrived at Chagrin river, and mistook it for the Cuyahoga. It was not always practicable to have provisions promptly delivered to the surveying parties, so that their work could go on without interruption. The axmen, chainmen, cooks, pack-horse men and boatmen, soon got over their first enthusiasm, which no doubt delayed their progress. After their experience in running the first four meridians, the romance of a life in the woods was very much dissipated. Every day was one of toil, and frequently discomfort. The woods, and particularly the swamps, were filled with ravenous mosquitoes, who were never idle, day or night. In rainy weather the bushes were wet, and in clear weather the heat was oppressive. They were not always sure of supper at night, nor of their drink of New England rum, which constituted an important part of their rations. Their well provided clothing began to show rents, from so much clambering over logs and through thickets. Their shoes gave out rapidly, as they were incessantly on foot, and were where no cobblers could be found to repair them. They had no special interest in the work, except their pay.

It does not appear that their discontent arose to an open rupture with the surveyors, but was sufficient to hinder the progress of the work. The agent and his subordinates, were obliged to make promises of lands to such as proved to be faithful, which the proceedings of September 30th, sufficiently explain.

Before they started homeward some of the party had selected lots in the capital city of New Connecticut. The allotment of the town and of the surrounding lots, was the work of all the parties. PORTER states that he ran the outline of the tract to be comprised in the new town. PEASE, STODDARD and SPAFFORD had a hand in it, and HOLLEY surveyed some of the one hundred acre lots. A rough map of the city was made during the survey, a copy of which is here given. A few lots were sold probably on the terms proposed by PORTER. Great expectations were formed of their projected settlement in Euclid, which, however, were not realized.

FIRST MAP OR PLAT OF THE CITY OF CLEVELAND, OCT. 1, 1796.

The original, of which this is a copy, reduced by photograph, was found among the papers of JOHN MILTON HOLLEY, at Salisbury, Connecticut, in charge of his son, Governor ALEXANDER H. HOLLEY. It is endorsed in the hand writing of AMOS SPAFFORD: "Original plan of the town and village of Cleveland, Ohio, Oct. 1st, 1796." The sheet is formed, by pasting several sheets and parts of sheets, of foolscap together, evidently extemporized in the field. It was the first rough sketch, used by the surveyors before their return to the east. Superior street was at first named "Broad" street — a very appropriate title, as it then had no equal in width. Miami street had the name of "Deer" street — probably from the appearance there, of one of those animals during the survey.

Maiden street, or lane, was ignored in the subsequent plat of SPAFFORD, in 1801, and thus abandoned. On this map there is no extension of Superior street to the river, which was done by SPAFFORD, under the name of Superior Lane.

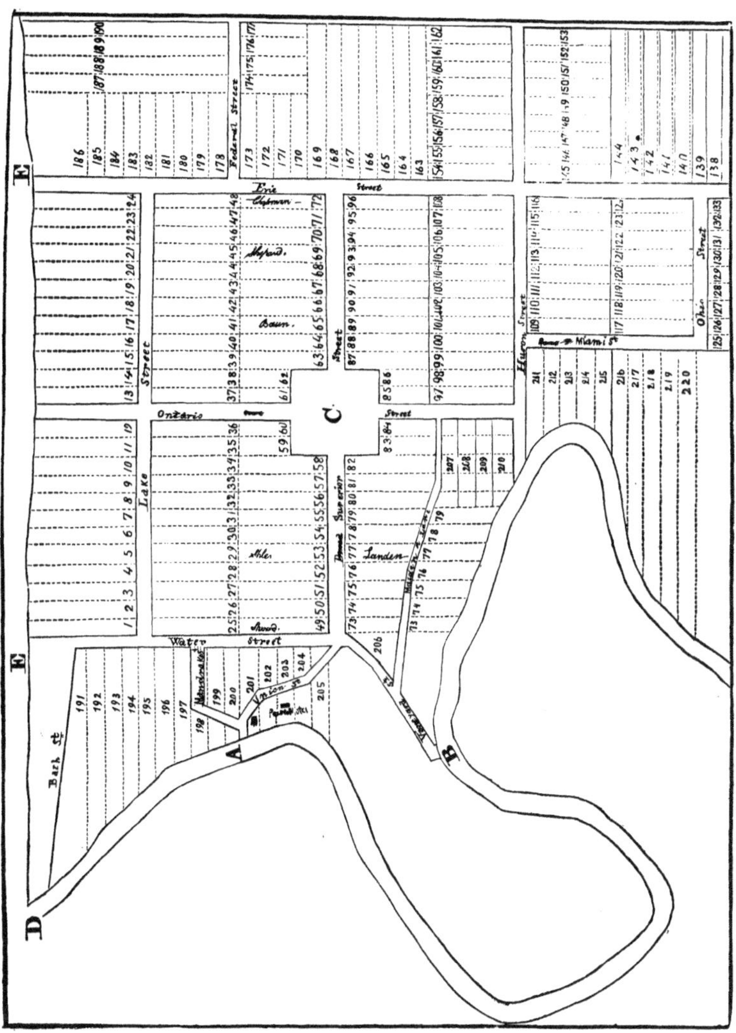

REFERENCES.

A, Lower Landing. *B*, Upper Landing. *C.* Public Square, of ten acres. *D*, Mouth of the River. *EE*, Lake Erie.

The Public Square is here indicated by a blank space, like an enlargement of the streets crossing each other at that point. Ontario had at first the name of "Court street," which is erased, and the present name inserted. The letters A, B, C, D, and E, on the copy, are introduced by me, for the purpose of reference. On the face of the original, there are the numbers of the lots — two hundred and twenty in number; the streets, Superior, Water, Mandrake, Union, Vineyard, Bath, Lake, Erie, Federal, Maiden, Ontario, Huron, Ohio and Miami — fourteen in number, and the names of the parties who had selected lots. These were: STODDARD, lot 49, north-east corner of Water and Superior streets; STILES, lot 53, north-east corner of Bank and Superior streets; LANDON, lot 77, directly opposite, on the south side of Superior street; BAUM, lot 65, sixteen rods east of the Public Square; SHEPHERD, lot 69, and CHAPMAN, lot 72, all on the north side of the same street.

"PEASE'S Hotel," as they styled the surveyors' cabin, is placed on the line between lots 202 and 203, between Union street and the river. Northwest of it, about ten rods, on lot 201, their store house is laid down. Vineyard, Union and Mandrake streets, were laid out to secure access to the upper and lower landings on the river. Bath street provided a way of reaching the lake shore and the mouth of the river.

After the return of the surveyors, regular field notes of the surveys of the city, were made out by Seth Pease, which are regarded as the official returns. With these notes is a map, styled on the face of it "Plan of the City of Cleaveland, 1796," which is substantially the same as the one here given. The river bluffs are slightly different, and the sand spit at the mouth is longer.

There are the same number of streets with the same names, and the lots are alike on both; but the name of the city is spelled on the field plat without the letter "a," probably through inadvertence. In the papers and correspondence of those times, and until after the war of 1812, it is spelled both ways. General Cleaveland, from whom the city was named, always signs with the letter "a" in the first syllable.

Several copies of the plat, were made on a scale about the same as the first draft, during the winter of 1796–97, for the use of the company, but it was never engraved. The first published map of the Reserve is that of Seth Pease, after his return in 1797. About the year 1816, soon after the organization of the village corporation, when some new streets were thought to be necessary, the authorized book of field notes, with its miniature plan, was brought here by James Root, Esq., brother to Ephraim Root, the secretary of the company.

This book remained until about the year 1856, since when, not being in official custody, it has disappeared. There is not now upon the Western Reserve a collection of the papers, maps, field books and proceedings of the company, from whom all our land titles are derived. A part of the Field Notes of PEASE, HOLLEY and WARREN are in my possession.

The survey of the city was commenced on the 16th of September, and completed about the 1st of October. HOLLEY's descriptions of their departure and journey homeward as far a Canandaigua are full and interesting, and are given without curtailment.

Monday, Oct, 17th, 1796.—Finished surveying in New Connecticut; weather rainy.

Tuesday, Oct. 18th. — We left Cuyahoga at 3 o'clock 17 minutes, for HOME. We left at Cuyahoga JOB STILES and wife, and JOSEPH LANDON, with provisions for the winter. WM. B. HALL, TITUS V. MUNSON and OLNEY RICE engaged to take all the pack horses to Geneva. Day pleasant, and fair wind about south-east; rowed about seven and a half miles, and encamped for the night on the beach.

There were fourteen men on board the boat, and never I presume, were fourteen men more anxious to pursue an object, than we were to get forward. Names of men in the boat:

AUGUSTUS PORTER,	JAMES HACKET,
SETH PEASE,	STEPHEN BENTON,
RICHARD STODDARD,	GEORGE PROUDFOOT,

JOSEPH TINKER,	JAMES HAMILTON,	
CHARLES PARKER,	NATHAN CHAPMAN,	Genesee.
WAREHAM SHEPHERD,	RALPH BACON,	
AMZI ATWATER,	MILTON HOLLEY.	

Walnut creek, a pretty stream twenty or thirty links wide, empties into the lake about seven miles east of the Cuyahoga; not navigable for boats. The township of Cleaveland lies on the lake shore, eight miles, four chains, seventy links. About one hundred and thirty chains east of the corner a stream, considerably larger than Walnut creek, empties into the lake. This is in the town purchased by the surveyors, and named (by MOSES WARREN, Esq.,) Euclid; in memory of the man who first made the principles of geometry known. About ten miles from the Cuyahoga, a rock shore begins and continues nearly a mile, then a good beach commences and continues to Chagrin river. This river is about fourteen rods wide at its mouth, and navigable for boats up three or four miles at all times, when there is no obstruction at the outlet, which however, is frequently the case, with this as well as most of the other rivers upon this lake, in consequence of the waves driving up a bank of sand.

Wednesday morning, 3 o'clock.—Clear and pleasant; moon shone bright, and we hoisted sail. About daybreak it began to thicken up in the west, and by sunrise the sky was hid from sight. Just before sunrise we passed the first settlement (except those made by ourselves) that is on the shore of the lake in New Connecticut. This is done by the Canandaiqua Association Company, under the direction of Major WELLS and Mr. WILDAIR. After the sun rose the wind got into the north and north-east, and came on to blow so fresh that we were obliged to run ashore on the beach and pitch our tent, about a mile east of the Chagrin.

Thursday, Oct. 20th, 1796.—Started half after six in the morning; no wind; against the ninth Range of towns. About nineteen miles by the lake shore from the Cuyahoga, a creek comes in, which forms a large marsh lying a mile along shore, and on average one hundred rods wide; at twenty-seven miles comes in Grand river. This stream is almost always a good harbor for boats, the outlet into the lake being about two or three rods wide and two or three feet deep. Just above the sand bar, made by the washing of the lake, the river is nearly twenty rods wide, and the depth sufficient for large vessels to anchor in. It continues this depth almost a mile, and is navigable for any boat four miles from the mouth, up to the Indian settlement, where are rapids which now obstruct the passage, but with some expense might be made navigable for boats a great distance, I suppose forty or fifty miles at least. The general course is north, till it approaches within eight miles of the lake, when it runs twenty miles nearly due west before it empties itself. About thirty-six miles is a burning spring in the lake, two or three rods from shore, which is very perceptible as you stand upon the beach, from its boiling motion. Mr. PORTER told me that he, with General CLEAVELAND and Mr. STOW, had made a trial to know if it really was inflammable, which they found to be the case, although it was a very unfavorable time when they did it. The waves ran high, and the wind blew hard. They held a torch well lighted very close to the water, when there appeared a flame like that of spirits burning, but as it was so much mixed with other air, and the water so deep over it, (four feet) the flame would go out immediately. About 11 o'clock the wind began to blow from the north-east, and came so hard that we put ashore, and encamped near the spring at 1 o'clock, P. M.

Friday, 21st. — Started about 2 o'clock; wind north-east, not strong; about 10 it lulled away, and we rowed to Conneaut; arrived about half after 12; took inventory of the articles left there, and about 4 o'clock in the morning, that is, on Saturday, the 22d, we hoisted sail for Presque Isle. We sailed and rowed prettily to the peninsula, unloaded, drew the boat across, and arrived at the garrison at 12 o'clock. Received a letter from my father of Sept. 16th, and one from MYRON of the 15th, by Esquire PAINE, of Onondaga county.

This place is settling considerably fast, and, I think, must be a place of consequence, as it affords a good harbor for vessels, has a good country around it, and is but fifteen miles by land from Le Beuf, which is on French creek, and about one hundred and fifty miles from Pittsburg, to which place from Le Beuf, is good boating through French creek and the Allegheny river all the way. The journey is performed often in two days. Settlers from the north-western part of Pennsylvania take this route to get on the Presque Isle lands. The peninsula is about seven miles in length, and from twelve rods to a mile wide. It is very little more than a bank of sand, although a great part of it is thickly timbered. The bay is about six miles in length and two miles wide. In the channel there is a sufficient depth of water for ships to anchor, but they cannot get near shore. With some expense, a wharf can be made out to the channel, which probably will be the case. Opposite the east end of the peninsula, on the main land, stands the fort. It has a commanding prospect and is agreeably situated, except a bad marsh between it and the lake, which in dry seasons is extremely unhealthy.

Sunday, Oct. 23d, '96.—Left Presque Isle at 35 minutes past one o'clock in the morning; a land breeze from the south-west. The wind continued, and we rowed till about 1 o'clock, P. M., when it came so fast from the west, from where it had hauled that we sailed till 4 o'clock; the wind then lulled, and we plyed our oars again; arrived in Buffalo creek at half after 10 in the evening. We struck a fire, and were asleep in less than thirty minutes from the time of landing.

Monday morning, Oct. 24th.—Left Buffalo creek at 9 o'clock in the morning. We ran down the river to Chipeway landing, which is twenty miles distant, at half after 12 o'clock. We were so fortunate, as to get our boat and luggage carried across the portage immediately, by some teams that came to the shore just as we did. We rode in a wagon to Queenstown. Came across Capt. DAVIS at Major INGERSOLL'S inn. With him, Mr. HUNN, Mr. BUTLER and Major PIXLEY, we spent a sociable evening.

Tuesday, Oct. 25th.—We left Major INGERSOLL'S at half past 7, and came to Newark. DAVIS came with us. We breakfasted at WILSON'S.

Newark is a pleasant village, situated on the west shore of Niagara river, just at its entrance into Lake Ontario. It is laid out in city form, and there are many very pretty buildings. I think it will not be a place of so much business as Queenstown. Opposite Newark stands the ancient fort of Niagara, built by the French. It appears to have been a place of considerable strength, though many parts are now tumbling to ruin. We left Newark at half after 10 o'clock, A. M.; wind north-east; about 1 o'clock the wind lulled, and we continued rowing till sundown, then encamped on the beach at the mouth of a creek, or marsh, called Key Harbor. The shore of the lake to this place is generally low and clayey. Just before we came to the harbor, a rocky shore commenced. The opening, where the marsh or creek comes in, is about fifteen rods, and about twenty miles from the fort.

Wednesday, Oct. 26th.—Started at 4 o'clock in morning; wind rather ahead. We rowed past Golden Harbor, the Eagle's Nest, and on to Oak Orchard; a creek of considerable size comes in here, supposed to be Tonawanda. From the appearance of the mouth, it never fills up with sand, therefore is a good harbor for boats, (the others mentioned were filled); arrived here about 12 o'clock. This is about forty-five miles from the garrison at Niagara.

Thursday, 27th.—Wind north-east, in consequence of which we are obliged to lie still. I had the headache this day. Towards evening the wind lulled away, and at a quarter after 6 o'clock we left our encampment, and determined to row all night. It was extremely cold; the waves ran high, and the wind came on to blow considerably hard against us. However, we continued rowing, and about sunrise passed the Genesee river.

Friday, 27th.—At 7 o'clock and 45 minutes we entered the mouth of Gerundicut bay, and found a fire burning here. We breakfasted, and pursued our way at 9 o'clock. This bay is about four miles in length, and from one-half to three-quarters of a mile wide. A great part of it consists of flags, marsh, or a kind of mossy grass, coming close to the top of the water. Towards the head of the bay, the navigation is so difficult that we were obliged to strip, jump into the mud up to our waists, and haul the boat thirty rods to get into the channel. We pursued the river to the head of navigation, which is about eight miles as the river runs, which is very crooked. PORTER, PEASE, STODDARD, and myself stayed at DUNBAR'S that night, the others went on.

Saturday, 29th. — We breakfasted, and then set out on foot for Canandaigua, where we arrived at sunset. Lodged at SANBORN'S.

JOHN MILTON HOLLEY.

Of him, Judge AMZI ATWATER, in his sketches of the personal appearance of the surveyors, says: "He was then a very young man, only about eighteen years of age, though he appeared to be older; tall, stout and handsomely built, with a fair and smiling face, and general good appearance. He was a beautiful penman."

Neither HOLLEY or PORTER returned to the survey in 1797. They eventually became brothers-in-law, PORTER removing, at an early day, to the banks of the Niagara river. HOLLEY settled in Salisbury,

Connecticut, the old home of the PORTERS. He was a brother of MYRON HOLLEY, prominent in New York, as one of the Canal Commissioners of that State. JOHN MILTON spent his days at Salisbury, leaving a large and respected family. His son, ALEXANDER H., once elected Governor of the State, still resides on the old homestead, near the famous Salisbury iron mine known as the "Ore Hill."

MOSES CLEAVELAND.

BY FREDERICK WADSWORTH, ESQ., OF AKRON.

"Mr. CLEAVELAND was a prominent and much respected citizen of Canterbury, Windham county, Connecticut; born about the year 1755. He graduated at Yale College in 1777. In 1788, he purchased a portion of the interest of SAMUEL H. PARSONS, in the Salt Spring tract, on the Meander creek. His profession was that of a lawyer, practising in his native town, where he died in 1806. He was a Brigadier General of militia, and a Representative in the Legislature.

His daughter, Mrs. FRANCES CLEAVELAND MORGAN, of Norwich, Connecticut, says the city of Cleveland was a decided pet with him so long as he lived. There were many papers and journals of her father, which have been scattered in the changes of the family. Mrs. MORGAN still treasures the pipe which PAQUA presented her father, at the conference on Conneaut creek."

Mr. ATWATER says General CLEAVELAND was "a short, thick set man, with a broad face, dark complexion and coarse features." In Judge PORTER'S letter of July, 1843, he states, that the General had furnished himself with an Indian dress, and being of a swarthy complexion, afforded an excellent likeness of an Indian Chief; and was honored thereafter by the party, by the name of "PAQUA," the name of the chief of the tribe referred to."

This resemblance to the aborigines, appears to have been patent to everybody. In Judge SPAULDING'S address before the Cuyahoga County Pioneer Society, in October, 1858, he refers to it as follows:

"It is said of him, that some years after he left college, he attended an annual commencement at New Haven, where he met certain members of his own class, with whom he was examining the triennial catalogue, that had then just issued from the press. It is usual, in this catalogue, to print the names of such of the graduates as have studied theology, *in italics*. Gen. CLEAVELAND, in running his eye over the names of his classmates, chanced to find the name of one then present, who made no great pretensions to piety, printed in the form to denote a clergyman. Fond of humor and ready at a joke, he snatched a pen, and wrote against the name of his friend—'Settled at Mohegan;' which was then and is now, a small Indian settlement on the bank of the Thames, between Norwich and New London. The catalogue thus amended, was passed around the company, amid roars of laughter, until it came into the hands of the innocent subject of their mirth, when he, with easy facility and wit, retorted upon our hero, by writing against his name—'Born at Mohegan.'"

By reference to the list of original proprietors already given, it appears that he was an owner of $32.600 stock in the Land Company. After the business of 1796 was closed, it is not known that he afterwards visited the Reserve. Of his Indian name-sake, PAQUA, or "PAWQUAW," Mr. ATWATER says: "He was not a large Indian, but straight and handsomely built, with a fair and pleasant countenance, lighter than most Indians."

JOB P. STILES.

JOB P. STILES and his wife had a cabin built for them on the hill, before the surveyors left. RICHARD LANDON, one of the surveying party, was left to spend the winter with them, upon this dreary spot. From some cause not yet explained, he soon after abandoned the place, and EDWARD PAINE took up his residence with the STILES family. During the winter a child is reputed to have been born in the cabin, which had only squaws for a nurse.

The Indians who were quartered here at that time, constituting by far the most numerous part of its population, treated these lonely settlers with great kindness.

PAINE was a trader with the Indians during the winter of 1796–'97, who afterwards became a prominent citizen of Geauga county. STILES left here in 1800, and survived to a good old age, dying in Leicester, Addison county, Vermont, about the year 1850. The courageous Mrs. STILES lived to a still later period, but when her death occurred I am not informed.

PEASE's Journal of the return from New Connecticut, agrees closely with HOLLEY's. In getting out of the river, on the 18th of October, he says: "It was much obstructed by a sand bar, occasioned by a violent gale from the northward the day before. It was with some difficulty we reached the lake.

"We put ashore where two small runs empty into the lake, in the eastern part of Euclid. I walked a short distance to a settlement begun by the Canandaigua Company, Major WELLS Agent, and received some provisions that had been lent them by us."

This is the settlement referred to by HOLLEY, whose history is not yet developed.

Mr. Pease met with many difficulties and discomforts, on the journey from Canandaigua to Suffield.

Friday, November 8th.—"Eight miles beyond Cayuga Lake, found difficulty in getting provisions on the road, the water being so low the mills could not grind."

Saturday, Nov. 9th.—"A little beyond the Onondaga river, a gentleman let me ride his horse, although he was bare back."

Sunday, Nov. 16th.—"Got *home* about 2 o'clock in the morning."

His "home" was at Suffield, on the banks of the Connecticut river, above Hartford.

After the surveyors returned in the fall of 1796, a meeting was called on the 17th of January, 1797, at which the Directors and Trustees, were required to urge the Legislature to erect a county comprising all the Western Reserve. A committee was appointed to enquire into the causes of the "very great expense of the Company during the first year, the causes which have prevented the completion of the surveys; and why the surveyors and agents have not made their reports.

A tax, or assessment, of five dollars per share, was also ordered, the number of shares being four hundred. A Committee of Partition was appointed consisting of Daniel Holbrook, Moses Warren, Jr., Seth Pease and Amos Spafford.

Another committee was raised to inquire generally into the conduct of the directors. At a subsequent meeting, on the 22d of February, 1797, this committee made their report, thoroughly white-washing the directors, and overwhelming the dissatisfied stockholders. They also "voted that MOSES CLEAVELAND's contract with JOSEPH BRANT, Esq., in behalf of the Mohawks, of Grand river, Canada, be ratified."

By this time the distressing fact became known, that the "Excess Company" had no land whatever.

AUGUSTUS PORTER, who had made a traverse of the lake shore, from the Pennsylvania line to Sandusky bay, ascertained that it bore much more to the south, than the old maps represented. Upon calculating the contents of the tract, including the Fire Lands, he discovered that the Land Company had less than three million of acres, the quantity for which they had paid.

QUANTITY OF LAND IN THE RESERVE.

A. PORTER'S REPORT TO THE DIRECTORS, HARTFORD, JANUARY 28, 1797, ON THE QUANTITY OF LAND IN THE RESERVE.

"I have surveyed the said Reserve, and found it to contain 3,450,753 acres, exclusive of the islands in Lake Erie, and including Sandusky bay, supposed to exceed the islands in quantity about 30,000 acres. (Presents a map.) Fixed the south-east corner at the forty-first parallel by celestial observations, and by measuring from the Pennsylvania monument on Lake Erie, fixed by a surveyor general of that state. Determined the lake shore by a traverse from the Pennsylvania line. Was not able to run the west line, on account of the Indian title not being extinguished. Owing to imperfections of the compass, there may be an error of a few thousand acres."

Mr. PORTER'S estimate proved to be as near the truth, as his means of computation would allow. The length of the west line, depended upon the accuracy of the meander of the lake shore, along a rugged coast from the Pennsylvania line, until the sum of the westings, should equal one hundred and twenty miles. Great was the astonishment of the "Excess Company," when his report was published. After 500,000 acres are subtracted from 3,450,753, the Land company had less than they bargained for, and the "Excess Company" had nothing.

PORTER's work was questioned, and a professor of mathematics from Yale College gave it a searching examination. No material error was discovered.

Not many years since, the late LEONARD CASE had the patience to go through each township, and determine the number of acres by the surveys. His figures are as follows:

	Acres.
Drafts east of the Cuyahoga, - -	972,861
Sales by the Directors east of Cuyahoga,	30,461
Drafts west of the Cuyahoga, - -	828,977
Islands in Lake Erie, - - - -	4,810
Fire lands, - - - - - - -	496,590
Total, - - - - - - -	3,333,699

The late General SIMON PERKINS has given the following, as the result of his investigations:

	Acres.
Salt Spring tract, - - - - - -	25,450
Conn. Land Co. east of Cuyahoga, -	2,002,970
Conn. Land Co. west of Cuyahoga. -	832,577
Islands in Lake Erie, - - - -	5,924
Fire lands, - - - - - - -	500,000
General PERKINS' total, - - -	3,366,921
LEONARD CASE's total, - - -	3,333,699
AUGUSTUS PORTER's total, - - -	3,450,753

The calculation of Mr. CASE being made in great detail, after all the lands had been disposed of, with all the surveys and drafts before him, may be regarded as very near the truth. Deducting the fire lands, 496,590 acres, from the whole Reserve, the Land Company, instead of 3,000,000 acres, only acquired 2,837,109 acres, from which a portion of the Salt Spring tract of about 4,000 acres sold by PARSONS should be deducted.

Probably some of the water courses and small interior lakes, were left out of the contents of the townships, as determined by Mr. CASE.

The south line of the Reserve is now considered as somewhat above the forty-first parallel, and is not strictly parallel with it. A close measurement, would probably extend the western boundary of the fire lands to the westward, due allowance not having been made, for the slack of the chain through, a tangled undergrowth.

When the valueless swamp land shall be added to the proper deductions, the company's purchase, amounted to little more than two and one-half millions of arable land.

Having determined to go on and complete the surveys of the town lines, and the townships to be allotted, and also to make partition among the owners, an assessment of ten dollars per share was levied, to be paid on the 26th of June, and another of fifteen dollars, payable September 15th, 1797.

At the annual meeting the directors and trustees, were empowered to take such measures, as should be deemed best calculated to procure a *legal and practical government*, over the territory of the company. As yet, the inhabitants who remained on their lands, were acknowledged or cared for by no legal authority. Most of them were at Cleveland, the extreme north-western point of the old county of Washington, erected in 1788. Their public business, as citizens of that county required them to travel to Marietta, on the Ohio. This they did not consider to be a practical government, and most of them doubted its legality. The seat of justice came a little nearer on the 29th of June, 1797, when Jefferson county was erected, with Steubenville as the county town. No magistrates were appointed for this part of the country, no civil process known, and no mode existed of making a legal conveyance. Citizens of the New England States, who have so much reverence for law, and such a constant use for it in the daily transactions of life, did not relish such a state of things. It was a lower civilization than their Indian neighbors possessed. For although there is no public authority, which the red man respects, he is his own executor of the customs of his tribe, under the simple law of retaliation.

The legislature of Connecticut, did not assume jurisdiction over her people in the western wilds, having already parted, with all shadow of right to the soil.

EXTRACTS FROM THE BARR MANUSCRIPTS.

"The Land Company in the fall of 1796, cleared about six acres of land at Conneaut, east of the creek, and sowed it with wheat, which was brought from the settlement on Genesee river, New York. This was the first crop of grain, produced by civilized men on the Western Reserve.

The sufferings of the families at Conneaut during the winter, were very great. The people at Cleveland were in a state of comfort, when compared with those at Conneaut, who were obliged to kill the cattle left by Mr. CHAPMAN in order to sustain life. The Indians supplied the Cleveland party with game, which was abundant, and they had the company's stock of provision, on which they could draw at any time. The savages were friendly and even kind. They deserved the appellation of friends, instead of savages; except when they were under the influence of intoxication.

Among them were "OGONCE" or OGONTZ, an Ottawa; SAGAMAW, a Chippewa, and SENECA, of the Seneca nation; all chiefs of their respective tribes.

SENECA was the most friendly, and is spoken of as a noble specimen of Indian character. In the fall, the Senecas, Ottawas, Delawares and Chippewas resorted here; and having procured what articles the traders had for them, dispersed to hunt through the winter, on the Cuyahoga, the Grand river, Mahoning,

Tuscarawas, Kilbuck, and Black rivers. In the spring they returned with their furs and game, and after trafficking away their stock, launched their bark canoes to repair to Sandusky plains and the Miami prairies, for the summer. Here they planted corn, beans and potatoes, around their villages.

While here the Senecas encamped at the foot of the bluff, between Vineyard and Superior lanes. On the west side were the Ottawas, Delawares and Chippewas. From the manner they had been hunted down by the Pennsylvanians, they called them Long Knives (swords), but the new comers, they called by the more complimentary term of "Sagamosh" or white men, and sometimes Bostonians.

SENECA was seen here in 1809, which is the last known of him. OGONTZ was at Sandusky in the year 1811."

JAMES KINGSBURY.

JAMES KINGSBURY was the first adventurer on his own account, who arrived on the Company's purchase. He came from Alsted, New Hampshire, with his wife, EUNICE, (ne WALDO,) arriving at Conneaut soon after the surveyors. There were also three children, whose fortunes were cast among the pioneers: ABAGAIL, who was afterwards Mrs. SHERMAN, of Cleveland, then at the age of three years, AMOS SHEPHERD KINGSBURY, about a year younger, and ALMON KINGSBURY, an infant.

EUNICE WALDO was also from Alsted. In November, after the surveyors had left, he found it necessary to return to New Hampshire. The journey was made by way of Erie, Buffalo, Canandaigua, and Albany, on horse back. He expected it would occupy four, perhaps six weeks. Reaching New Hampshire with no unusual delay or hardships, he was immediately attacked with fever, which run the usual course. From Buffalo one of his party returned to Conneaut, bringing the last news, the wife expected to receive until his return. Until winter, the Indians occasionally furnished her with meat. A nephew of the Judge, about thirteen years of age, was left at Conneaut, with a cow and a yoke of oxen. The expected husband did not return; no news arrived, and, in the height of her perplexity, a son was added to the household.

Mrs. GUN was at Conneaut at the birth of this child, the first white native of the Reserve. As soon as the Judge could safely ride a horse, he started for the shore of Lake Erie. He reached Buffalo nearly exhausted, on the 3d of December. The next day he set forward, although the winter snow covered the ground.

It was unusually deep, and fell without intermission every day for three weeks. In places it was up to the chin of a man, standing erect. Weak and distressed in mind, he moved forward every day, having only an Indian for guide, companion and purveyor, sometimes making only a few miles. It was the 24th of December when he reached the cabin. Mrs. KINGSBURY had finally recovered strength enough to move about, and had concluded to start with her family for Erie, the next day. Towards evening a gleam of sunshine, broke through the long clouded heavens, and lighted up the surrounding forest. Looking out, she beheld the figure of her husband approaching the door.

He was nearly exhausted, his horse having died of exposure. Mrs. KINGSBURY relapsed into a fever, which deprived her young child of its natural food. The provisions left by the surveyors, were nearly gone. Before Mr. K. had recovered from the effects of the journey, he was forced to return to Erie; and procure sustenance for his family. As there was no beaten track, it was impossible for the oxen to travel in so deep snow. He was obliged to drag a hand sled to Erie, and obtaining a bushel of wheat, to draw it himself to Conneaut. This they cracked and boiled. Soon after the cow died. The cattle had no other food, than the browse or small twigs of trees, which were cut for them to feed upon. The young lad did not know the difference, in different kinds of timber for this purpose. It was supposed the cow died, from eating the browse of oak trees. On the twigs of the elm, beech and linn which are tender and nutritious, cattle may live through the winter, as well as the deer and the elk. While the cow lived, there was a chance for the life of the infant, who was then less than two months old.

The child who had been named ALBERT, grew weaker from mere starvation, every day; its moans incessantly piercing the ears, and distressing the hearts of the parents, both of whom were sick. In about a month, after Mr. KINGSBURY reached home from the east; the child died. There was only Mr. K. and his young nephew at the place at the time.

They found a pine box which the surveyors had left, of which a rude coffin was made. As they carried the remains from the house, the sick mother raised herself in bed; following with her eyes the lonely party; to a rise of ground where they had dug a grave. She fell backward and for two weeks, was scarcely conscious of what was passing, or of what had passed. Late in February or early in March, Mr. KINGSBURY who was still feeble, made an effort to obtain something which his wife could eat, for it was evident that nutriment was her principal necessity. The severest rigors of winter began to relax. Instead of fierce northern blasts, sweeping over the frozen surface of the lake; there were southern breezes, which softened the snow and moderated the atmosphere.

Scarcely able to walk, he loaded an old "Queen's Arm," which his uncle had carried in the war of the revolution; and which is still in the keeping of the family. He succeeded in reaching the woods, and sat down upon a log. A solitary pigeon came, and perched upon the highest branches of a tree. It was not only high, but distant. The chances of hitting the bird were few indeed, but a human life seemed to depend upon those chances. A single shot found its way to the mark, and the bird fell. It was well cooked and the broth given to his wife, who was immediately revived. For the first time in two weeks she spoke in a natural and rational way, saying, "JAMES, where did you get this?"

When the surveyors under Mr. PEASE returned to their work in the spring, the family came with them to Cleveland, as their permanent home. On the west side of the river, at a point which cannot now be fixed with certainty, but probably near where Centre and Main streets cross, there was a dilapidated house.

The old settlers think it was erected by the French, but it was more probably done by the English, who were here soon after the peace of 1763. It was a better building than the French were in the habit of putting up in such remote places. It had been a comfortable and capacious log store-house. Very likely the French had built a cabin near the mouth of the river, which had disappeared.

Indians are universally destructive. Property, and especially houses that are not protected, remain but a short time after they are abandoned.

Probably this house was built about 1786, and used for storage. Mr. KINGSBURY occupied it while he put up a cabin east of the Public Square, near where the CASE block now stands. He determined, however, to locate on the bluff, south-east of Cleveland, which extends south from DOAN'S Corners to Newburg. His first trail was marked on the trees, near the line of Kinsman street. Finding a good spring near where he afterwards lived and died, another cabin was erected, and on the 11th of December, 1797, the family were fixed in their new home.

There were three children, ABAGAIL, (Mrs. SHERMAN,) aged four years, AMOS S., and ALMON. He was the first to locate on the hill. The year 1797 was so sickly about the mouth of the Cuyahoga, that the settlers sought the highlands to escape remittent fevers. During the next year there was a thriving settlement on the ridge, by which the city was materially diminished in population.

RODOLPHUS EDWARDS, NATHANIEL DOAN, ELIJAH GUN, EZEKIEL HAWLEY, and JAMES HAMILTON soon fixed their cabins along the bluff road, neighbors of the original pioneer.

Judge KINGSBURY now concluded to have a frame house, by way of aristocratic eminence. The logs were hauled to WILLIAMS' saw mill at Newburg, in the winter of 1799–1800. A freshet in the spring carried away the dam, and no sawing was done that season. His frame stood one year without covering, when he concluded to have a mill of his own, and erected one on KINGSBURYS brook near the the road, the remains of which may yet be seen. During the first winter on the ridge, they were obliged to pack their wheat from the city, pounding it by hand, and boiling it to a pudding.

The first crop raised by him was at his city cabin, east of the square.

In 1806 they had apples from their own trees, in in the venerable orchard which still graces the old homestead.

On the 10th of December, 1843, Mrs. KINGSBURY departed this life at the age of seventy-three years, and on the 12th of December, 1847, the old pioneer followed her, being nearly 80 years of age.

In the Cleveland *Plain Dealer* of December 15, 1847, there was published the following

OBITUARY.

Hon. JAMES KINGSBURY, who died at his residence in Newburg, on the 12th inst. in the eightieth year of his age, if not the last, was among the last of the few remaining pioneers, who bore a prominent part in the settlement of the lake shore. Like most of early settlers, he encountered hardships and trials which few of the present day can appreciate. Many of the incidents of his life are not only interesting in themselves, but intimately connected with the history of the Western Reserve; which, it is hoped, will yet be more fully written.

The subject of this notice, "the Judge," as he was usually denominated, was born in Norwich, Connecticut, December 29, 1767, He was the fifth son of ABSALOM KINGSBURY, who then resided in Connecticut, but soon after removed with his family to Alsted, New Hampshire. Several of the Judge's older brothers served under General WASHINGTON in the army of the Revolution. EBENEZER, the eldest brother, distinguished himself at the battle of Bennington, as one of the brave fellows who first scaled the breastworks of the enemy. The same old musket, or Queen's arm, with which he did such good execution, still remains in possession of the family at Newburg as a kind of heirloom.

JAMES, being at this time too young to engage in the public service, was employed at home in agricultural pursuits. In October, 1788, he was married to Miss EUNICE WALDO, a lady of New Hampshire, much esteemed for the amiableness of her disposition and moral excellence of her character. She lived to share with him his joys and sorrows as an affectionate wife, for more than half a century. In 1793 he received a military commission, with the rank of Colonel, from the Governor of New Hampshire—a mark of public confidence, as well as a distinction of some consequence in those days. But finding no occasion for the exercise of his military talents, and being stimulated with a love of adventure, he gathered his little family about him, consisting of his wife and three young children, and in June, 1796, with a few articles of household effects, a yoke of oxen, a horse and one cow, commenced a long and weary pilgrimage into the western wilderness. After some weeks of toil and hardship, he reached the shore of lake Ontario, near the site of the present town of Oswego. The facilities of navigation on the lakes at that early period, were comparatively unknown, and nothing better than a flat-bottomed open boat could be procured. In this he embarked with his family and household effects, while the oxen, horse and cow, were driven along the shore. He could only sail in calm weather, following the windings of the coast. When the emigrants reached the head of navigation on lake Ontario, the horse and oxen were very servicable in transporting the boat across the portage to Buffalo creek, a distance of about thirty miles, where the gallant little craft was launched with due ceremony upon the blue waters of lake Erie. Here the family were so fortunate as to meet with MOSES CLEAVELAND, Esq., agent of the Directors of the Connecticut Land Company, then on his way to join the surveying party who had preceded him.

The territory, within a few years after the Judge had made his location, became settled by the whites to a considerable extent, and his fellow citizens selected him to fill several important offices of trust. In 1800, the Governor appointed him a Judge in the Court of Common Pleas and Quarter Sessions of the Peace, for the county of Trumbull, which comprehended within its limits, at that time, nearly the whole of the Western Reserve. The seat of justice was at Warren, and the first session of the Court, for the want of a more convenient hall, was held with becoming dignity between two *corn cribs*, and the prisoners of the term, it is said, were placed within the cribs for safe keeping. At a subsequent period, the Judge held the office of Justice of the Peace and collector of taxes, under the district system. In 1805 he was elected a member of the Legislature, and having served one term was re-elected, and proved himself in all respects worthy of the trust.

In his politics, the Judge was always democratic. He supported the administration of JEFFERSON, MADISON, JACKSON and VAN BUREN, and gave his last vote in favor of President POLK. In 1812, he was engaged in forwarding supplies to the American forces, and in the communication of intelligence. Being on familiar terms with Commodore PERRY and General HARRISON, he was frequently admitted into their councils, and his opinions were treated with respect. On the day preceding the battle of Lake Erie, while Commodore PERRY was cruising in quest of the enemy, the Judge went on board the flag ship to pay his compliments to the Commodore, who in the course of conversation, asked him what he would do, if they should chance to fall in with the British fleet while he was on board? "What would I do," replied the Judge, "*Why sir, I would fight.*"

Of the Judge, it may be said with propriety, that he was the patriarch of the land—among the last of the brave pioneers on the lake shore. He possessed a noble heart—a heart that overflowed with kindness like the gush of a fountain. His generosities were never stinted in a good cause, nor his charities bestowed ostentatiously to be blazoned abroad among men. He regarded all mankind as his brethren and kinsmen, belonging to the same common household."

In commenting upon this obituary notice, J. W. Biddle, a pioneer of Pittsburg, made the following observations in his paper, the Pittsburg *American:*

"We knew thee well, good old Patriarch, when we were five and thirty years younger, and the hospitality of thy mansion extended to us then, is still fresh on our memory.

In 1812 Judge Kingsbury lived a little beyond the Mills, six miles from "the city" as Cleveland was even then called, and the youngest city and smallest even of its age, we had at that day seen. Kingsbury had been one of the earliest settlers—Major Carter was another, and occupied a red frame house on the top of the high plain which overlooked the Cuyahoga. A fine sample of pioneerism was this Major CARTER. He was a noble fellow—a fit cotemporary of KINGSBURY, but he was suffering at the time we knew him with a cancer on his lip, which we fear brought him to a premature grave. GEOEGE WALLACE and he, kept the only taverns then in Cleveland.

Dr. LONG was the only practising physician and a thorough bred one. There was no meeting house or established clergyman and but two stores, PERRY's and HIRAM HANCHETTS. The road to Sandusky crossed the Cuyahoga a quarter, or may be half a mile from the lake, opposite CARTER's house — the wild grass on the river bottom, below that road to the lake, being then undisturbed even by a scythe.

Our thoughts have often been recalled to the pleasant hours we have passed at Cleveland and at the farm and mansion, a good stout frame house, of our friend KINGSBURY—then with a family of adult sons and daughters, but whom until this notice struck us, we had supposed long since been gathered to his fathers."

SURVEYING PARTY OF 1797.

I have not yet discovered a full list of persons engaged in the expedition of 1797. The following names appear in Mr. PEASE's diary and accounts, in a way which shows they were connected with the surveys of that year, but there may have been others. Men were employed and discharged during the season.

Rev. SETH HART, *Superintendent.*
SETH PEASE, *Principal Surveyor.**

SURVEYORS. (8)

RICHARD M. STODDARD,*
MOSES WARREN,*
AMZI ATWATER,*
JOSEPH LANDON,*
AMOS SPAFFORD,*
WARHAM SHEPARD,*
PHINEAS BARKER,
NATHAN REDFIELD.

THEODORE SHEPARD, (or SHEPHERD,) *Physician.**

EMPLOYEES. (52)

Col. EZRA WAITE,
THOMAS GUN,
PELEG WATERMAN,
(or WASHBURN,)
Maj. WILLIAM SHEPARD,
HUBBARD T. LINSLEY,
DAVID ELDRIDGE, (drowned)
MINOR BICKNELL, (died,)

Josiah Barse, (or Barze,)
Jotham Atwater,
Oliver Culver,
Dan'l Holbrook, Explorer,
Stephen Gilbert,
Nathaniel Doan,*
David Clark,
Solomon Gidings,
Samuel Forbes,
James Stoddard,
Ezekiel Morley,*
Thomas Tupper,
Chester Allen,
James Berry,
Berry Nye,
Joseph Nye,
Asa Mason,
Eli Kellogg,
William Barker,
Shubal Parker, (or Park,)
Jacob Carlton,
Phil Barker,
Eli Canfield,
John Doane,
Joseph Tinker,*
Samuel Spafford, (son of Amos,)
Lot Sanford,
Alpheus Choat,
William Andrews, (died,)
Matthew L. Gilgore,
E. Chapman,
David Beard,*
Solomon Shepard,
William Tinker,
Alexander Allen,
George Gidings,
James Stoddard,
Enoch Eldridge,
Charles Parker,*
Job Coe,
Eli Rowley, (deserted,)
Clark Reynolds,
William Stoddard,
John Hine,
Sylvester Smith,

* These were of the party of 1796.

The names of the Shepherds are spelled both ways, interchangeably.

The outfit of the surveying party of 1797, and the funds were entrusted to Seth Pease. He left Suf-field on the 3d day of April, and proceeded to Schenectady, to organize his company.

Mr. Thomas Mather, of Albany, New York, assisted him in this business. It appears that the

Land Company did not supply them freely with money, for he says:

"*Thursday, April 14th.*—Spent the week thus far in getting necessary supplies. The want of ready cash, subjects me to considerable inconvenience. Mr. MATHER purchases the greater part on his own credit; and takes my order on Mr. EPHRAIM ROOT, Treasurer."

PEASE'S JOURNAL.

April 15th.—Helves were put into the axes, and they were ground. Rations began to be issued, and the camp utensils, left there by General Cleaveland, were again brought into use. Delayed on account of the compasses not being ready, which were to be made at Ballstown, by Mr. F. Young.

April 20th.—Six boats started up the Mohawk. Each mess of six men received for daily rations, chocolate, one pound; pork, five pounds; sugar, a small porringer; one bottle of rum; one-half bottle of tea; flour or bread, not limited. A man, his wife and a small child, taken on board one of the boats.

April 22d.—Warham Shepard, sent back to Ballstown for another compass. Doan, Holbrook and Forbes sick.

April 24th.—Arrived at the Little Falls of the Mohawk. Paid for lockage $12 07.

April 25th.—Reached Fort Schuyler, where Phineas Barker joined them, and also Mr. Harts boat.

April 26th.—The men very much fatigued.

April 27th.—Reached Fort Stanwix (Rome, New York.)

April 28th.—At Oneida lake, joined by Ezra Wait and Samuel Keeny.

April 30th.—Made the portage around Oswego Falls. Mr. Pease obtained his trunk, left at Three River Point, the year previous.

May 1st.—Passed Oswego Falls portage, with the freight, ran the boats over the rapids and reached the Fort. Detained by storms till Wedmesday, May 3d, and that day reached Salmon creek, one mile west of Great Sodus bay. The next day arrived at "Gerundigut" bay; and found their expected articles were not there. Oliver Culver, Samuel Spafford, and Daniel Clark joined the company.

"*Friday, May 5th.*—This morning Mr. Redfield took charge of the men and stores. I started for Canandaigua, on a horse hired of Dunbar. (Dunbar was a mulatto hunter or squatter at the bay). Went to Richardson's, where Mr. Hart was waiting for me, and we rode in company to Canandaigua."

"*May 6th.*—Found Moses Shepard (or Shepherd) at Sanborn's (or Sanburn's) who had procured pork, flour, cheese, whisky, horses and cattle. Conversed with Mr. Augustus Porter, about taking the superintendency of the surveys this summer, who concluded he could not attend to it; and advised me to proceed according to my instructions.

Sunday, May 7th.—Sent the hired horse by Mr. N. Doan to Gerundigut, and also Mr. Hart's; gave him a crown for expenses. One of our hands, by the name of Rowley, came to this place last night with his clothes, and inquired the way to Whitestown. It is reported he has left us, which I find to be so.

May 10th.—The land party, in charge of Major William Shepard are: Warham Shepard, Thomas Gun, Hubbard T. Lindsley, Peleg Waterman, (probably Washburn,) Amzi Atwater, David Eldridge, Josiah Barse, Minor Bicknell, Jotham Atwater, John Doane, Doctor Shepherd.

Thursday, May 11th.—Departed from Gerundigut a few minutes past 6 o'clock, A. M. Our fleet consisted of Major Amos Spafford, Seth Hart, Seth Pease, Joseph Tinker, David Beard, and N. Redfield, and six boats. I left one boat in charge of Moses Warren to bring on the whisky and other stores, expected this day. Reached Oak Orchard, forty to forty-five miles.

Sunday, May 14th.—Arrived at the garrison at Niagara, and gave the commanding officer, Captain Bragg, my letter. I went in, but we were not permitted to inspect the works, which were undergoing repairs, and went on to Queenstown.

On Monday we concluded to send boats No. 278 and 280 back to Gerundiugt, in charge of Beard and Tinker, for the rest of the stores. Put up at Ingersoll's.

Friday, May 19th.—Started from Chippeway with two boats, one for myself and one for Spafford. Reached Buffalo before night, and found the land party had been here since last Tuesday. They had bought and borrowed some flour and taken some fish, but lived very sparingly. Major Shepard, Dr. Shepherd and Warham Shepard came in this evening with three horses and a compass.

May 20th.—Major Shepard set forward with the horses and cattle by land; head winds.

Monday, May 22d.—Started at 6 o'clock, A. M. Reached Cataraugus about 4 o'clock, P. M., and tried to get an interpreter, but could not. The Indians stole eight to ten pounds of our pork and ham.

Friday, 26th.—Wind favorable and steady during the day. We kept our course outside of Presque Isle about 3 o'clock, and reached Conneaut before sunset, making no stop this day. Found the entrance good.

About 2 o'clock at night the wind shifted, rolled in a heavy sea, broke the painter of one of the boats, and set it adrift. There was a cry that our boats were all gone. As there was no living without them, we resolved to follow them, but happily they were not driven out of the creek, and were soon secured, setting a guard the rest of the night. We found that Mr. Gun's family had removed to Cuyahoga. Mr. Kingsbury, his wife and one child, were in a low state of health, to whom we administered what relief we could. Phineas Barker has not been able to do much for seven days, on account of fever and ague.

Monday, May 29th.—Major Spafford started at half past 10 o'clock, A. M., to run the line between towns 10 and 11, in the 1st, 2d and 3d Ranges.

May 30th.—Landon and Parker came on with their boats.

May 31st.—I left Conneaut about 10 o'clock, A. M., with our boat; the other, destined for Mary Easter's, was almost ready to start, and was to wait there for Major Spafford. The cattle were all ready but three, which the men were in search of. We had a fair wind till about 2 o'clock, P. M., when it came ahead. We partly unloaded the boat, and drew it into a small creek, about twenty miles west of Conneaut. Phelps and Parker put into the same creek.

Thursday, June 1st.—Started at 7 o'clock, rowed five or six miles, then had favorable wind; passed Grand river at 10 hours 55 minutes, Chagrin river at 12 hours 25 minutes, and entered Cuyahoga at 3 hours 22 minutes, P. M., landing at the store house at 4 o'clock. That night I was very unwell and had the toothache, from wading in the water and taking cold.

Found Mr. Stiles and Mrs. Stiles well, also Mrs. Gun. Mr. Gun had gone back to Conneaut. The men with me were Major Wm. Shepard, Dr. T. Shepherd, Ezekiel Morley, Nathaniel Doan, and —— Reynolds. Reynolds was set to chopping railcuts.

Saturday, June 3d.—Wind easterly. Two boats came in, and informed me that three of our boats, had reached Conneaut, and that Major Spafford's boat was at Mary Easter's, on Thursday. This night four of our boats arrived, viz: Spafford's, Warren's, Redfield's, and Hart's; property but little injured on the voyage. About 11 o'clock this day David Eldridge, one of our men, was drowned in attempting to swim his horse across the Grand river. He was nearly an hour in the water, before he could be got out. The boats put into the river, and Mr. Hart used every precaution to recover him, without effect. His corpse was brought to the Cuyahoga River.

Sunday, June 4th.—This morning selected a piece of land for a burying ground, the north parts of lots 97 and 98; and attended the funeral of the deceased with as much decency and solemnity as could possibly be expected. Mr. Hart read church service. The afternoon was devoted to washing.

Cleaveland, Monday, June 5th.—Began to clear land above the bank for a garden, and examined the stores to see if every thing was in condition.

June 6th.—Most of the men worked at the clearing got it cleared and fenced. Major Shepard and Esquire Warren, set out with Andrews as packhorseman, to explore the next township south of this, and the one next south of Euclid.

Wednesday, June 7th.—This morning Redfield started to run the line between Ranges 11 and 12, with ten days provision. Returning he is to begin at the south-east corner of Euclid, run north to the lake, and if necessary set off a piece to Wells township. Then go back, and run south to intersect the line between Towns 4 and 5.

Friday, June 9th.—Shepard and Warren returned, and report No. 6 in the 11th Range (Bedford) well watered and a plenty of mill seats. * * * They traveled over part of No. 7 in the 11th Range (Warrensville) and their whole route, was over choice land, with plenty of small creeks—about five of the lots they passed through in Cleaveland good land, then flat, inclined to swampy and bad water.

This day three parties, Shepard's, Warren's and Spafford's were delivered their supplies to start tomorrow if the weather permits. Warm south-west winds—articles delivered to each party; pork, flour, tea, chocolate, sugar, ginger, spirits, vinegar, cheese, pepper, empty bags, fire steel and punk, candles, a tent, axes and hatchets, pocket compass, measuring pins, salt, soap, horses. Major Shepard will receive his next supplies at the upper head quarters—has twenty days provisions. Moses Warren, Esq., will go to the south-east corner of No. 6, in Range 9, and run east to the Pennsylvania line, then travel to the ten mile post on the first meridian, (Coitsville) and run east to the State line, and then run west from said point. Provisions for thirty days.

To RICHARD M. STODDARD:—You will proceed up the river to our head quarters, though I am at a loss at present where it will be fixed, but you may take the line between the 10th and 11th ranges, and I will give you notice on that line, at the nearest corner. We shall go as far as possible with our boats. If I have an opportunity I will send a line here, after we have fixed our head quarters. If you should not arrive here, (Cleaveland) so as to be there in about thirty days from this date, I think you had better not go up the river, unless you receive another line from your humble servant,

SETH PEASE.

Saturday, June 10th.—Shepard and Warren's parties take their departure about 10½ o'clock, A. M. Spafford's and my party moved up the river about 4 o'clock, P. M. Got near Warren's line, and camped on the west bank. Left a frying pan.

Mr. JOS. TINKER:—I wish you to return and bring another boat load of stores as soon as possible. You will take four hands, and have such men return as are best pleased with the business of boating. I wish you a prosperous voyage.

SETH PEASE.

Mr. DAVID BEARD, *Sir*:—The surveyors have this day taken to the bush. We intend to build a store-house up the river. I wish you and those men who came with the boat, and are not to return with Mr. Tinker, to report to the head-quarters, and take charge of the stores. On our return from the Pennsylvania line, one or two of the surveyors will go exploring, and if you choose, you can accompany one of them. You will take a boat up the river, with three barrels of flour and two of pork, some chests, &c., which Mr. Hart will show you.

Yours, &c.,

SETH PEASE.

Sunday, June 11*th*.—Run a little beyond my line, and camped for the night on the east bank. We had to cut off some logs in order to pass.

Tuesday, 13*th*.—On the river, between Towns 4 and 5, (Boston and Northfield.) Spafford's party started out about noon, to run this parallel.

Wednesday, 14*th*.—Mr. Beard arrived from Cleaveland with news that both boats had reached there on Sunday night at 10 o'clock. They left one load at Conneaut, and brought on Mr. Kingsbury's family. We manned his boats and proceeded up the river, leaving Morley to keep the stores. Bicknall, (or Bicknell,) went in search of the pack-horses. Choat followed after Major Spafford, to have Atwater return. There came up the river with Beard, Wm. Barker, Choat, the two Allens, and two men, Mr.

Brown and Mr. Richey, who came to view the country. Last night made observations for variation one degree sixteen minutes east. Porter's compass had given just below the old town (Pilgerruh,) two degrees east. Mr. Porter called the variation at the mouth of the Cuyahoga one degree twenty minutes east. Water shallow and swift; found much difficulty in getting along. Camped opposite the peninsula.

Thursday, 15*th*.—Navigation better than yesterday. Arrived about 1 o'clock where we judged the line between three and four would come. Left Brown and Richey in charge of stores, and went down to Morley's camp. Bicknell had not found the horse. Jotham Atwater returned, and says that Choat lost the lines, and did not find them till 11 o'clock; and that Spafford had run three miles.

Friday 16*th*.—Sent Amzi Atwater with a boat load of provisions to the north-west corner of Town 4, Range 10, (Hudson). Started up the river, and got to the upper camp about 4 o'clock, P. M. Atwater came in before night, and said that Redfield had run to the place expected, and was about going to the river when he delivered him the message, and Redfield returned to his line. Took the level of the water at the peninsula. The ridge is twelve and a half feet above the water on the upper side, and eighteen and a half feet above it below, making six feet fall, and a rock bottom quite across the river.

Saturday, June 17th.—Mr. Beard took charge of one boat, and myself the other, and proceeded up the river, about a mile above where the stream from the south comes in, (Little Cuyahoga) to the head of boat navigation.

Sunday, 18th—After landing our stores, we took one boat and all hands went down to Morley's camp, in just three hours. Minor Bicknell had been to Cleaveland for the horse, and had returned with him. He lay out without fire or blanket, or much provisions, one night going and one coming. The horse got there before him. Redfield brought in his line north of our camp. Received letters from Messrs. Hart and Stoddard. Richard Stoddard had arrived with his brother, and wishes employment.

Monday, 19th.—Spend the day in washing and getting ready for the bush. Sent one boat down the river, by Thos. Tupper with Messrs. Brown and Richey. Wrote to Stoddard to survey more one hundred acre lots in Cleaveland. To Mr. Hart to have Dr. Shepard come up if he could be spared N. Redfields party fitted out with twenty-eight days provisions."

The field books and memoranda of Mr. PEASE are very full and interesting. They show the movements of the various parties of which he was the head, the general progress of the work, and the personal incidents of which such expeditions are fruitful. Although everything connected with the survey of the

Reserve, has some relation to the history of this city, I have not space to insert all of the transactions of year 1797.

Mr. PEASE and his party left the upper head quarters on the 25th of June, to resume the survey of the south line of the Reserve where it was left off the year previous, twenty miles west of the Pennsylvania line at the south-east corner of Berlin. They traveled along the great Indian trail which passed through Stow, crossing the Cuyahoga at Franklin Mills, or Kent, then known as the "Standing Stone," from a natural pillar of sand rock which stood in the middle of the stream, bearing a 'stinted pine. This ancient highway of the savages, passed up the valley of Breakneck creek, crossing the summit not far south of Ravenna, thence through Edinburg, Palmyra, and Milton to the Salt Spring, and thence down the Mahoning to the forks of Beaver.

PEASE arrived at the starting point on the 3d of July, and took observations for the variation, which he fixed at one degree, 30 minutes east. On the subject of the irregularities of the compass, he says:

"The south line was run as follows: From the Pennsylvania line to the fifth mile, one degree, twenty-one minutes, should have been one degree, twenty-five minutes. From the fifth to the ninth mile, one degree, twenty-one minutes, should have been one degree, thirty-three minutes. From ninth to thirteenth I expect was very near the truth. From thirteenth to fifteenth mile, two degrees, two minutes, ought to have been one degree, fifty minutes."

"From observations made on the various compasses, I find I cannot reduce them to a common standard, being differently affected at different places. Of two compasses on the Cuyahoga river, twenty miles south of the lake, one needle was to the left of the other ten minutes. At Cleaveland the one which was to the left stood fifteen minutes to the right, though they were not compared precisely at the same hour of the day. The magnetic needle is not always parallel to itself at the same place, which renders the compass an inaccurate instrument for running long lines. The variation is so irregular that it admits of no calculation, and must be determined by observations upon the heavenly bodies."

FROM THE FIELD BOOK OF MOSES WARREN.

Monday, July 17th.—Started from the upper head-quarters (on the Cuyahoga, above the forks,) at 1 o'clock, P. M., to continue the 2d parallel, and meet Mr. Pease from the south. (Pease was continuing the south line of the Reserve to the Tuskarawas). White and Reynolds, chainmen; Gun, pack-horse man and cook; Hamilton and P. Barker, axmen. Barker to return to-morrow. Having lent my compass to Mr. Redfield to run the seventh meridian, I took one of the Ballstown compasses that is not esteemed as good, but it traverses well with careful usage. Began at a post I set on the tenth meridian, (north-west corner of Tallmadge,) on the 30th of June. Ran west between Towns 2 and 3, Range 11, (Portage and Northampton.)

July 18*th.*—River fog prevented an observation of the polar star. Struck the right bank of the Cuyahoga river at three miles, forty-five links; thirteen chains, ninety-eight links from the Portage tree, which I traversed in three courses, the last crossing the river. I then traversed the path to course No. 23, and encamped at a run on course No. 7. Sent Barker back after crossing the river. By good observation of the polar star, I found the variation to be two degrees and 2 minutes east.

July 19*th and* 20*th.*—Continued the traverse to Tuskarawa landing, at course No. 74. At No. 72 is a large white oak, marked with many Indian hieroglyphics. In this vicinity are many Indian camps. The traverse from the second parallel by the path is 658.53; length of the portage, 644.55 chains.

July 21*st.*—Continued a traverse down the river, from which I was allured by Mr. Pease's pack-horse man, who sounded the Indian whoop, and being answered, refused to reply as we neared him. Mr. Pease connected his traverse with mine at No. 96, about forty chains south-west of the landing. Returned to the upper head-quarters with Mr. Pease and party, in the evening. Except the Cuyahoga hill, the Portage will admit of an excellent road, and that is not so formidable as the one at Queenstown, Upper Canada.

"*Aug.* 5*th*, 1797, 5 o'clock, P. M.—By the grace of God and good health, left Cleaveland with Joel Hawley, Thomas Tupper, chainmen; Matthew L. Gilgore and Enoch Eldridge, axmen; Sylvester Smith and Chester Allen, horsemen, with three horses; two hundred and sixty pounds of flour, one hundred and thirty pounds of pork, twelve pounds of sugar, four pounds of Chocolate, one and a half pound of tea, six quarts of rum, one half peck of beans, one camp kettle, one frying pan, and six tin cups, for a tour of thirty or forty days, to proceed to No. 1 in Range 10. Encamped about two and a half miles from head-quarters."

SURVEY OF THE TEN ACRE LOTS IN THE TOWN OF CLEAVELAND.

"CENTRAL HIGHWAY," OR EUCLID STREET.

"*August* 20*th*. — Began at the post at the east end of Huron street, (Euclid Street Church,) north-east side of the City of Cleaveland, run thence north eighty-two degrees east, setting a post at every tally, to the west line of the one hundred acre lots. Highway, one hundred and fifty links wide. Ran back on south side, south eighty-two degrees west, setting posts opposite the first at every tally, to the city line. The posts aforesaid are bounds of the highway and corner boundings of the lots, and are marked H. Numbers to be put on when the cross lines are run.

"SOUTH HIGHWAY," OR KINSMAN STREET.

August 21st.—Began at the end of Erie street, and ran south seventy-four degrees east, twenty-six tallies, one hundred and seven links, to the line of the one hundred acre lots, setting and marking posts at every tally; and then ran a line one hundred and fifty links south, sixteen degrees west of this, back and parallel to it, setting posts as before, each being marked like its opposite, to Erie street, west side.

"NORTH HIGHWAY," OR ST. CLAIR STREET.

Tuesday, August 22d.—Went to a post at the end of Lake (Federal) street, south-east side, and ran north fifty-eight degrees east to the one hundred acre lots, setting the posts on both sides as I went, the north side posts being at right angles from the others, and one hundred and fifty links therefrom. Land swampy and scalded; will require causewaying to make a good road, but can be passed as it is. Returned to the city."

On the 23d and 24th the middle lines, between the above roads, were run, and the posts set at the proper distance for the rear corners of the out-lots, generally known as the "ten acre lots," although there is no uniformity in the quantity. By opening these main highways from the outskirts of the city, spreading like a fan to the east, the lots fronting them increased in quantity as they receded from the town. This was done to make them of equal value, the most distant containing enough more land to make this equality, their fronts being equal.

STATEMENT OF AMZI ATWATER,

RELATING TO THE SURVEYS OF 1797, MADE IN AUGUST, 1850.

I was one of the first surveying party of the Connecticut Land Company, in the year 1796, and entered their service again about the middle of April, 1797. I joined the company at Schenectady. The company procured six boats and a sufficient quantity of suitable stores for the expedition. These boats were the common batteaux for the navigation of rivers and lakes, as practiced in those days. They were supplied with four oars, setting posts, paddles and a moveable mast and sail.

We ascended the Mohawk river through the old locks at Little Falls, up to the carrying place at Rome. The canal there was in progress, but not completed. The boats and stores were got across into Wood creek. Down that narrow, crooked stream, we got along somewhat easier than up the Mohawk river, which I may say was a sore job for raw and inexperienced hands like myself. In passing down this stream which had long been known by boatmen, we passed, in a small inlet stream, two large, formidable looking boats, or small vessels, which reminded us of a seaport harbor. We were told that they were the season before conveyed from the Hudson river, partly by water and finally on wheels, and to be conveyed to lake Ontario; that they were built of the lightest materials, and intended for no other use, than to have it published in Europe that vessels of those dimensions had passed those waters, *to aid land speculation.*

We passed down and across the Oneida lake, and past the Oswego Falls into lake Ontario.

At Oswego Falls the boats were unloaded, and were run down a slide into a natural basin, and a pilot employed to steer them to the lower landing. The stream looked dreadful (in my eye) to run a boat. But I considered that as we had a pilot who followed the business at fifty cents a trip, I would risk myself for once. I belonged to the first boat, and took my station in the bow strictly attending to the pilot's orders. We went quick and safe, and I was cured of all my former fears. I went back to attend my own luggage. I met the pilot on his return from his second trip, who requested me to go down with the other boats, and I accordingly did. We passed down to the lake and stayed some time for fair weather, then went on as far as Gerundigut bay and up to the landing, where the boats took in provisions. This was a slow and tedious way of conveyance, but it was the way which some of the early settlers of this country moved here for want of a better.

I was sent with a party of those men who could be best spared from the boats, to Canandaigua and its vicinity to collect cattle and pack horses for the use of the company. In a few days I was ordered with those men to drive to Buffalo, and take care of them until Maj. SHEPARD of the exploring and equalizing committee came on. We drove there and across the creek for safe and convenient keeping. In a few days the Indian chiefs came and demanded of me three dollars for pasturing the cattle and horses. I thought it unreasonable as the land all lay open to the common as I considered it, but I went with them up to Capt. JOHNSON, the Interpreter, and plead my case as well as I could, but I was no match for them in pleas and arguments. I concluded to pay their demand with their consent, that we might stay as long as we pleased. Soon after one of our horses strayed away up to the Indian village, and they sent it back without asking fee or reward.

In a few days Maj. SHEPARD came on and took the command, and we arrived at Conneaut the 25th of May.

After a short time of preparation, we went to the various stations assigned us. I went with Maj. SHEPARD to run the north lines of the townships of Monroe and Sheffield in Ashtabula county. A part

I ran under his direction and inspection. This was the first time I undertook to use a surveyor's compass.

After this I was ordered with a party of men to take the horses and cattle to Cleveland. We got along very well until we got to Grand river: we had no boat or other means of conveyance across, except we found an old Indian bark canoe which was very leaky—we had one horse which I knew was a good swimmer. I mounted him, and directed the men to drive the others after me. I had got perhaps half way when I heard the men on shore scream—I looked back and saw two men, with horses in the water but had parted from them—one of them got ashore, and the other, David Eldridge, made poor progress. I turned my horse as quick as I could and guided him up within reach of him, when I very inconsiderately took hold of his hand, as soon as I could. This turned the horse over, and we were both under the water in an instant; but we separated and I again mounted the horse, and looked back and saw him just raise his head above the water, but he sunk to rise no more,—this was June 3d.

We built a raft of flood-wood, lashed together with barks, and placing on it three men who were good swimmers, they with hooks drew up the body, but this took some time—perhaps two hours. We took some pains to restore the body to life, but in vain. Two of our boats came up soon after with a large portion of the men. They took the body to Cleveland and, buried it in the then newly laid out burying-ground.

We then went on with the cattle and horses, and arrived at Cleveland without any further difficulty.

After a few days of preparation, the two boats, with some of the surveyors, started up the river with the assistants and provisions. I, with one or two other men, was sent by land to get the horses up above the mouth of TINKER's creek, for the use of the surveyors. Not far above the creek, we found the remnants of some old huts, partly overgrown with thorn and plum trees, one or more fragments of doors were fastened with nails, which to me was a curiosity to see in such a place. I suppose they were the remains of the old Moravian settlement, but of this I may be mistaken. I found the boats, and gave up my charge of the horses to the surveyors, and went on board the boats. We got them along very slow, the river was very low, and in some places trees had fallen into the stream and obstructed the channel, and in others, stones had to be removed, and all hands had to join, lift by the sides, and get one boat up some distance, and then go back and get the other. When we got up to the north line of Boston, Mr. PEASE wishing to give some directions to Mr. REDFIELD, who was supposed to be near the north-west corner of Hudson township, I was sent up there with a back load of provisions and some directions for him. I passed the falls of Brandywine mills to the corner of Hudson. Not finding REDFIELD there, I erected a staging some ten feet high, and deposited the provisions and directions covered with a bark, which I had peeled for that purpose, and returned to the boats. After we got some distance above the Peninsula, we found it some better, but not very good there. The weather was very warm, with frequent showers of rain; I think my clothes were not entirely dry for near a week. We succeeded in getting the boats past the old Portage, and about half a mile above the south branch of Cuyahoga, where we established a camp. I was left there in charge of the provisions and stores, while some of the surveyors run lines to the Pennsylvania line, and others back. I erected a shed covered with barks, to cover the provisions, &c., and a tolerable good bark camp for myself. The surveying parties were frequently coming and going, and once in a while the boats came up, some sick and others well. While there, two or more Indian hunters were camped some distance, near the river, below us; one of them frequently visited us. He was very active, and more talkative than Indians generally, and could talk a little of our lingo. I had learned a little of the Indians, and between us both, by signs and motions, we could convey ideas tolerable well. We felt anxious to gain information respecting Indian paths and some of the streams, and from him we got some valuable information to us.

He showed a scar on his thigh, which looked as though it might be a gun-shot wound. I understood him to tell, how his horse was shot under him at the battle, when Gen. WAYNE defeated the Indians some years before; he made the motions how his horse plunged down, and he scrambled off in the bushes. He often repeated, "Capt. WAYNE very good man, Capt. WAYNE very great man." Mr. PEASE wishing to go to the salt spring and convey some provisions, employed this Indian to go with his horse and convey a load, who was gone but three days when he came back near night. I set before him some victuals I had cooked, when he handed me a few lines from Mr. PEASE, stating how he got along, and I must give him a quart of whisky, or more. I went and filled a junk bottle and presented it to him, with more ceremony than I am in the habit of using, as a present from the big Captain, (Mr. PEASE). He went off to his camp with many praises of us all. Next day he came back and presented a deerskin, for the big Captain, and then the bottle, "A little more whisky." I put on my most serious countenance, and told him we had but little, and our brethren would come in from the woods, some of them sick, and we should want it for medicine, but drew my finger across the side of the bottle, telling how full I would fill it, but he must not ask for any more; I accordingly did so. He next day came back and brought the bottle, but never asked for any more whisky, although he frequently visited the camp.

I think it was the 4th of July, Mr. WARHAM SHEPARD and I, were sent to run the 9th meridian, beginning at the north-east corner of Hudson, and running south to the south line of the Reserve. I commenced the line and run between Streetsborough and Hudson the first day, then SHEPARD took the compass and I the chain, thus we proceeded on, alternately to the south line of the Reserve, then returned to the camp. Next, we were ordered to the fifth meridian. (See General BIERCE's statement). After that was completed we all returned to head-quarters at Cleveland. Then we were directed to run out a few more of the remaining out lots of Cleveland, then to lot out the township of Warrensville, and a part of Bedford. This completed, my work was finished for that season, for I was taken sick with the ague and fever.

Sickness prevailed the latter part of the season to an alarming degree, and but a few escaped entirely. WILLIAM ANDREWS, one of our men, and PELEG WASHBURN, an apprentice to Mr. NATHANIEL DOAN, died of dysentery at Cleveland, in August or September.

All those that died that season, were of my party who came on with me, with the cattle and horses, in the spring, and were much endeared to me as companions, except TINKER, our principal boatman, who was drowned on his return in the fall. At Cleveland I was confined for several weeks, with several others much in the same situation as myself, with little or no help, except what we could do for ourselves. The inhabitants there, were not much better off than we were, and all our men were required in the woods. My fits came on generally every night, and long nights they appeared to me; in day-time, I made out to get to the spring, and get some water, but it was a hard task to get back again. My fits became lighter, and not so frequent, until the boats went down the lake as far as the township of Perry, which they were then lotting out. The cold night winds, and fatigue to which I was exposed, brought on the fits faster and harder. I considered that I had a long journey before me to get home, and no means but my own exertions, a large portion of the way.

I procured a portion of Peruvian bark and took it, it broke up my fits and gave me an extra appetite, but very fortunately for me we were short of provisions, and on short allowance. My strength gained, and I did not spoil my appetite by over eating, as people are in danger of in such cases. I soon began to recover my health, but soon after Maj. SPAFFORD started with a boat down the lake, with a sufficient number of well hands, and a load of us invalids to the number of fourteen in all. We passed on tolerable well down beyond Erie, opposite the rocky shore; there arose a dreadful looking cloud with a threatening, windy appearance; the wind was rather high, but some in our favor. Maj. SPAFFORD was a good hand to steer and manage a boat, they double manned the oars on the land side to keep off shore, and we went fast, till we got past the rocky shore; few or no words spoken, but immediately the wind came very heavy so that no boat could have stood it. There we staid three days without being able to get away. We got out in the evening, went below Cataraugus, where we were driven ashore again, where we lay about two days, still on short allowance of provision. The next time we had a tolerable calm lake, and safely arrived at Buffalo. By that time I had so recovered as to feel tolerably comfortable, and pursued my journey home on foot to Connecticut.

FROM AN ADDRESS BY GENERAL L. V. BIERCE.

On the 5th of July, 1797, WARHAM SHEPARD and ATWATER were sent to survey the 9th meridian from the 4th parallel south to the south line of the Reserve—one carrying the compass, the other the chain, alternately. Soon after their return to camp, after finishing that work, all the surveyors came in, and reported all the lower lines run, except the 5th, 6th, and 7th meridians. To complete these, Redfield was ordered to the 7th, STODDARD to the 6th, and SHEPARD and ATWATER to the 5th, which was the west line of Trumbull and Ashtabula.

STODDARD being lame, ATWATER took his compass and run his line ten miles, when he met STODDARD with one man, who took the line and finished it. ATWATER with one man then left that line, and met Mr. SHEPARD at the north-east corner of Palmyra. Here he found SHEPARD sick with the dysentery, and MINOR BICKNELL, the man who accompanied ATWATER, was taken with a violent fever. ATWATER took the compass and run seven miles, between Braceville and Windham, when BICKNELL became too unwell to ride on a horse. In the language of Judge ATWATER, in a letter before me, "here was a difficult case to know what to do. We were at a great distance from any comfortable place for the sick. Medicine we had none, and ignorant of its use if we had it. No guide but our compass, or township lines. To get him to Cleveland seemed most desirable if it were practicable. We were in hopes some of our boats were at our late camp, but how to get him there was the question. Necessity was the mother of invention." They took two poles and fastened them together with bark, so as to go by the sides of the horses like thills of a wagon, one horse following the other, so far apart as to admit a man to lie lengthwise between them.

With barks and blankets they made his bed as comfortable as possible, and by twisting bark ropes, lashed it to the pack-saddles. ATWATER left SHEPARD with one man to run the lines as best he could, and started with the sick man for Cleveland. They went south to the corner of Palmyra, then west on the third parallel. The next morning after they started, ATWATER sent a man ahead to have a boat ready at the Upper Head Quarters, to carry the sick man down the river. ATWATER proceeded west to the corner of Stow and Hudson, on the ninth meridian, then south to the old Indian trail from Fort McIntosh to Sandusky, where he met his messenger with the disagreeable intelligence, that the camp was broken up and the boats gone. ATWATER then directed him to go to Cleveland, and get a boat to come up and meet him at the south line of Independence. ATWATER then proceeded on the west line of Stow to the north line of Summit county, then west to the place for meeting the boats. In this litter they had thus conveyed BICKNELL, about five days and a distance of fifty miles. He had a high fever all the time, and had his reason but a little part of it. They arrived at the river early in the forenoon of July 25th, and BICKNELL died about two hours after. TINKER, with the boat and Dr. SHEPHERD, arrived a little after noon. ATWATER urged to have the corpse carried to Cleveland, but the boatmen would not consent, and he was buried near the river, on the south line of Independence, on land since cleared by Esquire FRAZER.

This, says Judge ATWATER, in the letter I have before referred to, "was the most affecting scene of my life. My feelings I cannot attempt to describe. My fatigue was great during the whole distance. My anxiety stimulated every power I possessed of body or mind.

I was in perfect health, and in the most active part of life, but when I had got through and the man was dead, and my extreme fatigue was at an end, it seemed as if every nerve was unstrung; and in ordinary circumstances, I should have thought myself entitled to a few days' rest. But we were obliged immediately to leave there, to return and find Mr. SHEPHERD."

ATWATER and his company followed the marked line east to the north-east corner of Portage county, where they found he had got the line up there, and he and his party were in good health.

The whole company then proceeded to run the line to the lake, which completed the township lines. Thus was completed the survey of the Western Reserve, east of the Cuyahoga.

Towards the latter part of the season sickness prevailed to an alarming extent. Boat loads of sick were sent off early in the fall. Says Judge ATWATER in the letter referred to, "I was at Cleveland in a sad situation—and all others were about as bad as I was. When the fit was off, I with a great deal of exertion could go to the spring and get a little water, and set it by the side of my old bear skin and blanket, where I lay through the long nights of ague and fever, and all around were much in the same situation. Oh! these were days and nights of sorrow and affliction."

TINKER, the principal boatman, was discharged in the fall, and in going down the lake, with three others, the boat was capsized near the mouth of Chatauque creek, and TINKER and two of the other men were drowned.

It appears in the field notes, that some of the meridians were run from the north southerly, and some of the parallels from the west easterly, as was most convenient. The parallels in the first four Ranges south of Town 6, were not run in 1796, which thus formed a part of this years work. In running the first five miles from the State line, they generally began at the 1st meridian, and ran east to the Pennsylvania line; fixing the town corners wherever the intersection took place.

Thus the several parties pursued their work during the summer and fall. The equalizing committee, was very busy exploring and surveying, comparing notes and arranging the parcels for a draft; fully determined that the work should be closed that season. Cleveland was the central point of all operations, and particularly as a general hospital. "On the 6th of August, at half past one, P. M., Peleg Washburn, the apprentice to Doan, died of dysentery, and was buried the same evening. (PEASE's Journal.)

Tuesday, Aug. 8th.—Sick list: Major Spafford, Sol. Giddings, Canfield, Barse, Hanchett, Linsley, Clark. On the 10th Samuel Spafford and Lot Sanford started to do my settling duties in Euclid, and the same for Dr. Shepard. 14th, Solomon Shepard came in sick. 16th, Esquire Warren and party, came in from running the four southern tiers, all well 18th, went out to explore a road to the southward.

Sunday 18th.—Mr. Hart started for town 5, in the 11th Range, where Redfield is at work. Warren is running out the ten acre lots.

Wednesday, 23d.—Reynolds taken sick. The committee is busy comparing notes. 26th, I took the oversight of the new house, (south of Superior street,) and shingled it this day.

Sunday, Aug. 27th.—Jotham Atwater, from Shepards and Atwater's party, came in sick with fever and ague. Green set out to take his place, but returned at night, sick. What men were well, worked on the house. Sick list this day: Sol. Giddings, Hine, Canfield, Green, Sol. Shepard, Doctor Shepard, Mr. Hart, Reynolds, Hamilton, Clark and Linsley. The Committe concluded to have Esquire Warren go up to the Portage, and explore there and some towns on the river.

Monday, Aug. 28th.—Esq. Warren set out with Mr. Abbott and Mr. ——, of Pennsylvania, whom the Committee hired; also, Chester Allen and James G. Stoddard, who had liberty to change berths with Allen; and take provisions to Stoddard's party. This morning I was very unwell, but attended to business part of the day; had chills, head-ache, back-ache and fever. Took a sweat and felt somewhat relieved, slept comfortably. 29th, more comfortable; preparing a place for the Committee to transact business; in the afternoon fever and chills again. 31st, Tinker arrives with the boat, Choat and Coe left on account of sickness. Weather very rainy.

Saturday, Sept. 2d.—Majors Spafford and Shepard are to survey and explore some towns east of the Chagrin river. Escaped the fit last night; twelve persons sick.

Monday, 4th.—Doctor Shepard went to see Mrs. Parker, (probably the wife of Charles Parker in Mentor.) Andrews very sick of dysentery. 5th, I have another fit, which lasted till 10 o'clock, at night. 7th, I had a violent fever. Andrews died about 8 o'clock, at night.

Friday, 8th.—Andrews interred. I am weak, but better than yesterday. Cannot furnish hands for Shepard's and Atwater's party, till more arrive. Warren and party return from the Portage. Abbot sick of fever and ague.

(Here Warren takes up the journal.)

Saturday, 9th.—Mr. Pease had a hard fit of fever and ague. Shepard and Atwater surveying the ten acre lots.

Monday, 11th.—Pease took four large doses of bark, (Peruvian.) At 10, he had a paroxysm and slow fever. Alex. Allen comes in from Redfield unwell. Their horse strayed away.

Tuesday, 12th.—Our invalids are Sol. Gidings, Eli Canfield, Josiah Barse, Thos. Green, Luke Hanchet, Sol. Shepard, John Hine, Sol. Sanford, and Jotham Atwater, who took their discharges, and started for home on a boat, to be taken as far as Gerundigut. Spafford arrives this afternoon.

Wednesday, 13th.—The committee sat. Redfield came in at night.

Thursday, 14th.—The men cleaning their clothes. Redfield's party made search for their horse to no purpose. They are jealous of the Indians about there, and think they have stolen him.

Friday, 15th.—Stoddard and his party came in all well but one, and he able to move about.

Saturday, 16th.—Shepard, Atwater and Redfield start to lot No. 6, in the 11th Range, (Warrensville.)

Tuesday, 19th.—Stoddard and party could not find their pack-horses.

Wednesday 20th.—He started early to help the other surveyors, in No. 6, Range 11.

(Here Pease resumes the Journal.)

Wednesday, 27*th*.—Three parties came into camp in pretty good spirits, having finished No. 6, Range 11, which they find to be a most excellent township. Landon is shoeing the horses.

Friday, 29*th*.—Three parties made up, and are to go with the committee in the boat. The horses assigned by lot. Mr. Redfield has the "Hannah" horse, Mr. Shepard the "Morton" mare, Mr. Stoddard "Mary Esther," and Mr. Landon the "Stow" horse. Sick Roll: Amzi Atwater, Chester Allen, Alexander Allen and Clark Reynolds. Tupper is not well, but able to cook. Linsley and William Barker sick.

Saturday, 30*th*.—Four parties of surveyors start this afternoon. Expect to be at Grand River in nine days.

Sunday, October 1*st*.—Had a touch of fever and ague: not violent.

Monday, 2*d*.—Paid Samuel Spafford towards four and a half days' clearing, in Euclid, at 5 shillings, three crowns, $3,30. Gave Mr. Hart a purse containing four dollars, left with me, supposed to be Minor Bicknall's. Nathan Chapman credit by two bushels of wheat, $4,50.

Tuesday, 3*d*.—Started from Cuyahoga with one boat, Major Spafford taking the helm; also Esquire Warren, Col. Wait, Samuel Spafford, Phineas Barker, David Clark, Wm. Barker; passengers, Doan, Reynolds and Forbes. Stores: Three bbls. pork, five bbls. flour, four or five lbs. sugar, a trifle of whisky and rum. We had chests and baggage enough with our stores and men, who were mostly sick, to load the boat. Left the mouth of the river about 10 o'clock, A. M., wind fair. In the afternoon run ashore and spoke with some strangers, from Harpersfield, in New York. Col. Moss, who appeared to be the principal man, rode on to Cleveland; with him was Capt. Harper and another gentleman. Capt. Harper took passage in our boat to Chagrin river. Passed Major Spafford and his party, who started from Cleveland, by land, about the same time we did, and were going to Grand river. Entered the Chagrin about dusk, with some difficulty on account of shoal water, pitched our sail for a tent, ate our supper and stretched ourselves before a good fire for sleep.

Wednesday, 4th.—Violent storm during the night and all this day. Upset our camp and disturbed the river so the boats were moved to a safer part of the harbor. Major Spafford came on with his party, Tupper and Culver, and four horses. Concluded to go with him by land; rode to Mr. Parker's and lodged there. Light frost.

Thursday, 5th.—Wind fair. Before our horses were saddled, our boat passed the house under fine headway. We rode to Grand river, and Captain Harper accompanied us on foot. Found the boat safe in the river; took dinner and moved up stream above the Indian settlement and encamped on the west side.

Friday, 6th.—The three gentlemen we saw the other day going to Cleaveland, hailed us. As they contemplated becoming settlers, we furnished them with a loaf of bread. Capt. Harper went with them, and all bid us good bye. Shepard took Tupper and went to explore No. 11 in Range 6, and No. 11, Range 5, to return in two or three days. Spafford and Warren returned from exploring No. 11, in the 8th Range.

Saturday 7th.—Shepard and Kellogg came in sick. Appropriated Grand river township.

Sunday, 8th.—Opened the second barrel of pork and found it very poor, like the first, consisting almost entirely of heads and legs, with one old sow belly, teats two inches long, meat one inch thick.

Monday, 9th.—Determined to lot No. 11, Range 7, and to appropriate gore No. 12, Range 6. Shepard came in.

Tuesday, 10th, Grand river.—Stoddard returned a little before sunset. Had finished his work except a line in No. 11, Range 8, on which, through mistake, he started wrong.

Wednesday, 11th.—Stoddard went back to finish his line. Mr. Redfield's pack-horse man came in with news that Redfield would be here before night.

Tuesday, 12th.—Spafford and Shepard start on an exploring expedition, to meet us at Conneaut.

In the afternoon I started for Conneaut in the boat. Encamped at the mouth of Grand river.

Friday, 15*th*.—Warham Shepard and Reynolds we left at the middle of No. 11, Range 7, to guard stores, which we landed. Camped at the burning springs, about three miles further. I tried one of them with a candle; the bubbles would flash like spirits, which I repeated three times, and the candle was put out by water.

(The party impeded by head winds.)

Conneaut, 22*d*.—Mr. John Youngs called on us, and says that Joseph Tinker, —— Peirce and Capt. Edwards were drowned on the 3d inst., in the night, near Shaddauque, (Chatauque,) in a violent gale, upsetting the boat. Joel Hawley escaped, but gave only an imperfect account how it happened. The boat belonged to Mr. Abbott, who was not on board. There was some loss of property, of which three hundred dollars, in bank bills, belonged to Mr. Abbott, and the boat was much injured. The bodies of Tinker and Peirce were found, near the shore, on the 16th, and interred at Sixteen-mile creek. We learn further, that a man by the name of George Clark, was murdered on the 25th of September, on the Big Beaver; supposed by the Indians, who were seen with him the evening before the body was found. He was wounded in the head with a rifle, and stabbed in the left side, with a knife. One of the Indians had a rifle, and the other a knife.

The Indians were arrested by Mr. Youngs, and another gentleman and committed to prison at Pittsburg.

Monday, Oct. 23*d.*—Had a fit of ague and fever, which continued until night.

Tuesday, 24*th.*—Sold the roan mare and saddle to Nathaniel Doan, and took his note for thirty-two dollars. Mr. Youngs, Mr. Warren and Mr. Doan set out for Buffalo creek, this morning. Mr. Hart arrived with his boat.

Conneaut, Oct. 25*th.*—We are short of pork, not having more than three-quarters of a barrel, and receiving none by Mr. Hart's boat, must send one boat over to Chippewa. Accordingly fitted out one under Major Spafford. She took on board all the men, sick and well, except Mr. Hart, Wm. Barker and myself. They were Colonel Ezra Wait, Amzi Atwater, Doctor Shepard, George Giddings, Samuel Spafford, David Clark, Eli Kellogg, Alexander and Chester Allen, H. F. Linsley, James Berry and Asa Mason. Major Spafford to wait at Queenstown for the other boat. Major Shepard started by land, for Buffalo creek, with Warham Shepard and Thomas Tupper. Parker agreed with Mr. Hart, to take the Stow horse to Buffalo creek.

October 31*st,* 1797.—Mr. Hart and myself started from Conneaut, after sunset. Our hands were Landon, Goodsel, Smith, Kenney, (Keeny,) Forbes, Chapman and James and Richard Stoddard, with a land breeze and our oars, got within two miles of Presque Isle. (Redfield's party left in the woods.)

Nov. 1st.—Near Lowrey's Creek, Richard and James Stoddard took their route by land. Had a slight fit of the ague.

Nov. 2d.—At Lowrey's creek got a quart of milk, which Mr. Hart paid for; and bought two oars.

Nov. 3d.—Arrived at Buffalo creek at 4, P. M., found Major Shepard, Esquire Warren, and several of the sick men. Major Spafford came in yesterday.

Sunday 5th.—The two Allens, Eli Kellogg, and Thomas Tupper, started for Genesee. Samuel Forbes, E. Chapman and the two Parkers, accompanied them; the two Parkers having arrived, with the Stow horse, from Cleveland.

Nov. 6th.—This day the rear guard came up. Mr. Redfield, the two Nyes, Enoch Eldridge, the two Barkers, Shubal Parks, (or Parker,) Jacob Carlton, Clark Reynolds, and Richard and James Stoddard, with four horses; snowing moderately all day."

It does not appear, from the field notes, that the latitude of Cleveland was determined, either in 1796 or '97, or that the instruments were brought here for that purpose. In fact, the position of this place was not fixed, astronomically, until January, 1859, when the late Lieutenant Colonel J. D. Graham, of the United States military engineers, in charge of the light houses on the lakes, determined the latitude of the new court house to be forty-one degrees, thirty minutes, five seconds, north; and the longitude from Greenwich, eighty-one degrees, forty-two minutes, six seconds, west; equal to five hours, twenty-six minutes, forty-eight and one-tenth seconds, time. As the longitude was determined from Cambridge, Mass., by telegraph, and that is the best established point in America, from Greenwich, by chronometer, this may be regarded as correct; unless there shall be a correction for Cambridge; since the Atlantic cable has connected it with the prime meridian in England.

Neither do any of the field notes, letters or reports, connected with the surveys of the Land Company, refer to the existence of iron ore, or coal, on the Reserve. The south line, as far west as the Tuscarawas, was run over beds of coal, and the east line, for about thirty miles. All the townships east of the Cuyahoga, were explored in 1796 and '97; of which about one third were underlaid by strata of ore and coal, without being discovered. The first coal worked, to my knowledge, was taken from the bed of a small run, a mile west of Talmadge center, in 1810, and was used by blacksmiths only. In 1828 it was first brought to Cleveland, in small quantities, for the same purpose. As late as 1838, only a small amount was mined in the Mahoning valley, near Youngstown.

Mr. Pease, with the other surveyors and committee-men, remained at Canandaigua to finish the partition, and make up their reports; a work which the stockholders expected would have been concluded a year sooner. On the 13th of December, 1797, the committee reported upon the four townships, each of which had been surveyed into one hundred lots, containing one hundred and sixty acres.

The surveyors for these towns were: NATHAN REDFIELD, RICHARD M. STODDARD, PHINEAS BARKER and JOSEPH LANDON.

The towns selected by the committee, as the most valuable, were Nos. 5, 6 and 7, of Range 11, and No. 11, of Range 7; now Northfield, Bedford, Warrensville and Perry.

At a meeting held at Hartford, January 23, 1798, FARMERS BROTHER and RED JACKET received a douceur of fifteen dollars each for expenses, ten dollars in cash and five dollars in goods.

"*Whereas*, The Directors have given to TABITHA CUMI STILES, wife of JOB P. STILES, one city lot, one ten acre lot, and one one hundred acre lot; to ANNA GUN, wife of ELIJAH GUN, one one hundred acre lot; to JAMES KINGSBURY and wife, one one hundred acre lot; to NATHANIEL DOAN one city lot, he being obliged to reside thereon as a blacksmith, and all in the city and town of Cleaveland. Voted, that these grants be approved."

Another tax of twenty dollars a share was laid. The Company having given up all ambitious hopes of being one of the powers of the Union, now offer their political title to the Congress of the United States, and in case it is accepted, they empower Mr. SWIFT to desire Governor ST. CLAIR to lay off a new county comprising the Western Reserve.

Donations of land to actual settlers were authorized. The committee on roads, report in favor of constructing a road near the lake, from Erie to Cleveland, with a branch from Township 10, Range 3, (Lenox, Ashtabula county,) to the Salt Spring, on the Meander creek.

As the Six Nations claimed a part of the fifteen hundred dollars promised to the Mohawks, at Buffalo, June 24th, 1796, "it is ordered that this sum be paid to ISRAEL CHAPMAN, Superintendant of Indian Affairs, to be distributed by him." At the same meeting a committee was appointed, authorized to prosecute or settle with the heirs of SAMUEL H. PARSONS for their claim to the Salt Spring tract.

MEMORANDA OF JUDGE BARR.

Major LORENZO CARTER, who came here in 1797, was a great acquisition to the settlement. He was perfectly fearless, and otherwise peculiarly fitted to meet the perils of the wilderness. He was an expert marksman, and an enthusiastic hunter; the terror of the deer and bear of the neighborhood.

On the west side of the river, at the mouth, was a natural mound, covered with trees, (see GAYLORD'S sketch.) Strange as it may seem, in the early days, and as late as 1820, persons have walked across the mouth on a sand bar, the channel being frequently closed up by storms. KINGSBURY and GUN, came here from Conneaut, early in 1797, remaining that season, when they removed to the ridge, in what was afterwards Newburg. EZEKIEL HAWLEY, came to Cleveland the same year. KINGSBURY built a shanty east of the Public Square, and GUN occupied one of the Company's cabins, until one was built on River street, north of St. Clair, near the cupola opposite WINSLOW's warehouse, (1842, late HUSSEY & McBRIDE.) HAWLEY built on the hill, on the north-east corner of Water and Superior, now (1842,) owned by NATHAN PERRY. The Land Company, the same season, put up a double log cabin, on the south side of Superior, east of Vineyard lane. CHARLES PARKER and EBENEZER MERRY, settled in Mentor the same year, and each sowed a crop of wheat, from seed obtained at Conneaut.

Mr. ELDRIDGE, one of the employees of the Land Company, who was drowned in crossing Grand river, was the first person buried in the city of Cleveland. The first burying ground was on lot 97, between Prospect and Huron streets, east side of Ontario, which was removed to Erie street in 1835. PELEG WASHBURN, who was an apprentice to NATHANIEL DOAN, as a blacksmith, died of dysentery in 1797. At this time, a death or two excites little attention;

but when we reflect how few there were in this country at that time, their distance from home: destitute of the necessaries and comforts of civilization, a death and a burial, was an occurrence of no small moment.

This was a sickly season. The old settlers have often remarked, in reference to those melancholy times, they could not have got along without the game which Major CARTER killed, and the attentions of his generous wife."

BIOGRAPHICAL SKETCHES.

The history of every member of the surveying parties of 1796–7, has a deep interest for their descendants, a large number of whom reside in the country, of which they were the first thorough explorers. They pursued their toilsome way, during those years, over all that part of the Reserve, east of the Cuyahoga, leaving perpetual evidence of their track through the forest, in measured lines, marked upon the trees.

Only a few of the hands employed by the company on the surveys of 1796, returned to the work in 1797. Of those who passed that year in the field, but a small portion became settlers. The formal compact of Sept. 30, 1796, in reference to the settlement in Euclid, was carried out, by not more than two. Probably the severe labors of the survey, cooled their admiration of the new country. Many of them underwent the ordeal of fever and ague, which was abundantly sufficient to damage their faith in the "promised land."

A courageous man, who might be willing to encounter this miserable disease, which prostrates every form and grade of ambition, would not willingly expose his family to it. They saw that no civil government existed, or was likely to exist. Some of the surveyors, like Spafford and Atwater, determined to take their chances, and spend their days in New Connecticut. Doan, Gun and Clark, also became settlers. Of those who returned to New England, very few were again heard of here.

At the recent pioneer meetings, the private history of a small number of them has reached us. Sanford, Culver and Morley, survived long enough to hear of those movements, to rescue from oblivion the enterprises of their youthful days.

EZEKIEL MORLEY.

BY ALFRED MORLEY.

Kirtland, Ohio, June 7, 1858.

Mr. Whittlesey:—In reply to your enquiries in regard to Ezekiel Morley, I will answer as nearly as I can. He was an uncle of mine, not my father. He was born in Glastenbury, Connecticut, in 1758; died in Chester, Geauga county, Ohio, August 6th, 1852, lacking nine days of ninety-three years.

Emigrated from Genesee county, New York, to Chester, Ohio, in 1832. He was a Revolutionary soldier, and drew a pension of ninety-six dollars a year. Was one of the surveying party in running the lines of the Western Reserve in 1796—'97, and assisted in erecting the first log cabin that was built in Cleveland. He supposed himself to be the first white man that saw Chagrin Falls. Enclosed you will find his signature.

My father was seventeen months older than uncle EZEKIEL, and was a Revolutionary soldier. He died where I now live, aged eighty-six years and six months, having lived with the wife of his youth sixty-three years.

Yours Truly,

ALFRED MORLEY.

LOT SANFORD.

STATEMENT OF A. W. PERRY, HIS SON-IN-LAW, AND OF R. W. PERRY, A GRANDSON.

SHOREHAM, VT., November 21, 1859.

We have consulted with LOT SANFORD, who was not in the surveying party of 1796, but in that of 1797.

He was born September 5th, 1773, and was one of the party who went out to survey the Western Reserve. AMOS SPAFFORD was the chief surveyor of this party. No particular incident happened on the outward journey, except the accidental death of DAVID ELDRIDGE. He undertook to swim his horse across Grand river, although strongly advised to the contrary, and the animal proving unequal to the task, ELDRIDGE was drowned and his body carried on to Cleveland, and buried on the banks of the Cuyahoga. SANFORD assisted in digging his grave, thus performing the office of sexton to the first white man who was buried in Cleveland.

The company arrived and established their head quarters, building a log house, and enclosing a garden for the purpose of raising their vegetables. SANFORD laid a fence around this garden, being the first fence ever built in the town.

There had been a log hut built at this place the year previous, by the same party.

SETH HART, the agent of the company, was left in charge of the head quarters. No incidents are mentioned while the party was out surveying, except the death of MINOR BICKNELL, who was taken sick with fever, and was carried through the woods fifty miles before he died. He was buried near the Cuyahoga, probably about thirty miles from the present site of Cleveland.

Soon after arriving at head quarters, two more of the party—ANDREWS and WASHBURN—died, and were buried by the side of ELDRIDGE. Several members of the company are mentioned, among whom are SAMUEL SPAFFORD, (son of AMOS,) and OLIVER CULVER, who were chainmen; ANDREWS was flagman, and SANFORD—the subject of this sketch—went as axman. He, with eleven others, left Cleveland the 12th of September, 1797, and returned to Orwell, Vermont, where he then lived, arriving the 3d of December. In April, 1804, he removed to a farm which he had purchased in Shoreham, Vermont, where he has since lived, being now in his eighty-sixth year.

The two BARKERS, ALPHEUS CHOAT, DAVID CLARK, OLIVER CULVER, the two NYES and AMOS and SAMUEL SPAFFORD were from Vermont; the two GIDDINGS were from Connecticut. SANFORD and SAMUEL SPAFFORD chopped four acres of timber in Euclid, the first ever chopped for settlement duties.

About eight or ten years ago JOB STILES died in the town of Leicester, Addison county, Vermont. My brother has heard STILES boast of putting up the first house in Cleveland. SANFORD retains his mental faculties in a good degree, but is infirm from a paralytic stroke he had about two years since, and therefore he cannot write you, but I send you his autograph, written before. He feels a lively interest in the historical articles published in Cleveland, which are read to him. You cannot better compensate him and his wife, who still lives, than by sending him such articles."

Mr. SANFORD died at Shoreham, April 20, 1860, on the farm he had cultivated since 1804, being eighty-six years and seven months of age. He there acquired a competence, living for more than fifty years in communion with the Congregational church, of which he was a liberal supporter. His wife died in June, 1865, at the age of eighty-two.

OLIVER CULVER.

At the pioneer celebration of October, 1858, Oliver Culver, of New York, one of the surveying party of 1797, was present, supposed to be the only survivor. Lot Sanford was, however, then alive. The following letter gives a brief history of Culver, who may still be living.

Rochester, July 29, 1860.

John Barr, Esq.—Mr. Oliver Culver, of Brighton, to-day called on me, and handed me your letter of March 27th, 1860, in which you request him to state the date and place of his birth, and to send his autograph, for the Pioneer society of Cleveland. Mr. Culver would willingly send his autograph, but he can not, because for some time past, his sight has so much failed, that he does not write, even his own name. In all other respects, his health continues robust and good. Mr. Culver was born at East Windsor, Hartford county, Connecticut, September 24th, 1778; and will be eighty-two years old on the 24th of September next.

When he was five years of age, soon after the peace of 1783, his father removed from East Windsor, to Ticonderoga, N. Y. After a short residence there, he removed to Orwell, Vermont, where Mr. CULVER remained with his parents, until the spring of 1797, returning home, occasionally, until 1805. In February, 1797, he hired, with his father's consent, to AMOS SPAFFORD, to accompany him with a party of surveyors to the Connecticut Company's Lands.

Early in March, 1797, he was sent by AMOS SPAFFORD, with his son SAMUEL SPAFFORD, on foot, from Orwell, Vermont, to Schenectady, New York, to arrange for boats, and ascertain when they would be ready to carry the party on, from there up the Mohawk. SAMUEL SPAFFORD wrote back to his father, that the Mohawk would not be clear of ice, and the boats ready to start, before the first of April: and that he and Mr. CULVER would go on to Irondequoit bay, and there camp, and hunt, until the surveying party arrived. They did so, traveling by land, on foot, well provided with arms, ammunition and provisions. At Irondequoit bay, they camped, and boarded with ASA DUNBAR, and family, a trapper, who was a mulatto man, from the Mohawk country, of whose location they were informed at Schenectady. They remained there hunting, and curing the skins taken, about six or seven weeks, until the surveying party under Mr. SPAFFORD arrived, about the last of April.

At Queenstown their boats were drawn over land, on carriages, with teams, by some Canadians, and launched at Chippeway, from whence they crossed to the mouth of Buffalo creek, and coasted up from there along the south shore of lake Erie. At Cleveland the party erected a log house. Mr. CULVER was a chain bearer, that season at twelve dollars a month.

When cold weather arrived, the party returned to Vermont. Mr. CULVER, and SAMUEL SPAFFORD stopped a few weeks at DUNBAR'S, and continued their hunt, with the object of collecting peltries.

Late in Decmber, after the snow became too deep for hunting, they traveled on foot to Orwell. In 1798, Mr. CULVER went to Cleveland, in a party of eighteen men, employed as before, to assist in cutting out a road, to the Pennsylvania line, on which they worked that season. In 1800, he bought his present farm in Brighton, Monroe county, New York, cleared seven acres, and sowed it to wheat, and got a good crop.

Up to 1804 he was emploped three years at Irondequoit landing, by AUGUSTUS GRISWOLD; superintending an ashery. In 1804 he went to Cleveland, with a boat load of salt, dry goods, liquors, and tobacco, &c., and opened a store. The vessel was loaded at Black Rock, freight paid, three dollars per barrel. She was built at Erie, by SETH REED, and commanded by Capt. DOBBIN. In 1805, Mr. CULVER, married and settled on his farm. His wife died a few weeks since. I write this by his direction.

Respectfully, yours, &c.,

J. M. HATCH.

When CULVER, re-visited the city fifty-four years after his mercantile trip, its identity with the sickly and scattered town of 1804, could scarcely be traced. He was conveyed through long and compactly built streets, covering nearly all the ample space allotted by the surveyors for city and out-lots. When he last saw them, they were not distinguishable from the surrounding forest, except by an occasional horse trail, and by blazed lines upon the trees.

SETH PEASE.

The personal history of Mr. PEASE, the most prominent of the surveyors, of the Land Company, is but imperfectly transmitted to us. According to Mr. ATWATER, he "was above medium height, slender and fair, with black, penetrating eyes. In his movements he was very active, and persevering in his designs, with a reflecting and thoughtful air. He was a very thorough mathematician."

FROM A LETTER OF RALPH GRANGER.

FAIRPORT, LAKE CO., O., Sept. 27, 1843.

"SETH PEASE was my uncle. He was very precise in his business. Besides the minutes necessarily returned to the Company, he kept a full private journal. This I have seen, containing records of personal adventures with colored landscapes, one of which is the first residence of the surveyors at Conneaught. He also brought to Connecticut, from

Ohio, specimens of minerals, which I have seen, among them some beautiful alabaster from Sandusky. He died at Philadelphia. His wife died in Connecticut. The only children now living are Mrs. NOAH A. FLETCHER, of Washington City, and ALFRED PEASE, his youngest son, at Dayton, Montgomery county, Ohio. This journal may have been lost or mislaid."

His journals, of which a portion for the years 1795 to 1799, inclusive, are before me, show excellent penmanship, and precise business habits. In 1795 he surveyed for the State of Massachusetts, in the province of Maine. After the close of the surveys east of the Cuyahoga, in 1797, Mr. PEASE, engaged with PORTER, ATWATER, and others of his enterprising old friends of the woods, in the allotment of the "Holland Purchase," in western New York. This service occupied two years, '98 and '99. The elections of the year 1800, resulted in the success of the "Republican," or JEFFERSON party, over that of the Federalists. Under JEFFERSON'S administration, GIDEON GRANGER, became Post Master General, and Mr. PEASE, who was a brother-in-law, was made Assistant Post Master General. Judge CALVIN PEASE, of Warren, Trumbull county, Ohio, was his brother. In 1806, when the Indian title to that part of the Reserve west of the Cuyahoga, was extinguished, SETH PEASE, was directed by the Government, to extend the southern boundary along the

41st parallel, west of the river, which he did. There is still hope of recovering more of the memoranda, to which the Hon. RALPH GRANGER refers. His skill as a draftsman and sketcher, and his facility in description will give them great interest.

NATHANIEL DOAN.

NATHANIEL DOAN, was one of those of the first surveying party, who volunteerd for the second year's work. He was so well pleased with the new country, that he emigrated with his family in 1798, and became one of the permanent settlers. In 1799 they fled from the miasma of the river bank, like the majority of the early residents, and settled on the Euclid road, four miles from the Cuyahoga, at the corners; where the road from Newburg intersects Euclid street. This gave rise to a hamlet, which has increased to a village, and which, until recently, was known as "Doan's Corners."

Mr. DOAN was the blacksmith of the Land Company, whose business it was, during the progress of the survey, to keep their pack horses well shod. In 1798 he erected a rude shop on the south side of Superior street.

A blacksmith is a very important member of a pioneer settlement. He is soon brought into personal acquaintance, with all the neighboring people. His shop becomes a central point for gossip, and for more serious discussions upon public affairs. Mr.

Doan appears to have been an useful smith, and a good citizen. His name appears frequently, in the proceedings at elections and town meetings. In 1804, he was made a lieutenant in the first militia company organized here. Nathan Chapman, who was not personally connected with the surveyors, but who appears to have been on the Reserve, from the year 1796, as a purveyor of beef, and a trader, was a friend of Doan. Chapman had no family, and died at Doan's Corners in 1814. Doan died at the same place, in 1815. The widow of the late Edward Baldwin, of Cleveland, once the sheriff and treasurer of Cuyahoga county, is the daughter Nathaniel Doan.

The late Seth Doan, who was his nephew, in a statement made to James S. Clark, Esq., in January, 1841, remarks, "that a boat was despatched in the fall of '98, down the lake, to a mill ten miles west of Erie, at Walnut creek, for flour; but it was beached and destroyed, at Euclid Point. They had occasional communications with Detroit, through straggling Frenchmen and Indians. There was, as yet, no settlement at Buffalo or Black Rock, nor any between Cleveland and the Ohio river. The one at Presque Isle, or Erie being the nearest. When we arrived, there were three or four clearings, of about two acres each. One between Water street and the bluff, just north of St. Clair street; another near Stiles' house, on Bank street, and one near Haw-

LEY's at the end of Superior street, where the "Central Buildings," (Atwater Block,) are now standing."

ELIJAH GUN.

Although GUN, like STILES, came to Ohio with the surveyors, and spent a large part of his life in the vicinity of Cleveland, his personal history has not been well preserved. On the approach of old age, he left the pioneer homestead, in Newburg, and removed to the Maumee river, to the residence of his son, near Napoleon, Ohio. Little has come down to us, of his occupations, and of his trials at Conneaut during the winter of 1796–'7. Both himself and his wife, appear to have endured the hardships of those days better than many of their cotemporaries. His cabin, at Conneaut, was about a mile above Stow Castle, on the creek. He reached a very advanced age, nearly or quite, four score and ten, dying among his kindred, on the banks of the Maumee.

AUGUSTUS PORTER.

Although AUGUSTUS PORTER survived all the other surveyors, and lived on the shore of lake Erie; his personal history is here imperfectly known. He appears to have attached much value, to the water power at Niagara Falls, and at the head of Niagara river, where the navigable waters of the lake terminate. After spending about ten years in the woods as a surveyor and explorer, principally in the western part of New York, he established himself for life on the Niagara river. One reason why we are not better informed in regard to him, is given in the following extract from his letter to Judge BARR, dated at Niagara Falls, Jan. 10th, 1843.

"Had I all my original papers connected with the subject above named, such as my journal, original field notes of the survey taken on the ground, calculations on contents, geographical remarks, of persons employed, &c., &c., I should be able to give you such information, and it would give me much pleasure to do so. But unfortunately all these documents were lost in my dwelling house at this place, destroyed in 1813 by British troops."

This letter is quite lengthy, going over in much detail, the operations of 1796 in the field, which he conducted. I have made less use of it than other writers upon the pioneer times, because, being entirely a production of the memory, after the lapse of forty-seven years, it is occasionally contradicted by written evidence of the same date. Of what relates to himself he should be the best authority. He says:

"That in the early part of the year 1789, being the next year after Messrs. GORHAM & PHELPS, had made their great purchase of the State of Massachusetts of about six millions of acres of land, lying in the western part of the State of New York, then known as the Genesee country, I being in the twentieth year of my age, went into the country a surveyor, and continued in the business until the winter of 1796, most of the time in the employ of OLIVER PHELPS. During the time from 1789 to 1796, my business led me to become particularly acquainted with most of that section of country, the navigable streams and small lakes, and the south shores of lake Ontario, and lake Erie as far west as Presque Isle, (now Erie) in Pennsylvania, and I had had considerable experience in the navigation of those streams, and the shores of lakes Ontario and Erie, in small boats."

"In running up the first four meridians, PEASE had delivered his provisions to other surveyors, excepting a small quantity sufficient to subsist on until I should meet them, which was now all exhausted, and of course we had nothing but the flour I had procured. I returned to the point where Mr. PEASE had run the line, and took the direction of the survey, and continued the line to the lake. On the evening of the first day, we very fortunately, discovered one of the finest bee trees I ever saw. We encamped, cut down the tree, ate to our satisfaction, each man filled his canteen, and the residue we put in the bags of flour. Excepting for two or three days, while our honey lasted we lived on bread alone. On our arrival at the lake, we took the beach and went east to our camp at Conneaut; and what was remarkable, on our way there, we fell in with all three of the parties, who had each finished their lines, and joined our party."

"All things being thus arranged, and about to muster our men for a start, we found some disposition in camp to mutiny, or, what would now be called a strike for higher wages. For the purpose of settling this difficulty, Gen. CLEAVELAND agreed that before the close of the season, and after some of the township lines should have been run, a township should be selected and set apart, to be surveyed into lots of one hundred and sixty acres each, and each individual of the party who should choose, might have the privilege of purchasing a lot on a long credit, and at a stipulated price named, what that price was, I do not recollect. This settled the matter, and all became satisfied. The township during the season was set apart, and called Euclid; and as I am informed, still retains that name."

"On the north side of Sandusky bay, about opposite where the City of Sandusky now stands, there was a Frenchman residing with his family, and also several Indian families. On our first arrival at the bay we went to this place, remained a short time, then returned to the mouth of the bay, and resumed our traverse. Before we had reached the upper end of the beach, or sand bar, lying between the lake and bay, we fell in with a party of Indians whose actions and looks we did not much like, yet they offered us no injury, and we passed on and concluded our traverse."

"Having returned from Sandusky bay to Cuyahoga, I remained there some time, perhaps two or three weeks, and surveyed the outlines of a piece of land designed for the town. Its dimensions I do not recollect—probably equal to about a mile square, bounding west on the river and north on the lake. I made a plat of this ground and laid it off into streets and lots. Most or all the streets I surveyed myself, when I left it in charge of Mr. HOLLEY to complete the survey of the lots."

Mr. HOLLEY's minutes, as far as we have them, make no reference to surveys by him on the city lots. On the fly leaf of one of the field books, in Mr. PEASE's hand writing, are brief minutes of the lots, their position on the streets, and their contents. As yet these are the only original notes discovered, and they may have been transcribed by PEASE, from the work of some of the other surveyors. Mr. PORTER mentions the loss of a boatman belonging to his party, at Spraker's rift, on the Mohawk, killed by a fall from the mast, while he was adjusting a sail. This accident is not referred to in the journals of PEASE or HOLLEY.

"Immediately after this I commenced the traverse of the Cuyahoga river, with the intention of pursuing the whole line of boundary, as described in WAYNE's treaty with the Indians, as far as the south line of the Reserve. This line began at the mouth of the Cuyahoga, thence up the same to the portage, thence across the portage to the Tuscarawas branch of the Muskingum, thence down the same, &c. I accordingly traversed the Cuyahoga up, until it began to lead me off to the north; having kept two or three men, looking out continually along the west side of the river for the portage road, but without discovering it. The leaves having fallen and obscured the path it could not be found, and I returned to the mouth of the river."

Mr. Porter lived to a very advanced age, and died on the banks of the Niagara. He was a prominent citizen on the frontier, as most of the old surveyors were. The intelligence and energy, which are necessary to make a good surveyor in the western wilds, furnish an excellent foundation for an influential character. A large number of the leading men in the new States, and in the Indian wars, belonged to this profession, which then not only required knowledge and sense, but a reasonable stock of warlike skill and courage, to deal successfully with the aborigines. Gen. Peter B. Porter was a brother of Augustus. I regret not being able to do better justice, to the eventful life of the man who determined upon the plan of this city, and who must have surveyed some portions of it. Neither his name, or that of any of the first surveyors, has been perpetuated, in any street or place within our limits.

According to his contemporary, ATWATER; PORTER "was full middling in height, stout built, with a full face, and dark or rather brown complexion. In a woodsman's dress, any one would see by his appearance that he was capable, and determined to go through thick and thin, in whatever business he was engaged. By the bursting of a gun, he had lost the entire thumb of his left hand."

Mr. PORTER received for his services as principal surveyor, in 1796, five dollars per day, and Mr. PEASE for the same services, in 1797, three and one-half.

LORENZO CARTER.

BY THE LATE ASHBEL W. WALWORTH.—1842.

Major CARTER was a friend of liberty to the utmost. He was always found on the side of the weak and oppressed. His language was, "I hate negroes, and do not want them about me." But for all that, he did have them about him, most generally those that did him the least good. He used them as well as he did other people, if they were civil and decent.

To illustrate his goodness of heart, I will relate the following facts:

Early in the spring of 1806, a canoe containing a white man, his wife and some children, and a colored man, were coming down the lake. The canoe was upset, and all drowned but the colored man, called BEN, between this place and Rocky river. BEN was a large man, and reached the iron bound shore, where there was an old tree which had tumbled down the rocks; he climbed up it so far as to be clear of the water, and then stayed until he was discovered by some boatmen. When taken off he was almost insensible, his feet and limbs were much frozen, and he was brought to Major CARTER's house in that situation. He had no money, and all the clothes he had were not worth three dollars. The Major took care of him, as he would one of his children, all summer. The rheumatism drew his limbs out of shape, and I think his toes were frozen off. Although he hobbled about a little in the fall, I do not think he was able to render the least assistance to the Major.

Some time in October, 1806, there came to Cleveland two Kentucky gentlemen, well mounted, and stopped at Major SPAFFORD's, who lived where the Merwin, or Mansion House used to stand. They stated that one of them was the lawful owner of BEN. The Kentuckians walked over to CARTER's and made their business known. He told them of BEN's misfortunes, and also what he had done for him; said he did not believe in slavery, and he did not like negroes. The owner said he wanted to see BEN, and if he did not want to go back, he might stay where he was; that BEN would say that his master was kind to him, and that he could say that BEN was a good boy, but had been enticed away.

The Major told him that BEN was away, and he did not know where he was, but at all events you can never see BEN, without he wants to see you. The Kentuckians agreed to that, and told the Major to see BEN, and he might have his choice to stay or go at his option, but wanted to see him face to face. The owner and the Major had a number of interviews, and finally it was agreed that the owner and BEN, should see each other near enough to converse. BEN was to stand on the west side of the river, on a piece of land now owned by Mr. SCRANTON, covered with the heaviest kind of timber, the owner to be on the east side, a little below where the widow COLAHAN now lives, near the end of Huron street. At the time they were in conversation, I was passing along the top of the bluff, and heard them converse. The owner said, "BEN, have I not always used you well, and treated you as well as the rest of my family?" BEN answered in the affirmative. Many inquiries and answers passed, but the conversation was marked by good feeling on both sides. Nothing further occurred to my knowledge until the next morning, or the next but one, when I saw BEN mounted on one of the Kentuckians' horses, with holster and pistols, &c., and the man on foot, on the road to Hudson, about a mile from Major CARTER's, talking in the most friendly manner.

Now comes the most inexplicable part of the story. It would seem that the Major showed no dissatisfaction to BEN's going with his master; but two white men, one called JOHN THOMPSON, and the other JAS. GEER, hangers on at the Major's tavern, and nearly as useless as BEN had been to him, preceded, or followed and passed the Kentuckians; for when they had got about three miles from Newburg Mills, (then called Cleveland Mills,) on the old "Carter road," they appeared, one on each side of the road, each with a rifle; and as the Kentuckians and BEN were passing, BEN still mounted; one of the men says, "BEN, you d—d fool, jump off of that horse and take to the woods." BEN obeyed, the hunters also ran, and it may be supposed, though not known, that the Kentuckians were somewhat astonished. However, they never returned to tell of their bad luck. The men and the Major kept the secret, but it was found out in this way. In the winter, a son of Major SPAFFORD, and a younger brother of NATHAN PERRY, Esq., of this place, were out on the west side of the river hunting. They got lost, and wandered around till nearly worn out. At last they struck a horse's track, and followed it until it brought them to a hut, and who did they meet but poor BEN, who told them the story and enjoined secresy, which they kept as long as was necessary. There was not at that time any road on the west side of the Cuyahoga, not a white person living east of Huron or north of Wooster, and perhaps none there. BEN's hut must have been in Brecksville or Independence.

What became of BEN is not known by me, but he was probably sent to Canada.

In the spring of 1807, (I think it was,) a man, perhaps forty-five years old, talkative, forward and rather singular, came into the place, stopped with Major SPAFFORD and worked for him two or three months. One morning Major SPAFFORD came to Major CARTER's and inquired about the man. He said he was at his house last night, and was not now to be found, and he did not know but he might have walked over to CARTER's house. Major CARTER had not seen him, but says he, "the rascal has run away." Major SPAFFORD says, "I think not; he brought nothing with him to my house, and I do not know as he has carried anything away; and further, I think I must owe him about four dollars." "Well," says Major CARTER, "there shall nobody run away from this place, and I'll go after him; I can track him out."

He immediately started down what is now Water street, to the lake. There was then a number of log and brush fences across the street. When he got to the lake he found the track, and followed it down about two miles, when it turned off towards the road that leads to Euclid. The Major followed to the road, and thence toward Euclid, to near where Mr. J. K. CURTIS now lives, (Willson Avenue,) where he overtook the man. The Major told him he must go back to Cleveland. He said, "he would not go, that he did not owe anybody there, and had not stolen anything, and the Major had nothing to do with him." The Major told him "he did not care whether he went back or not, but one of two things you shall do, either you must go with me peaceably, or be killed and thrown into this cat swamp, to be eaten by the wolves and turkey buzzards." The Major had a peculiar manner of suiting actions and looks, to words. "Oh!" says the man, "if you are in earnest, I don't care if I go back." The Major brought him to Major SPAFFORD, who asked him "What made him go off in such a manner; you know I owe you something." He answered, "I suppose you owe me a little, but I will tell you how it is with me. I have been a roving character, and don't stay but a little while in a place. I have been in the habit when I left a place to run away." Major SPAFFORD told him "it was a bad one, and that he had better give it up; besides, you cannot run away from this place." The man said "he saw it would not do here, and he thought he would not try it again." Major SPAFFORD told him "to eat his breakfast, and he would see in the meantime how much he owed him, and then he might go when and where he pleased." The man said "he had about given up the idea of going, and if the Major would let him work he would stay," which was agreed to, and he stayed two or three months.

Sometime in the fall of 1798, Major CARTER said to me, "When I was living in my old log house under the hill, I saw an Indian coming up the river in a canoe. He landed opposite my house, fastened his canoe, and with his paddle walked up to where I stood. After the usual salutation, he asked, 'What stream do you call this?'" The Major replied, "the Cuyahoga." "No, no, this is not the Cuyahoga. I was here when a boy so high, (placing his hand about the height of a boy ten or a dozen years old,) and the Cuyahoga was like this," making a plan with his paddle on the ground, which corresponded with what we call the old river bed. [It must be kept in mind, that from the point where the parties stood, they could not have a view of the old river bed as we can now, on account of the forest.] The Major said he had not any doubt, that the river used to empty itself at the west end of the pond. The Indian appeared to Major CARTER to be seventy or seventy-five years old.

Subsequently I learned that in the year 1798, an old Oneida Indian, whose name was SCANODEWAN, who had been a faithful friend to the Americans during their struggle for independence, and was much attached to the HARPERS, of Harperstown, State of New York, followed Col. ALEX. HARPER and family to Harpersfield, in this State.

SCANODEWAN made himself useful to the Colonel,

by hunting and procuring game for the support of his family and others.

Col. HARPER died in the fall of 1798, and soon after SCANODEWAN became uneasy, and told the family of Col. HARPER that he would go to the lake, build a canoe, and go up the lake. He returned to the widow HARPER's, and reported to them the changes that had been made since he had been there before, more especially the alteration of the mouth of the Cuyahoga river. There can be little doubt that SCANODEWAN, was the same man who conversed with Major CARTER on the subject.

The facts relating to the Indian, I have recently obtained from Mrs. TAPPEN and her brother, Col. ROBERT HARPER, of Harpersfield, Ohio, who is the youngest child of the late Col. ALEX. HARPER, and who was eight years old when his father died.

Major CARTER was far from a quarrelsome man. I never heard of his fighting unless he was grossly insulted, and as he would say, "driven to it." It was a common saying in this region, that Major CARTER was all the law Cleveland had, and I think he often gave out well measured justice. It was not unfrequent, that strangers traveling through the place, who had heard of the Major's success in whipping his man, who believed themselves smart fighters, thought they may gain laurels by having it said that they whipped him. I never heard it asserted by any one, and never heard of any one boasting, that such an act had been performed.

He was kind and generous to the poor and unfortunate, hospitable to the stranger, would put himself to great inconvenience to oblige a neighbor, and was always at the service of an individual or the public, when a wrong had been perpetrated. In all the domestic relations he was kind and affectionate.

In the year 1812 he was afflicted with a cancer on his face, and went to Virginia in 1813 for medical aid, which proved useless. He died February 8th, 1814, aged forty-seven, after enduring the most excruciating sufferings for months, previous to his death. Mrs. Carter survived him till October 18th, 1827, aged sixty-one.

AMOS SPAFFORD.

BY JUDGE HOSMER.

Perrysburg, April 11th, 1843.

My Dear Sir:—Of Major Amos Spafford I have been able to learn but little. He emigrated from Vermont to Cleveland in 1800 or 1801. He received the appointment of Collector for the District of Miami, and of Postmaster, in 1810, at the commencement of which year he moved from Cleveland to the foot of the rapids, and built a small log house under the table of land, which forms the present site of Fort Meigs.

His first return to the Government shows that the amount of exports from this district, at the expiration of the first quarter, was three thousand and thirty dollars. It consisted of three thousand dollars worth of coon, bear and mink skins, and thirty dollars worth of bear's oil. Major SPAFFORD cultivated a piece of land, including Fort Meigs, built several out houses, and acquired considerable property here previous to the war. He was a man very much esteemed by the American and French inhabitants, was indeed an adviser and friend to all the early settlers.

At the time the war broke out, there were sixty-seven white families living on the twelve mile square Reserve, and some nine or ten families in the immediate neighborhood. The first actual notice the settlers had, that hostilities had commenced after HULL's troops had marched through to Detroit, was the appearance of about forty Delaware Indians and as many British, at the foot of the rapids one bright morning in July, 1812. The Indians, under command of their war chief SACAMANC, by direction of the British, entered every house on the north side of the river, and after a friendly salutation, took all articles of any value which they could find, loaded them into the canoes, pirogues and flats belonging to the settlers, and then passed over to the south side. They met Major SPAFFORD in his cornfield, and were about to subject his house to pillage, but were prevented by a salvo of twenty dollars, paid them by the Major, which was all the money he had.

With the exception of their chief, SACAMANC, and four other Indians, they together with the British, left with their plunder by water, for Malden. The Maumee river was in those days inhabited by a species of hybrid, half human, half animal, better known at the present time by the name of Canadian French. These creatures united in their character the cunning of an Indian, and the sagacity of the white. They were principally friends to the British interest. One among them, who had long been an Indian trader, was, however, a true American in feeling. His name, PETER MANOR, should ever be remembered, for he was a true friend of the Americans. He knew SACAMANC, pretended a friendship for him and for the British, and learned from him that in the space of eight or ten days, it was the intention of the confederated tribes in the British interest to hold a council near Malden, and in six days thereafter to make a general descent upon Monroe, Maumee and the other places on their trail to Fort Wayne, whither they were going, with about fifteen hundred British, to aid the beseigers of that fort, for the purpose of pillage, massacre and rapine.

SACAMANC and his four men left for the interior of our State, the day after the others had gone to Malden. Manor visited Major Spafford the next day, asked him what he intended to do; and was informed that he intended to remain on the river and attend to his business. Manor then told him of the conversation he had had with Sacamanc, at which the Major took alarm, and concluded to make preparations to go down the lake. As the contemplated attack was some two or three weeks distant, he was in no hurry. About five days after this, at or near ten o'clock in the morning, a man, who was brought up among the Indians, and who had been befriended by Major Spafford, came running to his house in breathless haste, with the astounding information, that a party of some fifty Pottawatomies were within six miles of the foot of the rapids, and that they were massacreing every Yankee they met with. The Major spread the news among his neighbors. They immediately launched an old barge, which was built by the army a year previous at Fort Wayne, and used by Col. Undermick and other officers, to come down the river on their way to Detroit.

Having put on board of this crazy hulk, what few articles of provision and furniture they could, the little party consisting of the Major's family and three other families, set sail for Milan, in Huron county. Scarcely had they got under cover of the point, below the amphitheatre at the foot of the rapids, ere the Pottawatomies made their appearance. They inquired after the Yankees, and were told by MANOR that they had been gone a week. The Indians stole what money and other property the fugitives had left, and started for Malden. Meantime, the little barge, favored by prosperous gales, reached Milan in safety. Major SPAFFORD established his office as collector there until after the war, at the close of which he and his old companions returned to old Fort Meigs. When they left they had dwellings, horses, fine corn-fields, and comfortable homes. On their return they found their fields destroyed, and their horses and cattle stolen by the Indians. Government promised redress for the injuries committed by our army. Their families obtained a small compensation, for the supposed quantity of corn taken from the fields by Gen. HARRISON'S army.

This small sum was obtained through the energy of Major SPAFFORD, who, on behalf of himself and neighbors, made two trips to Washington, and spent much time there before aught could be accomplished. Nothing disheartened he commenced repairing his ruined homestead. Of the old arks that were used to transport provisions to our army during the war, from Fort Amanda and other places on the Auglaize and St. Marys rivers, he constructed a comfortable farm house and office, both of which are still standing in front of Fort Meigs. He received a grant from Government of a tract of land next above and adjoining the Fort, which is now owned by his son,

Judge AURORA SPAFFORD, of this place. He retained his office of Collector until 1818, when he died at his residence. Major SPAFFORD took an active part in all the early affairs of this county. He named our town Perrysburg, in honor of the hero of lake Erie. I have several letters of his in my possession, one to General HARRISON and one to President MADISON, setting forth in the most graphic language, the losses to which he and his neighbors had been subjected by the war, and asking for redress. He was a sound headed, pure hearted man, as all say who knew him, and as his papers abundantly prove.

Yours, faithfully,

HEZ. L. HOSMER.

In Judge ATWATER's description of the personal appearance of the surveyors, he says of SPAFFORD, "he was more than medium in height, very straight, broad in the forehead, with a sober, serious countenance; rather slow in his motions, and on the whole was an excellent man."

1798.

The committee on partition, PEASE, SPAFFORD, WARREN and HOLBROOK, having reported from Canandaigua, the directors called the stockholders together at Hartford, to receive their lands. All the territory east of the Cuyahoga was included in the partition, except the six townships reserved for sale. These were Chapin, now Madison, Geauga county; Mentor, Lake county; Charlton, afterwards Chagrin, now Willoughby, Euclid, Cleveland, then including Newburg, and Weathersfield, or the "Salt Spring Township," in Trumbull county. On the 29th of January, 1798, the long expected draft took place, consisting of ninety-three equal parcels, embracing a township or more. On the next day the four allotted towns were drawn, in four hundred parcels, one for each share in the company. These were, Northfield, Bedford and Warrensville, in this county, and the township of Perry in Lake county.

As the subject of civil government made no progress, a petition was again laid before the general assembly of Connecticut, reciting their numerous failures in Congress, and most earnestly praying for relief. This was in October, 1798. In December an agent was appointed, to urge upon Congress speedy attention to their condition, in case the assembly should fail them.

At this meeting, Gen. CLEAVELAND's contract with the surveyors, made at Cleveland, Sept. 30th, 1796, was ratified and assumed by the company. Three hundred dollars was appropriated for the improvement of the Salt Springs, with a view to leasing the same. A bounty of two hundred dollars cash, or a loan of five hundred dollars, was offered to such persons as would put up certain grist mills, and two more assessments of ten dollars per share levied.

On the first of May, 1799, no relief had been obtained upon their petitions for a civil government, the losses and delays of their enterprise on this account were again presented to the State of Connecticut. This had been so embarrassing to their operations, that in the following year, the State was asked to abate the interest due upon their payments.

MSS. OF JUDGE BARR.

"RODOLPHUS EDWARDS from Chenango county, New York, came to Cleveland this season; also NATHANIEL DOAN and family, from Chatham, Middlesex county, Conn. His journey from Chatham occupied *ninety-two days.* At Utica, N. York, he was joined by his nephew, SETH DOAN, at the urgent request of the latter, who was an ambitious boy of thirteen. In 1801 SETH'S father, TIMOTHY DOAN, moved into Euclid, as his future home. NATHANIEL DOAN went at first into the cabin built by STILES, and immediately put up a blacksmith shop on the south side of Superior street, not far east of the end of Bank street. JOSEPH LANDON and STEPHEN GILBERT cleared some ground and sowed it to wheat, on what was afterwards the HORACE PERRY farm. Major CARTER planted two acres of corn on Water street, just south of the light house.

In the latter part of the summer and all the fall, every person in the colony was at some time sick with fever and ague or billious fever. DOAN'S family was attacked on the way, and were obliged to stop at Mentor, from whence PARKER and CHURCH brought them here. It consisted of nine persons, every one of them sick. SETH DOAN was the only one with strength enough to do anything, and he had shakes every day himself. He was able, when the fit subsided to bring a pail of water, and gather firewood. For two months this boy made the trip to Mr. KINGSBURY'S after his daily fit was over, and brought a little corn for the sick, which they mashed in a hand mill at Newburg. The nearest water mill at that time was on Walnut Creek, in Pennsylvania. When SETH was unable to go, their only vegetable food was turnips.

When Major CARTER had an intermission of the disease, he and his hounds generally secured a deer, which was liberally shared with the other sick families. CARTER's family being somewhat acclimated, suffered less than the new comers. There was no physician to prescribe, and few medicines.

In the place of calomel, they used an infusion of butternut bark, and for quinine and Peruvian bark, they substituted dog wood and cherry. For tea and coffee they burned corn, wheat, rye and peas. The families of KINGSBURY and GUN, on the ridge, were in good health, and visiting the city as often as possible, were untiring in their attentions to the sick. EDWARDS, who had moved to the ridge, was sick, and continued so all winter. As the cold weather came on, the invalids gradually recovered strength, so that by the first of January, 1799, they were in reasonable health.

About the middle of November, four of the settlers who had a respite of one or two days between fits, started for Walnut Creek to get flour. As they were coasting along the shore below Euclid creek, their boat was wrecked in a storm, and they were obliged to return. During the winter and spring they were without flour, subsisting upon wheat and corn, ground in the hand mill and made up Graham fashion.

The Land Company caused a road to be surveyed and partially worked this year, from Cleveland to the Pennsylvania line, about ten miles from the lake, which was the first road opened through the Reserve. David Abbott, from Fort Stanwix, New York, settled at the Chagrin river, and Joseph Burk and family, in Euclid. Burton, Harpersfield and Youngstown were also occupied for the first time as settlements."

1799.

"Mr. N. Doan, moved to Doan's corners in January, where he lived both beloved and respected until his decease in December, 1815. After his removal Major Carter's was the only white family in Cleveland until April, 1800. In the spring of '99 Wheeler W. Williams, of Norwich, Conn., and Major Wyatt commenced building a mill at the Falls, in Newburg. This being the first mill on the Reserve, its completion was celebrated by the pioneers with great joy and festivity. During the following winter our citizens enjoyed the luxury of bolted flour, made in their own mills, from wheat raised by themselves.

Seth Doan is the only denizen of the city at that time, who still (1842) resides in it. Only *four* out of a population of *fifteen* survive. These are Sarah Doan, the widow of Nathaniel, Lucy Carter, widow of James Strong, Alonzo Carter, of Newburg, (still living, 1866) and Seth Doan, the heroic boy.

The season of 1799 was very healthy. With the exception of Messrs. Williams and Wyatt, and two or three young men who came to Newburg, no settlers arrived this year. TURHAND KIRTLAND, father of Prof. J. P. KIRTLAND, was made Agent for the Land Company and visited the Reserve."

1800.

In the year 1800 the inhabitants of the Western Reserve found themselves in the enjoyment of a civil government. The discussions between the State of Connecticut and the United States were composed, by the transfer of the State claim of jurisdiction to the Federal Government, and the claim of the Government to the soil, to the State. Governor ST. CLAIR established the county of Trumbull, and issued a a proclamation for elections, to be held under the Territorial system; which was dated Sept. 22d, and directed to DAVID ABBOTT, Sheriff, commanding him, "That on the second Tuesday of October, he cause an election to be held for the purpose of electing one person to represent the county in the Territorial Legislature." All elections by the existing laws, were to be held at the respective county seats of the counties in the Territory. Of course this election was held at Warren, the seat of justice for Trumbull county. The manner of conducting the election was after the English mode. That is, the sheriff of the county assembled the electors by proclamation, he presided at the election, and received the votes of the electors orally, or *viva voce.* It will readily be conceded, that in a county, embracing as Trumbull then did, a large Territory, only a portion of the electors would attend. The number convened at that election was *forty-two.* Out of this number General Edward Paine received 38 votes, and was the member elect. General Paine took his seat in the Territorial Legislature in 1801.

Immediately after the organization of Trumbull county, at the first Court of Quarter Sessions in August, the county was organized into eight townships. The townships were named Youngstown, Warren, Hudson, Vernon, Richfield, Middlefield, Painesville and Cleveland.

Cleveland embraced the townships of Chester, Russell and Bainbridge, now in Geauga county; all of the present county of Cuyahoga east of the river, and all of the Indian country from the Cuyahoga to the west line of the Reserve. When the townships west of the river were organized, after the county of Cuyahoga was erected, the channel of the river formed the western boundary of Cleveland. The City of Ohio and the City of Cleveland, were organized in March, 1836, without changing this boundary; but the dividing line between the cities followed the new or artificial channel, made in 1827 by the construction of a harbor.

A portion of Cleveland township, embracing about seven acres at the mouth of the river, remained in Ohio City until the township organization was given up.

On the 2d of October, 1800, the election was held at Warren, where the electors assembled, after the English fashion, for the first and the last time. None were present from Cleveland. The appointment of township officers was vested in the Court of Quarter Sessions, composed of Justices of the Peace of the quorum, appointed by the Governor. Efforts had been made by the Territorial Legislature to change this mode of appointment, to an election by the people, but the sturdy old Governor applied his veto to all such innovations. In 1802, he so far relaxed as to allow of election districts, or precincts, of less size than a county.

In Cleveland township, KINGSBURY was the first Justice of the Quorum, AMOS SPAFFORD a Justice not of Quorum. STEPHEN GILBERT and LORENZO CARTER were the first constables.

"Early in the spring, DAVID HUDSON passed here, in company with THADDEUS LACY and DAVID KELLOGG and their families, to settle in Hudson, Summit county, Ohio. Capt. ALLAN GAYLORD, of Newburg, was of this party. (1866, Capt. GAYLORD is still living). A school house was built this season, near KINGSBURY'S, on the ridge road, and Miss SARAH DOAN, daughter of NATHANIEL DOAN, was the teacher. DAVID CLARK and Major AMOS SPAFFORD, with their families, arrived from Vermont, and became settlers in Cleveland. Major SPAFFORD occupied the Merwin lot, south of Superior and east of Vineyard streets, near the corner. Mr. CLARK built on Water street, west side, near the Mansion House. [The Mansion House of 1842 stood nearly opposite VINCENT's furniture store.] JOHN WALWORTH and EDWARD PAINE settled at Painesville, BENJ. TAPPEN at Ravenna, and EPHRAIM QUINBY at Warren, during this year."—(BARR.)

LETTER OF J. A. ACKLEY.

PARMA, July 29th, 1858.

HON. JOHN BARR,

Dear Sir:—LORENZO CARTER was a half brother of mine, but he, being the eldest of six children by the first, and myself the youngest of three children by the second husband; and our mother having lived a widow six years, brings us quite a distance apart. He was a man, and gone from home before I was born. Consequently I can say little of him from my own knowledge, but must rely on what I have heard from my mother, brothers and sisters. LORENZO CARTER was born in the year 1766, at Warren, Litchfield county, Connecticut, and consequently was about ten years of age, at the commencement of the revolutionary war, at which time, he had the misfortune to lose his father. He was then left to the care of a widowed mother, in moderate circumstances, with a family of six children, all young; to pass through that turbulent period. LORENZO was a strong, athletic self-willed boy, and it could not be expected that a mother would guide and direct him like a father. But our mother was a thorough going woman, and managed to get along reasonably well, until the close of the war, when she married again, and soon after moved to Castleton, Rutland county, Vermont; then almost a wilderness.

LORENZO was about eighteen years of age, a very natural age to become fond of a dog or gun, hunting and fishing. The country being new, and game plenty, he soon became quite a Nimrod. Arrived to manhood, he bought a lot of new land, took to himself a better half, and settled on his land. But farming, or at least clearing a new farm, was not exactly to his mind. He soon became restless and wished for a change. About this time the Ohio fever began to rage, and CARTER, in company with a man by the name of HIGBY, started for the Western wilds. Their course was through western Pennsylvania, to Pittsburg, down the Ohio river as far as the Muskingum river. They then turned north and struck the lake at Cleveland, from thence by the nearest route home. CARTER arranged his affairs as soon as possible, and the next year, in June, started with his family and effects for the west, and arrived at Cleveland in the summer of 1797.

Many stories are told of Major CARTER, some are true, and many that are not true. He was the man for a pioneer, with strength of body and mind, but not cultivated. His maxim was not to give an insult, nor receive one, without resenting it, and the insulter generally paid dear for his temerity. With all his faults, his heart was in the right place, and he was as ready to avenge a wrong done to the weak, as one done to himself.

Respectfully, Yours,

JOHN A. ACKLEY.

LETTER OF COL. JAMES HILLMAN.

YOUNGSTOWN, OHIO, Nov. 23, 1843.

JUDGE BARR, *Cleveland:*

Dear Sir —Yours of the 15th came duly to hand, making enquiries of the early times and settlement of Cleveland.

In the spring of 1786, Messrs. DUNCAN & WILSON entered into a contract with Messrs. CALDWELL & ELLIOTT, of Detroit, to deliver a quantity of flour and bacon at the mouth of the Cuyahoga river to a man by the name of JAMES HAWDER, an Englishman, who had a tent at the mouth of the river, for the purpose of receiving it. In May, 1786, I engaged with DUNCAN & WILSON, at Pittsburg, as pack-horseman, and started immediately. We took the Indian trail for Sandusky, until we arrived at the "Standing Stone," on the Cuyahoga, a little below the mouth of Breakneck creek, where the village of Franklin is now. There we left the Sandusky trail and took one direct to the mouth of Tinker's creek, where was a little town built by HECKEWELDER and ZEISBERGER, with a number of Moravian Indians. They were Moravian preachers. Here we crossed the Cuyahoga, and went down on the west side to the mouth. In going down we passed a small log trading house, where one MEGINNES traded with the Indians. He had left the house in the spring before we were there. I understood he had some difficulty with the Indians and left, but whether any were killed I do not recollect.

We made six trips that summer. On the second trip, one HUGH BLAIR, a packhorseman, in crossing Breakneck creek, fell backwards from his horse and broke his neck. His horse got his foot fast in some beech roots. We called it "Breakneck creek," a name I believe it has always retained.

The mouth of the Cuyahoga was then about the same as when I last saw it, in 1813. In 1786 there was a pond of water west of the mouth, which we called "Sun Fish Pond," where we caught sun fish. We carried axes to cut our wood, and I remember, we at one time undertook to open the mouth of the river, which was choked up with sand. We made wooden shovels and began to dig away the sand until the water ran through, which took away the sand so fast that our party was divided, a portion being left on the east side where Cleveland now is. CALDWELL & ELLIOTT had a small sail boat to carry the flour and bacon to Detroit. We used to cross the river by means of the "Mackinaw," that being the name of the sail boat. By opening the mouth of the river, she could sail up to where there was a spring, near where Main street comes to the river. We made collars of our blankets for some of the horses, and took our tent ropes, made of raw elk skin, for tugs, drew small logs and built a hut at the spring, which I believe was the first house built on the Cleveland side. [No mention of this is made by the surveyors.]

On the west side the bottom was in woodland, except Sun Fish Fond, which had the appearance of an old outlet to the lake. At that time there were no traders about the mouth of the river, only HAWDEN'S (or HAWDER'S) tent, who was there to receive the flour and bacon. As fast as we delivered it, it was forwarded by the Mackinaw to Detroit. There was no trading at Grindstone brook, where MEGINNES formerly traded.

In the year 1785, DUNCAN & WILSON sent some kettles and some Indian goods to the Salt Springs, on the Mahoning river, in Trumbull county, with a view of making salt. Government ascertained that fact, and in the same year, there being troops at Fort McIntosh, at the mouth of Big Beaver, sent a Lieutenant and some soldiers, with an order to

DUNCAN & WILSON to quit the enterprise, which they did, as the Indian title had not been extinguished.

DUNCAN & WILSON left a man at the Salt Springs by the name of JOHN KRIBS, to take care of their property. In the summer of 1786, when we were on our way to Cleveland, near where the Mahoning crosses the State line, an Indian came to us and said that KRIBS (or KRIPS,) had been murdered by an Indian named NEMAHAHE, which means "Great Wolf." We left our horses and loading near the State line, and went that night to the Salt Spring, about eighteen miles. We found him very much eaten by wolves. We went back to our horses, and when we came on we then buried KRIBS.

I am now eighty-five years old. As to the meaning of Indian names for rivers and water courses, I am not able to give any information that would be useful to you.

Resp'y, your very ob't serv't,
JAMES HILLMAN.

BOUNDARIES OF CUYAHOGA COUNTY.

That part of Cuyahoga county which lies east of Cuyahoga river, had its first organization as a part of Washington county, erected July 27, 1788, with the county seat at Marietta. Lake Erie was the northern boundary of Washington county, and the Cuyahoga river, the old portage path, and the Tuscarawas river its western boundary, on the Reserve. The city of Cleveland was thus situated at the extreme north-west corner, of the first county erected in Ohio. That part of Cuyahoga county which lies west of the river was embraced in the county of Wayne, with the county seat at Detroit, erected August 15, 1796. On the 29th of July, 1797, that part of the Western Reserve which lies east of the Cuyahoga river, and the old portage path, became a part of the county of Jefferson; with the county seat at Steubenville. The county of Trumbull was erected July 10, 1800, and embraced all the Western Reserve, including the Fire lands, and the Islands opposite. All these organizations were effected by proclamation, prior to the existence of the territorial legislature. By an act of the State legislature, dated December 21st, 1805, which took effect March, 1806, the county of Geauga was set off from the county of Trumbull, including a large part of the present county of Cuyahoga; and extending west as far as Range 14. Huron county was erected February 7, 1809, covering the Fire lands. The counties of Cuyahoga, Portage and Ashtabula were authorized February 10, 1807. By this act the county of Cuyahoga was declared to embrace so much of the county of Geauga as lay west of the 9th range of townships. The organization of the county of Cuyahoga did not take place till January 16, 1810. The boundaries of this county, by the Act of 1807, were as follows. On the east side of Cuyahoga rivers, all north of Town 5, and west of Range 9; on the west side of the river, all north of Town 4, and east of Range 15; a space between Ranges 14 and 20 on the west; and the county of Huron, being attached to Cuyahoga county for judicial purposes.

One of the commissioners for fixing the county seat presented his bill for services, in the following words:

"COLUMBIANA COUNTY, OHIO,
October, 1809.

Deir Sir:—I have called on Mr. PEAIES for my Pay for fixing the Seat of Justis in the County of Cuyahoga and he informt me that he did not Chit it. Sir, I should take it as a favour of you would send it with Mister PEAIES at your Nixt Cort and In so doing will oblige Your humble Sarvent R. B**R.

ABRAHAM TAPPIN Esq.

A Leven Days Two Dollars per day, Twenty two Dollars."

On the 25th of January, 1811, the line between Huron and Cuyahoga counties was changed on the west. Beginning at the south-west corner of Strongsville, No. 5, in the 14th Range, it was carried westward, to the south west corner of Eaton, No. 5, in the 16th Range; thence north to the north-west corner of Eaton township; thence west to the middle of Black river, and northerly, following its channel, to the lake. When the county of Medina was erected, February 18th, 1812, another alteration took place in the western boundary of Cuyahoga county. From the north-west corner of Eaton, the line extended north to the north-west corner of Ridgeville, No. 6, Range 16; thence west to Black river, and with the river to the lake. Until the 1st of April, 1815, when Huron county was organized, legal proceedings in that county, were prosecuted in Cuyahoga. Lorain county, which was organized on the 1st of April, 1824, took from the south-west part of Cuyahoga, Town 5, of Range 15, (Columbia,) and the west half of Olmsted, in that Range. By the Act of January 29th, 1827, this half township was restored to Cuyahoga County.

Changes in the outline of the county, were not yet at an end. When Lake county was organized, March 20th, 1840, the township of Willoughby, on the north-east was dissevered from Cuyahoga.

Afterwards, January 29th, 1841, a strip ninety rods wide, in the north-east part of Orange township, extending from the north-east corner down the east line, to the east and west center road, was annexed to Geauga county.

In compensation for this, lots 17, 18 and 19, in the south-west corner of Russell, Geauga county, were transferred to Cuyahoga, in order to accommodate the thriving village of Chagrin Falls.

On the 11th of January, 1843, the tract taken from Orange was restored. Since then the county lines have remained without change.

E
D
C
B
A

CLEVELAND UNDER THE HILL,

EARLY IN THE SPRING OF THE YEAR 1800, FROM A RUDE SKETCH MADE AT THE TIME BY ALLEN GAYLORD, OF NEWBURG.

A. Surveyors' cabin, or "PEASE'S Hotel." *B.* Log store-house of the surveyors. *C.* LORENZO CARTER'S first cabin. *D.* Mouth of the river. *E.* Old river bed and natural mound beyond it.

Although this is only a rough outline taken by one of the pioneers, who was wholly unskilled in the use of the pencil, it must be regarded as a reasonably correct picture of the lower town at that time. The trail or road up the hill, is no doubt more conspicuous and street like than it should be, although it was then used by teams. During the same year, DAVID BRYANT became a settler, and commenced building a small distillery at the mouth of the ravine, between the cabins, as his son more fully relates in the following letter:

LETTER OF GILMAN BRYANT.

MOUNT VERNON, OHIO, June 1st, 1857.

ALEXANDER C. ELLIOTT, Esq.—*Sir:* According to your request, I will inform you about the first settlement of Cleveland, Ohio, according to my best recollection.

My father, DAVID BRYANT, and myself, landed at Cleveland in June, 1797. There was but one family there at that time, viz: LORENZO CARTER, who lived in a log cabin, under the high sand bank, near the Cuyahoga river, and about thirty rods below the bend of the river, at the west end of Superior street. I went up the hill to view the town. I found one log cabin erected by the surveyors, on the south side of Superior street, near the place where the old Mansion house formerly stood. There was no cleared land, only where the logs were cut to erect the cabin, and for fire-wood. I saw the stakes at the corners of the lots, among the logs and large oak and chestnut trees. We were on our way to a grindstone quarry, near Vermillion river. We made two trips that summer, and stopped at Mr. CARTER'S each time. In the fall of 1797, I found Mr. RODOLPHUS EDWARDS in a cabin under the hill, at the west end of Superior street. We made two trips in the summer of 1798. I found Major SPAFFORD in the old surveyor's cabin. The same fall Mr. DAVID CLARK erected a cabin on the other side of the street, and about five rods north-west of SPAFFORD'S. We made two trips in the summer of 1799, and in the fall, father and myself returned to Cleveland, to make a pair of mill stones for Mr. WILLIAMS, about five miles east of Cleveland, near the trail to Hudson. We made the mill stones on the right hand side of the stream as you go up, fifteen or twenty feet from the stream, and about half a mile from the mill, which was under a high bank, and near a fall in said stream of forty or fifty feet. If any person will examine, they will find the remains and pieces of the rock, the said stones were made of. The water was conveyed to the mill in a dugout trough, to an under-shot wheel about twelve feet over, with one set of arms, and buckets fifteen inches long, to run inside of the trough, which went down the bank at an angle of forty-five degrees, perhaps. The dam was about four rods above the fall; the mill stones were three and half feet in diameter, of gray rock. On my way from the town to Mr. WILLIAMS' mill, I found the cabin of Mr. R. EDWARDS, who had left the town, about three miles out; the next cabin was Judge KINGSBURY'S, and the next old Mr. GUNN, thence half a mile to Mr. WILLIAMS' mill.

On my return to Cleveland in the fall of 1800, my father and myself came there to stay. He took a still from Virginia, and built a still-house under the sand bank, about twenty rods above L. CARTER'S and fifteen feet from the river. The house was made of hewed logs, twenty by twenty-six, one and a half stories high. We took the water in a trough, out of some small springs which came out of the bank, into the second story of the house, and made the whisky out of wheat.

My father purchased ten acres of land about one-fourth of a mile from the town plat, on the bank of the river, east of the town. In the winter of 1800 and spring of 1801, I helped my father to clear five acres on said lot, which was planted with corn in the spring. Said ten acres were sold by my father in the spring of 1802, at the rate of two dollars and fifty cents per acre. Mr. SAMUEL HUNTINGTON came to Cleveland in the spring of 1801, and built a hewed log house near the bank of the Cuyahoga river, about fifteen rods south-east of the old surveyors's cabin, occupied by Mr. SPAFFORD.

I attended the 4th of July ball, mentioned in the History of Ohio. I waited on Miss DOAN, who had just arrived at the Corners, four miles east of town. I was then about seventeen years of age, and Miss DOAN about fourteen. I was dressed in the then style—a gingham suit—my hair *queued* with one and a half yards of black ribbon, about as long and as thick as a corncob, with a little tuft at the lower end; and for want of pomatum, I had a piece of candle rubbed on my hair, and then as much flour sprinkled on, as could stay without falling off. I had a good wool hat, and a pair of brogans that would help to play "Fisher's Hornpipe," or "High Bettie Martin," when I danced. When I went for Miss DOAN I took an old horse; when she was ready I rode up to a stump near the cabin, she mounted the stump and spread her under petticoat on "Old Tib" behind me, secured her calico dress to keep it clean, and then mounted on behind me. I had a fine time!

The Indians scattered along the river, from five to eight miles apart, as far as the falls; they hauled their canoes above high water mark and covered them with bark, and went from three to five miles back into the woods. In the spring, after sugar making, they all packed their skins, sugar, bear's oil, honey and jerked venison, to their crafts. They frequently had to make more canoes, either of wood or bark, as the increase of their furs, &c., required. They would descend the river in April, from sixty to eighty families, and encamp on the west side of the river for eight or ten days, take a drunken scrape and have a feast. I was invited to partake of a *white dog*. They singed part of the hair off and chopped him up, and made a large kettle of soup. They erected a scaffold, and offered a large wooden bowlful, placed on the scaffold, to "Manitou," and then they presented me with one fore-paw well boiled, and plenty of soup, the hair still between the toes. I excused; they said, "a good soldier could eat such." They said "God was a good man and would not hurt anybody." They, in offering the sacrifice to Manitou, prayed to him for their safety over the lake, and that they might have a good crop of corn, &c.

Yours, &c.,

GILMAN BRYANT.

CLEAVELAND, OHIO, 17th July, 1800.

Gen. M. CLEAVELAND, Canterbury, Conn.,
to be left at Norwich Post Office.

Dear Sir:—On my arrival at this place, I found Major SPAFFORD, Mr. LORENZO CARTER and Mr. DAVID CLARK, who are the only inhabitants residing in the city, have been anxiously waiting with expectations of purchasing a number of lots, but when I produced my instructions, they were greatly disappointed, both as to price and terms. They assured me, that they had encouragement last year, from Colonel THOMAS SHELDON; that they would have lands at ten dollars per acre, and from Major AUSTIN at twelve dollars at most; which they think would be a generous price, for such a quantity as they wish to purchase. You will please excuse me, for giving my opinion, but it really seems to me good policy to sell the city lots, at a less price than twenty-five dollars, (two acres) or I shall never expect to see it settled.

Mr. CARTER was an early adventurer, has been of essential advantage to the inhabitants here, in helping them to provisions in times of danger and scarcity, has never experienced any gratuity from the company, but complains of being hardly dealt by, in sundry instances. He has money to pay for about thirty acres, which he expected to have taken, if the price had met his expectation; but he now declares that he will leave the purchase, and never own an acre in New Connecticut. Major SPAFFORD has stated his wishes to the company, in his letter of January last, and I am not authorized to add any thing. He says he has no idea of giving the present price, for sixteen or eighteen lots. He contemplated building a house, and making large improvements this season, which he thinks would indemnify the company fully, in case he should fail to fulfill his contract; and he is determined to remove to some other part of the purchase immediately, unless he can obtain better terms than I am authorized to give. Mr. CLARK is to be included in the same contract, with Major SPAFFORD, but his circumstances will not admit of his making any advances. I have requested the settlers not to leave the place, until I can obtain further information from the Board, and request you to consult General CHAMPION, to whom I have written, and favor me with despatches by first mail. * * *

Mr. EDWARDS has gone to see the Governor. Crops

extraordinary good, and settlers healthy and in good spirits. They are increasing as fast as can be expected, but the universal scarcity of cash, in this back part of the country, renders it extremely difficult to sell for money, and the vast quantity of land in market will prevent a speedy sale of our lands. The people have been encouraged that the Company would have a store erected, and receive provisions in payment for lands, for money is not to be had. Mr. TILLITSON, from Lyme, wants two, one hundred acre lots, and would pay for one in hand if horses, cattle or provisions would answer, or would take them on credit, if he could have sufficient time to turn his property, but has no cash to advance.

I have given a sketch of these circumstances, in order that you may understand my embarrassments, and expect you will give me particular directions how to proceed, and also, whether I shall make new contracts with settlers, whose old ones are forfeited. They seem unwilling to rely on the generosity of the company, and want new writings. * *

I have the pleasure of your brother's company at this time. He held his first talk with the Smooth Nation, at Mr. CARTER's this morning. Appearances are very promising. I flatter myself he will do no discredit to his elder brother, in his negotiations with the aborigines.

I am, dear sir, with much esteem, yours, &c.,

TURHAND KIRTLAND.

Samuel Huntington, Esq., of Norwich, Conn., visited Ohio, reaching Youngstown in July. He made a horseback tour through the settlements on the Reserve, keeping daily memoranda, which are preserved by his descendants, at Painesville.

In this diary he says: "*Thursday, October 7th*, 1800. — Left David Abbott's mill, (Willoughby,) and came to Cleveland. Stayed at Carter's at night. Day pleasant and cool. *Friday, 3d.* — Explored the city and town; land high and flat, covered with white oak. On the west side of the river is a long, deep stagnant pond of water, which produces fever and ague, among those who settle near the river. There are only three families near the point, and they have the fever. *Saturday, 4th.*— Sailed out of the Cuyahoga, along the coast, to explore the land west of the river. Channel at the mouth about five feet deep. On the west side is a prairie, where one hundred tons of hay might be cut each year. A little way back is a ridge, from which the land descends to the lake, affording a prospect indescribably beautiful. In the afternoon went to Williams' grist and saw mill, (Newburg,) which are nearly completed. *Sunday 5th.*—Stayed at Williams'. *Monday, 6th.*—Went through Towns 7, 6 and 5, of Range 11, to Hudson."

Mr. Huntington continued his journeyings during the season, embracing the settlements on the Ohio as low as Marietta. Here he made the acquaintance of Governor ST. CLAIR, the Territorial Judges, and principal men of Ohio. He returned to Norwich, Conn., in the fall, having concluded to become a citizen of New Connecticut.

The ridge, of which so many of the first comers speak, is a natural terrace or bluff, the edge of the upland country, fronting towards and parallel with the lake, from which side it has the appearance of an elevated range. It extends easterly from Newburg to and beyond Painesville, the crest rising from one hundred and sixty to two hundred feet above lake level, broken only by steep and deep gullies where the streams pass through it.

1801.

"TIMOTHY DOAN arrived at Cleveland in the spring, and in the fall removed to Euclid. He died in the fall of 1828, at the age of seventy. SAMUEL HAMILTON and family settled at Newburg. About five years after he was drowned in Buffalo creek, on his return from a visit to the east. At Cleveland the people were unusually healthy. This year became notorious, on account of a Fourth of July celebration and ball. It was held in one end of Major CARTER's double log house, on the hill near the corner of Union and Superior lanes. JOHN WOOD, BEN WOOD and R. H. BLINN were managers. Major SAMUEL JONES was chief musician and master of ceremonies. About a dozen ladies and twenty gentlemen constituted the company. Notwithstanding the floors were of rough puncheons, and their best beverage was made of maple sugar, hot water and whisky, probably no celebration of American independence in this city was ever more joyous than this.

ELISHA NORTON opened a store in CARTER's house, under the hill, and DAVID BRYANT built a log distillery, on the ground afterwards occupied by MATTHEW WILLIAMSON as a tannery. [The distillery stood where M. B. SCOTT's warehouse is now.]

Previous to this year, the people had no laws but those of GOD and their own consciences, yet they lived in great harmony. A bond of union existed in their common pleasures, as well as in their misfortunes. During the days of club law, very few disputes occurred, such was the universal good feeling that prevailed. Not a single case of Lynch law occurred from 1796 to the organization of the State government, and only one of "club law." This happened between Major CARTER and the Indians, and was caused by alcohol.

Both old LEATHERSTOCKING and the red men, were very good and generous friends in the absence of this demon." (Judge BARR.)

The Rev. JOSEPH BADGER, a soldier of the Revolution, came to the Reserve in 1800, as a missionary from the Connecticut Missionary Society. He was at Cleveland on the 18th of August, 1801, when he lodged at LORENZO CARTER'S. On the 6th of September, he says: "We swam our horses across the Cuyahoga by means of a canoe, and took an Indian path up the lake; came to Rocky river, the banks of which were very high, on the west side almost perpendicular. While cutting the brush to open a way for our horses, we were saluted by the song of a large yellow rattlesnake, which we removed out of our way."

SPAFFORD'S re-survey of the streets and lanes of city took place in November. He planted fifty-four posts of oak, about one foot square, at the principal corners, for which he charged fifty cents each, and fifty cents, for grubbing out a tree at the north-east corner of the Square.

SAMUEL HUNTINGTON, who was an attorney, removed with his family to Youngstown early in the summer of 1801. He soon determined to establish himself at Cleveland, and contracted with AMOS SPAFFORD to superintend the erection of a well built block house, of considerable pretensions near the bluff south of Superior street, in rear of the site of the American House. HUNTINGTON was then about thirty-five years of age. He was the protege and adopted heir of his uncle and name-sake, Governor SAMUEL HUNTINGTON, of Connecticut. His education was very complete for those times. It would appear from his correspondence with Frenchmen, his knowledge of the French language, and the polish of his manners, that he had spent some time in France. His family consisted of his wife, Miss MARGARET COBB, a companion and governess; and two sons, JULIUS C. and COLBERT, who still survive. HUNTINGTON belonged to the more moderate republicans, and does not appear to have lost the confidence of the Federalists. Governor ST. CLAIR soon appointed him Lieutenant Colonel of the Trumbull county regiment, and in January, 1802, one of the Justices of the Quorum. The only time when the Governor is known to have visited the Reserve, was at the trial of McMAHON, at Youngstown, charged with the murder of an Indian named SPOTTED GEORGE, at the Salt Springs. Mr. HUNTINGTON acted as counsel in the case, but on which side, I am not informed.

The extreme Jeffersonian Republicans, like JOHN S. EDWARDS and Judge TOD, looked favorably upon HUNTINGTON, who was ambitious and popular; and who entered at once upon the career of a public man. He took by common consent, priority on the bench of Quarter Sessions. In November, 1802, he was elected a delegate to the convention to form a State constitution, which appears to have been well received by ST. CLAIR. After its adoption, he was elected Senator from Trumbull county, and on the meeting of the first Legislature at Chillicothe, was made Speaker. On the 2d of April, 1803, he was appointed a Judge of the Supreme Court, his commission, which was signed by Governor Tiffin, being the first issued under the authority of the State of Ohio. A character so prominent and successful, no doubt, had a favorable influence upon the place of his residence, which, in 1801, was nearly depopulated. In person he was small, but exceedingly active. His manners were affable, though somewhat after the French style, in business his habits were correct and efficient.

1802.

Carter built a frame house on the hill west of Water street and north of Superior Lane, which was burned almost as soon as finished. Amos Spafford put up the second frame house, near the west end of Superior street, on the south side. In the latter part of July Mr. Badger again took Cleveland in his circuit. He does not give a very favorable report of the morals of the place.

"Mr. Burke's family in Euclid, had been in this lone situation over three years. The woman had been obliged to spin and weave cattle's hair, to make covering for her children's bed. From thence I went to Cleveland, visited the only two families, and went on to Newburg, where I preached on the Sabbath. There were five families here, but no apparent piety. They seemed to glory in their infidelity. On the way from Cleveland here, I fell in company with a man from Hudson, who wanted to know if I was going to form a church there. I replied, if I found suitable characters I should. 'Well,' said he, 'if you admit old Deacon THOMPSON, (and some others,) it shall not stand, I will break it down and have an Episcopal church.'"

In 1802 the Territorial Legislature had so far prevailed over the old system, that citizens of the townships were allowed to elect trustees, appraisers, supervisors of highways, fence viewers, overseers of the poor, and constables, *viva voce*. They had not yet attained to the election of justices of the peace and militia officers. At the February term of the Quarter Sessions, it was ordered that the house of JAMES KINGSBURY be the place for holding the first town meeting in Cleveland. Here is the result of the first election held in "Cleaveland, Trumbull county, Ohio."

"Agreeably to order of the Court of General Quarter Sessions, the inhabitants of the town of Cleaveland met at the house of JAMES KINGSBURY, Esq., the 5th day of April, A. D. 1802, for a town meeting, and chose

Chairman, RODOLPHUS EDWARDS.

Town Clerk, NATHANIEL DOAN.

Trustees,
AMOS SPAFFORD, Esq., TIMOTHY DOAN, WM. W. WILLIAMS.

Appraisers of Houses,
SAMUEL HAMILTON, ELIJAH GUN.

Lister,
EBENEZER AYRS.
Supervisors of Highways,
SAM'L HUNTINGTON, Esq., NATH'L DOAN, SAM'L HAMILTON.
Overseers of the Poor,
WILLIAM W. WILLIAMS, SAMUEL HUNTINGTON, Esq.
Fence Viewers,
LORENZO CARTER, NATHAN CHAPMAN.
Constables,
EZEKIEL HAWLEY, RICHARD CRAW.

A true copy of the proceedings of the inhabitants of Cleaveland at their town meeting, examined per me,

NATHANIEL DOAN, *Town Clerk*."

According to a widely circulated tradition, Mr. HUNTINGTON, about this time, came near being devoured by wolves, not far from the Euclid street station. He was coming in from Painesville, on horseback, alone, and after dark, floundering through a swamp, which occupied what is now the corner of Willson avenue and Euclid street. A gang of hungry wolves had taken up their nights lodging in this swamp, who made a combined attack upon the judge and his horse. His only defensive weapon was an umbrella, with which he charged them right and left. The horse, in a terrible fright, performed his part nobly, by a rapid movement along the trail towards town, outstripping the ferocious animals, and brought up, with his rider, at the door of the double log house south of Superior street.

At the August term of the Quarter Sessions, Lorenzo Carter and Amos Spafford were each licensed to keep a tavern at Cleveland on paying *four* dollars. George Tod, (afterwards Judge Tod) of Youngstown, was appointed appraiser of taxable property.

The sale of the six reserved townships, and of the city lots in Cleveland, did not come up to the expectations of the Company. City lots had receded from fifty dollars cash in hand, to twenty-five dollars on time. The treasury of the association, instead of being filled by the proceeds of sales, had to be replenished by the disagreeable process of assessments. By individual exertion, the private owners under the previous drafts, had disposed of limited amounts of lands, on terms which did not create very brilliant expectations of the speculation. In truth, the most fortunate of the adventurers realized a very meagre profit, and more of them were losers than gainers.

Those who were able to make their payments and keep the property for their children, made a fair and safe investment. It was not until the next generation came to maturity, that lands on the Reserve began to command good prices. Taxes, trouble and interest, had been long accumulating. Such of the proprietors as became settlers, secured an excellent home at a cheap rate, and left as a legacy to their heirs, a cheerful future.

At this time, however, it was considered better

for the property to be wholly in private hands, and on the 28th of December, 1802, another draft was made of the six townships, which had been divided into ninety parcels. This included all of the lands east of the Cuyahoga, except a few city lots in Cleveland. Some had been sold, but most of them were assorted to the stockholders as part of the draft.

The names of the original owners are here given.

ORIGINAL OWNERS OF LOTS IN CLEVELAND BY DRAFT, OR FIRST PURCHASE.

NUMBER OF CITY LOTS, 220.

Samuel Huntington, 1 to 6, 61, 75, 76, 78, 80 to 84, 190 to 194, 206, 210
Caleb Atwater, 7 to 24, 31 to 36
Lorenzo Carter, 25 to 30, 54, 197 to 205
Ephraim Root, 37 to 47
Elijah Boardman and others, 48
Ezekiel Hawley, 49 to 51
David Clark, 52 and 53
Joseph Howland, 55 to 57, 62
Charles Dutton, 58
James Kingsbury, 59 and 60
Samuel W. Phelps, 63
Joseph Perkins and others, 64 to 72
Austin & Huntington, 73 and 74
Wyles and others, 77
Judson Canfield and others, 79
Samuel P. Lord, Jr., 85 to 87, 97 to 99, 211 and 212
William Shaw, 88 to 96, 100 to 133
Samuel Parkman, 134 to 138

1803.

"A healthy year, marked by increased emigration and the organization of the state of Ohio. The first indictment found on the Reserve was against Mr. CARTER, the pioneer, for an assault upon JAMES HAMILTON, of Newburg. A second frame house was erected by Major SPAFFORD on the brow of the hill, between Superior and Vineyard Lanes, at the end of Superior street. Postmaster DANIEL WORLEY once occupied the same building as a residence."—(BARR.)

ELECTION OF 1803—STATEMENT OF WARREN YOUNG, ESQ., OF WARREN, MARCH 27th, 1848.

"I am unable to find the canvass sheet of this year. The election was held in Cleveland, Oct. 11th, and there were *twenty-two* votes given. For the two representatives, DAVID ABBOTT had twenty-two votes; EPHRAIM QUINBY, nineteen; AMOS SPAFFORD, one; and DAVID HUDSON, one. TIMOTHY DOAN, NATHANIEL DOAN and JAMES KINGSBURY, Judges of election. Rodolphus Edwards and Stephen Gilbert, Clerks. Sworn in by Timothy Doan, Justice of the Peace.

Bryant's log distillery, of course, attracted the attention of such Senecas, Hurons, Chippeways, and Delawares, as had a weakness for fire-water. Alexander Campbell, who was doubtless a Scotchman, saw that here was a good place to traffic with the stoic of the woods. He built a rude store a little further up the hill, near the spring, but more towards the junction of Union and Mandrake Lanes. St. Clair street was an improvement of much later times. The same spring, afterwards supplied the tannery of Samuel and Matthew Williamson's establishment, on lot 202, the vats of which were directly across River street.

In this cluster of log shanties, the principal traffic of Cleveland was transacted. Here the red man became supremely happy over a very small quantity of raw whisky, for which he paid the proceeds of many a hunt. If anything remained of his stock of skins after paying for his whisky, the beads, ribbons, and trinkets, of Mr. Campbell's store absorbed the entire stock. Here the squaws bartered and coquetted with the trader, who in their eyes was the most important personage in the country. Here the wild hunter, in his dirty blanket, made the woods ring with his savage howls, when exhilerated with drink. He shone forth for a moment in his native barbarity, ferocious alike against friend and foe.

THE MURDER OF MENOMPSY.

The first murder committed within the limits of this city, occurred at the cabins under the hill. The parties were Indians. There are three persons now living who were in Cleveland at the time, and saw the combatants. They are ALLEN GAYLORD and ALONZO CARTER, of Newburg, and JULIUS C. HUNTINGTON, of Painsville. As to the precise time when it was committed, they do not agree, but place it in 1802 or 1803.

NOBSY, MENOBSY, or MENOMPSY, was a medicine man, either a Chippewa or an Ottawa. Among Indians, a medicine man is a conjuror, priest, prophet and warrior, as well as a doctor. MENOMPSY had prescribed officially for the wife of BIG SON, who was of the tribe of the Senecas, and she had died.

BIG SON was brother to SENECA, a noted Indian and friend to the whites, sometimes called STIGONISH or STIGWANISH.

At the time of the murder, DAVID BRYANT had in operation his still for making whisky, under the hill.

ALEXANDER CAMPBELL, was also at his trading house; that must have stood in River street.

In the dusk of the evening, BIG SON and MENOMPSY, somewhat elevated by the fire-water of BRYANT'S still, had an altercation respecting the case of mal-practice, by which BIG SON claimed that his wife had been killed. Retaliation is the Indian law of justice. He had threatened to kill the Indian doctor, but MENOMPSY claimed that he was a charmed man and no bullet could hurt him. "Me no fraid," said MENOMPSY, as they walked out of the store and took the trail that wound up the bluff, along Union lane.

The Senecas were encamped on the east side of the river below CARTER's, and the Chippewas and Ottawas on the west side, partly up the hill.

As they went along the path, BIG SON put out his hand as though he intended a friendly shake, after the manner of white men. At the same time he drew a knife and stabbed MENOMPSY in the side. The blood spirted from his body, which CARTER tried to stop with his hand, as the Indian fell. "NOBSY broke now, yes, NOBSY broke," were his last words. In a few minutes he was dead. The Chippewas took up the corpse and carried it to their camp on the west side.

Major CARTER knew full well what would happen, unless the friends of MENOMPSY were appeased. During the night the valley of the Cuyahoga echoed with their savage voices, infuriated by liquor and revenge.

The Chippewas and Ottawas were more numerous than the Senecas. In the morning the warriors of the first named nation, were seen with their faces painted black, a certain symbol of war. Governor HUNTINGTON resided here at that time, and AMOS

SPAFFORD, who, with Major CARTER, constituted the principal men of the place. The murder of MENOMPSY was compromised for a gallon of whisky, which BRYANT was to make that day, being the next after the killing. One of the stipulations was that the body should be taken to Rocky river before it was "covered," or mourned for, with the help of the whisky. BRYANT was busy and did not make the promised gallon of spirits. The Chippewas waited all day, and went over the river decidedly out of humor. They were followed and promised two gallons on the coming day, which reduced their camp halloo, to the tone of a mere sullen murmur. But CARTER and his party well knew, that in this suppressed anger, there was as much vengeance as in the howlings of the previous night. They fulfilled their promise, and upon receiving two gallons, the Chippewas and Ottawas took up the corpse, according to agreement, went to Rocky river and held their pow wow there. CARTER did not sleep for two nights, and few of the residents enjoyed their beds very much, until the funeral procession was out of sight.

Such is the substance of the statements of Captain GAYLORD, Mr. CARTER, and Mr. HUNTINGTON, all of whom remember the event.

BIG SON was a half brother of STIGONISH, STIGWANISH or SENECA, and previous to the murder had been regarded as a coward. SENECA refused to acknowledge him on this ground, until his heroism had been demonstrated in this way. By the Indian code of honor, a successful trick against an enemy, takes rank with high personal bravery.

STATEMENT OF ALONZO CARTER.

NEWBURG, June 14, 1858.

My father came here on 2d of May, 1797. He was from Rutland, Vermont, but stayed the winter previous in Canada. I was seven years old then, going on eight. We built a log cabin under the hill, five or six rods from the river, and about twenty rods north of St. Clair street. There was an old trading house on the west side of the river, which stood not far from the corner of Main and Center streets.

It was a double log house, quite old and rotten, which the traders used only during the trading season. JAMES KINGSBURY and his family came here two or three weeks after we did, and stayed a while in that house.

In July, 1797, our hired girl was married to a Mr. CLEMENT, from Canada. They were married by Mr. SETH HART, who was a minister, and the agent of the company.

I remember seeing the cabin where the crew of the British vessel wintered, after it was wrecked. It was about two miles down the river, on the bank of the lake. The vessel had two brass guns on board, which were buried on the shore. My father used to go to the wreck, and get bolts, spikes and other pieces of iron. Some of this iron is in the gate at my house now.

In the year 1798 my father brought on some goods to trade with the Indians. I remember when MENOMPSY, the Chippewa medicine man was killed; it was towards evening. MENOMPSY had doctored BIG SON's wife, who said he had killed her with his medicine. They were in CAMPBELL's store, under the hill, which stood between the surveyors' cabin and store house. BIG SON threatened to kill the doctor in the store, but MENOMPSY said, "me no 'fraid." They went out and walked along the road up Union lane. It was getting pretty dark. BIG SON pretended to make friends, and put out one hand, as though he would shake hands. With the other hand he drew his knife and stabbed MENOMPSY who fell down and died. The Chippewas were encamped on the west side of the river, and the Senecas and Ottawas on the east side. Every body expected there would be an Indian fight. The west side Indians painted themselves black, and threatened the Senecas very severely. My father did not sleep for two days and nights.

My father built a new frame house in 1803, near the junction of Superior lane and Union lane. Just as it was finished the shavings took fire, and it was burnt. He then built a block house on the same spot in the same year.

I knew AMOS SPAFFORD ten years; he was a surveyor and came here to live in 1799. He and my father set the big posts at the corners of the streets in 1801, or 1802. I and my brother were boys with his boys, and in 1799 we went about the streets a good deal, and sawed the corner stakes. SPAFFORD took up the stakes, and put down the posts which he cut in the woods near by. The stakes had been there three or four years. Superior lane was a sharp ridge where we could not get up or down. Traveled up and down to the river, on Union lane. In 1800, or 1801, a vessel landed one hundred barrels of salt on the beach, which was carried off on horses, or carried up the beach. My father built his warehouse there in 1809 and '10. General TUPPER, an army contractor, used it in 1812 to store provisions, and also MURRAY'S warehouse. In 1813 they moved everything two miles up the river, to Walworth's Point, to keep the stores from the British.

My father's warehouse was washed down in 1816 or '17. The remains were there in 1823 and '24. It was a double log house, and was undermined by the lake.

Persons were buried in the old burying ground in 1797. A Mr. ELDRIDGE was drowned at Grand river, and his body was brought here. We got some boards and made a strong box for a coffin. We put him in, and strung it on a pole with cords, to carry him up to the burying ground. Built a fence around the grave.

The water rose in 1813—overflowed all the low ground. Bank begun to slide in 1818. Ontario street was cut out at the time of the war.

The Connecticut Land Company built two buildings between Superior and Union lanes.

The general landing was near foot of Superior lane. Vessels could seldom get into the river. They anchored off and had lighters. When they came in they landed at the foot of Superior lane.

My father died in 1814. They began to work Superior lane very early—soon after I came here.

The Indians had been camping on the beach at the Point, and left a cat there which my mother wanted. It was in 1798, I went with her to catch the cat, who ran under the logs back of the beach, and as I jumped over after her I went plump into the water, on this side where the swamp was.

In 1806, the channel was three rods wide, and ten inches deep. My brother went in there to bathe, and got on the bar. I was across the river in the field topping corn. I saw his hands out of the water and ran there as fast as I could. He was never seen any more. The river has never been so far east as it was then.

In 1803 and '04, the hill road was traveled to Painesville. It crossed the Cuyahoga at the foot of

Union and Mandrake lanes where the Indians used to cross. They swam their horses.

In 1802, a man killed a bear with his hoe on Water street, near the Light House.

1804.

MILITARY ELECTION AND REMONSTRANCE.

"*To* ELIJAH WADSWORTH *Maj. Genl. 4th Division:*

Agreeable to General orders, the Qualified Electors of the fourth Company district, in the second Brigade, of the fourth Division of the Ohio Militia; met at the house of James Kingsbery, Esq., at eleven o'clock forenoon, and maid choice of three Judges and a clerk, and when duely sworn proceded and made choice of Loranzo Carter Captain, and Nathaniel Doan Lieutenant, and Samuel Jones Ensign for sd Company given under our hands and seals at Cleveland Trumble county; this seventh day of May one thousand eight hundred and four.

JAMES KINGSBERY,
NATHANIEL DOAN,
BENJAMIN GOLD, } Judges of the Election."

REMONSTRANCE.

"*To* ELIJAH WADSWORTH, *Major General of the 3d Division of Militia of the State of Ohio:*

SIR:—We, the undersigned, hereby beg leave to represent that the proceedings of the company of

Militia, on Monday, the 7th day of instant May, in choosing officers, in our opinion, illegal and improper. *Firstly.* By admitting persons under the age of eighteen years to vote, and *Secondly.* By admitting persons not liable to do military duty to vote. *Thirdly.* In admitting men to vote who did not belong to the town. *Fourthly.* By not comparing the votes with the poll book at the close of the election. We also consider the man who is returned as chosen Captain ineligable to the office. *Firstly.* By giving spiritous liquors to the voters previous to the election. *Secondly.* On account of having frequently threatened to set the savages against the inhabitants. All which charges we consider proveable and able to be substanciated by good and sufficient witnesses. We therefore beg leave to request that the appointment of officers in the township of Cleveland may be set aside, and the said company led to a new choice.

THADEUS LACEY,	WILLIAM W. WILLIAMS,
RODOLFUS EDWARDS,	AMOS SPAFFORD,
JOEL THORP,	ROBERT CARR,
JAMES HAMILTON,	ABNER COCHRAN."

It does not appear that this remonstrance produced any effect. At the next election CARTER withdrew or was dropped, though he was present and acted as one of the judges.

1805.

"Major CARTER's son, HENRY, a smart boy of about eleven years, was drowned at the mouth of the river. Search was made along the beach for the body, many days without effect. DAVID ABBOTT built the "Cuyahoga Packet" at Chagrin river, a schooner of twenty tons, which sailed on lake Erie until the war, when it was captured by the British."—(BARR.)

Judge HUNTINGTON about this time abandoned his hewed log house, the most aristocratic residence in Cleveland city, and removed to the mills he had purchased at the falls of Mill creek. This was probably owing to the same cause, which induced other families to prefer the highlands, the prevalence here of the detestable ague. What is now Newburg was then much the largest settlement.

This was the year of the final settlement with the Indians, for their claims to lands west of the river. WM. DEAN, on his return from the treaty ground, writes to Judge HUNTINGTON as follows: The letter is superscribed to "The Hon'l. SAM'L. HUNTINGTON, at the mills near Cleaveland," and is dated "On board the sloop Contractor, near Black river, July 7, 1805."

"*Dear Sir*:—On the 4th instant, we closed a treaty with the Indians, for the unextinguished part of the Connecticut Reserve, and on account of the

United States; for all the lands south of it, to the west line. Mr. PHELPS and myself pay about $7,000 in cash, and about $12,000 in six yearly payments, of $2,000 each. The government pays $13,760, that is the annual interest, to the Wyandots, Delawares, Munsees, and to those Senecas on the land, forever. The expense of the treaty will be about $5,000, including rum, tobacco, bread, meat, presents, expenses of the seraglio, the commissioners, agents and contractors. I write in haste, being extremely sorry I have not time to send you a copy of the treaty. You will see General CHAMPION, who will be able to give you further information.

Having some intention of making a purchase of considerable tracts of land, in different parts of the Reserve, amounting to about 30,000 acres; I beg of you to inform me what I should allow per acre, payments equal to cash; and address me at Easton, Pa. From thence, if I make a contract, I expect, with all speed, to send fifteen or twenty families of prancing Dutchmen."

ABRAHAM TAPPEN, of Unionville, Ashtabula Co., O., among many reminiscences of the surveys and settlements, thus refers to this treaty.

"Owing to various causes, a treaty for the extinguishment of the Indian title to the Company's land west of the Cuyahoga, and also the Sufferers', or Fire Land, was not held until June, 1805. Cleveland was designated as the place for holding the treaty.

The Indians to the west, having claims to the lands in question, were invited to attend in council at that place. The Indians residing in Western New York, having some claim to the land, sent a deputation of not far from thirty of their number, to attend the treaty at Cleveland. They arrived at that place in June, accompanied by JASPER PARISH, their interpreter. The treaty was to be held under the auspices of the United States Government. Commissioners from the different parties interested in the treaty, were promptly and in season at the contemplated treaty ground. On the part of the General Government, Col. JEWET was the Commissioner, a very large muscular man. On the part of the Connecticut Land Company, Gen. HENRY CHAMPION appeared as Commissioner. General CHAMPION was also of more than common size, and a man of good sense.

"For some cause the Indians living to the west, and interested in the subject matter of the treaty, refused to meet the Commissioners in council at Cleveland. And, if we except the deputation from New York, few or no Indians appeared at that place. After staying a few days at Cleveland, and being well assured that the Indians would not meet them in treaty there, the Commissioners proceeded westward; and after some delay, and a show of great reluctance on the part of the Indians, they finally succeeded in meeting them in council. The treaty was held at the Ogontz place near Sandusky City."

[Other authorities have it at Fort Industry, on the Maumee.]

"It is said by those who attended this treaty, that the Indians in parting with and making sale of the above lands to the whites, did so with much reluctance, and after the treaty was signed, many of them wept. On the day that the treaty was brought to a close, the specie, in payment of the purchase money, arrived on the treaty ground. The specie came from Pittsburg, and was conveyed by the way of Warren, Cleveland, and the lake shore to the place where wanted. The treasure was entrusted to the care of LYMAN POTTER, Esq., of Warren, who was attended by the following persons as an escort: JOSIAH W. BROWN, JOHN LANE, JAMES STAUNTON, JONATHAN CHURCH, LORENZO CARTER, and another person by the name of CLARK, all resolute men and well armed. The money and other property as presents to the Indians, was distributed to them the next day after the signing of the treaty. The evening of the last day of the treaty, a barrel of whisky was dealt out to the Indians. The consequent results of such a proceeding were all experienced at that time."

Prof. KIRTLAND, in an introductory lecture delivered at the opening of the term in the Cleveland Medical College a few years since, related the following incident, connected with this attempt at holding a treaty:

"While waiting their tardy movements, the company collected one afternoon on the bank of the lake, near the present location of the light-house, and were observing the descent of the sun, into the broad expanse of waters at the west. The gorgeous displays of light and shade, heightened by the brilliant reflections from the lake, unsurpassed by the brightest scenes ever exhibited by Italy's boasted skies, served, in connection with concurring circumstances, to add interest to the occasion. One of the company, the Hon. GIDEON GRANGER, distinguished for talents, enterprise and forethought, uttered, to his astonished associates, this bold and what was then deemed, extraordinary prediction:

"'Within fifty years,' exclaimed he, 'an extensive city will occupy these grounds, and vessels will sail directly from this port into the Atlantic Ocean.'

"A prophecy so specific and decided, coming from such a source, though received with a share of skepticism on the part of some, made a deep impression on the great body of his hearers."

CHARLES JEWET, was the Commissioner on the part of the United States, HENRY CHAMPION for the Land Company, and I. MILLS, for the Sufferers by fire, or the Fire Lands Company.

At the election in the fall of 1805, the poll book for Cleveland was rejected for two very good reasons. The certificate to the oaths of the clerks and judges was not attached, neither were the signatures of the judges of election. The number of votes cast was twenty-nine, of which JAMES KINGSBURY had twenty-seven for State Representative. In the county of Trumbull there were given for EDWARD TIFFIN, for Governor; (the second term) three hundred and seventy-nine votes, and none against him. JAMES KINGSBURY received for Representative three hundred and seven votes, and HOMER HINE three hundred and fourteen.

MILITARY ELECTION IN CLEVELAND.

To ELIJAH WADSWORTH *Maj. Genl. 4th Division:*

We, the Judges of an election Holden in the seventh Company of the second Battalion of the First Regiment of the fourth Division of the Ohio Melitia do Certify that the persons here after named is just and truly elected in sd Company to the different posts atached to their names, given under our hands. This the twentyeth day of May said eighteen hundred and five.

NATHANIEL DOAN, Captain.
SAMUEL JONES, Leuftenant.
SYLVANUS BURK, Ensign.

LORENZO CARTER,
WM. WR. WILLIAMS, } Judges.
WILL'M. ERWIN,

Done in presence of RODOLPHUS EDWARDS, Clerk.

ELECTORS' NAMES.

JACK F. MASON,	NEHEMIAH DILLE,
DAVID KELLOG,	TIMOTHY DOAN,
EB. CHARTER,	SETH DOAN,
JACOB COLEMAN,	STEVEN GILBERT,
BEN WARDEN,	SAMUEL HURST,
DANIEL PARKER,	RICHARD BLIN,
CRISTOFER GUN,	EPETA[RY] ROGERS, ?
WILLIAM COLEMAN,	SAMUEL JONES,
JOHN DOAN,	NATHANIEL DOAN,
THOMAS THOMAS,	WILLIAM ERWIN,
HENRY NORTON,	BEN WOOD,
HARRY GUN,	SYLVANUS BURK,
JONATHAN HUBBARD,	SAMUEL DILLE,
MASON CLERK,	MEAGE DATA,
NATHAN CHAPMAN,	CHARLES PRARD. ?

NATHANIEL DOAN, Captain, 29 votes for Captain.
SAMUEL JONES, 29 votes for Leuftenant.
SYLVANUS BURK, 24 votes for Ensign.
SAMUEL JONES, one vote for Leuftenant.
EZEKIEL HOLLEY (HAWLEY) six votes for Ensign.

These returns are in the hand writing of RODOLPHUS EDWARDS. It is very difficult to decypher some of the names which are given literally. In this way the names of families are subject to such changes that the originals cannot be recognized. "HAWLEY," has now become "HOLLY" or "HOLLEY" which is identical with the HOLLEY's of Salisbury, without any relationship.

The name of Mr. WILLIAMS, of Newburg, the builder of the first mill is in the early papers written

WHEELER W., WM. W., and WILLIAM WHEELER. Our immediate ancestors were not as well versed in orthography as they were in penmanship. The disturbances of the Revolution, had a depressing effect upon education, even in New England.

1806.

"Early in the spring, Mr. HUNTER, his wife and one child, with a colored man, called BEN, and a colored boy, were driven ashore in a skiff, a short distance east of Rocky river. The shore at that place is a rocky cliff, nearly perpendicular. They held as fast to the rocks as possible, the surges breaking over them continually.

"The wreck occurred on Friday, and the storm continued to increase that night. On Saturday there was no abatement, and the children died. Mrs. HUNTER expired on Sunday, and Mr. HUNTER on Monday. Some traders were passing along the coast for Detroit on Tuesday, and discovering BEN, who was the only survivor, brought him back to Cleveland. He was almost naked, having for three days and four nights kept his position on the cliffs, without a morsel to eat, by means of some bushes which grew in the crevices of the rocks. Major CARTER took care of BEN, and treated him kindly, for a year or more, while he was an invalid. The flesh came off from his lower limbs, rendering him a very disagreeable object.

"Surveys were commenced this year on the lands west of the Cuyahoga river. This brought many strangers to the place, which contained more white people than ever before. The year was rendered conspicuous by the holding of a militia training. They marched and countermarched to the lively roll of Joseph Burke's drum, which he had used in the Revolutionary War, and to the soul-stirring strains of Lewis Dille's fife. They were all undoubtedly brave, many of them bearing on their shoulders the old fire-arms of the Revolution."

"The little settlement sustained a severe loss in the death of David Clark, and received a valuable accession in Judge Walworth and Major Perry, Senior."—(Barr.)

Abraham Tappen, an old surveyor, proposed to run the town lines. The following extracts are from a full account of the survey by himself, published in the *Cleveland Herald*, in January, 1851:

"I had spoken to Mr. Amos Sessions to join with me, and endeavor to obtain a contract for surveying the new purchase the coming season. Mr. Sessions was not a surveyor, but he was a man then in the prime of life, and possessing energy of character, and great perseverence in business he undertook, would make him a safe and trustworthy partner. We accordingly made the following proposals to be laid before the Directors:

'PAINESVILLE, August 20th, 1805.

'To GEN. HENRY CHAMPION: — We will survey the land belonging to the Connecticut Land Company, west of the Cuyahoga river, at the rate of dollars, cents per mile. We will survey it into townships, and make other sub-divisions as shall be directed by the Company. We will plainly blaze and accurately chain the lines; will map, and return field book, &c. We will begin and finish the survey next season. For the purpose of furnishing provisions and other necessaries for said survey to receive dollars in hand at the commencement of the survey; remainder at the close. For the well and faithful performance of such survey, we will bind ourselves in bonds with sufficient security.

'ABR'M TAPPEN,
'ANSON SESSIONS.'

The contract was made, the work commenced and vigorously prosecuted during the season.

"From the west side of the Reserve, five hundred thousand acres of land, was to be measured off by the surveyor of the Fire Land Company. ALMON RUGGLES, Esq., was the surveyor of that Company. The balance of the Reserve, from the east line of the Fire Land to the Cuyahoga river, was comprised in our contract for surveying, amounting to some eight hundred and thirty thousand acres. We agreed to and did meet in Cleveland on the 15th of May, together with our men, chain carriers, pack-horses and their drivers. Capt. JAMES HARPER, of Harpersfield, was engaged as surveyor. The names of the men employed were JAMES ARBUCKLE, IRA WRIGHT, AUGUSTUS STAUGHTON, GUY CARLTON, JOHN ROSS, SAMUEL PARKER, Mr. MCMAHAN and his two sons, ALEX. MCMAHAN and WM. MCMAHAN, and a young man by the name of HEWIT, and an Englishman, a worthless fellow, whom we soon discharged. Also, for a short time, an active young half-breed Indian, who took charge of a very vicious Indian horse, hired as a pack-horse. The horse had once been the property of the noted Indian chief OGONTZ. As before stated, our party assembled at Cleveland on the 15th of May, and our boat with flour, tents, and other necessary articles, came into the river on the same day. We were prepared to send out two surveying parties immediately; but the surveyor designated by the United States Government to run the south line had not yet arrived. We had notified Judge KIRTLAND at what time we should be at Cleveland to commence the survey. He accordingly met us at that place on the day of our arrival. As it could not be known the precise time when the Government would commence running the south line, Judge KIRTLAND proposed that our surveying parties should commence, and should measure off their own meridians, taking care to commence so far south that when the south line was run, it would be sure to cross our ranges. The Government surveyor did not commence running the south line until the 24th of June, at which time we had nearly finished our meridians.

"The south line of the Reserve, as surveyed in 1796 by SETH PEASE, measuring from the Pennsylvania line, ended at Tuscarawas river, a distance of fifty-six miles. A further distance of sixty-four miles was yet to be run, making the whole distance, to the south-west corner of the Reserve, one hundred and twenty miles. From the south-west corner a line was to be run to the lake, parallel to the west line of Pennsylvania. The running of these lines was to be done by a surveyor, under the direction of the Secretary of the Treasury, at Washington. The surveyor selected by the Treasurer was SETH PEASE, then a principal clerk in the post office department at Washington, and who, ten years before, had run the eastern section of the south line, to the Tuscarawas."—(A. TAPPEN.)

The same process was gone through with to obtain a division west of the Cuyahoga as had been east of it. TAPPEN and his assistants, of whom Capt. HARPER was the principal one, completed their meridians and parallels during the season of 1806. An equalizing committee was out with the surveyors, whose track among the towns is shown upon a map now before me, by dotted lines. The parties in the woods suffered from want of water, there being an unusual droughth that summer. On the 16th of June a total eclipse of the sun occurred, which for a short time, produced in the shady forest the darkness of night.

A commission, consisting of AMOS SPAFFORD, of Cleveland, and ALMON RUGGLES, of Huron, was organized to establish the division line, between the Fire Lands and the Land Company. Their directions were, to lay off half a million of acres from the west end of the Reserve, using the meridian one hundred and twenty miles west of Pennsylvania, as the farther side, and the forty-first parallel as a base. Their measurements did not agree with those of Mr. PEASE, and the dividing line was not established until sometime in the winter of 1806–7.

This left an unsurveyed space on the margin of the Company's tract. These difficulties protracted the work of survey and of the final draft. The Government not being satisfied with the southern boundary, ordered it to be re-surveyed in 1808.

The committee on equalization reported to Judge KIRTLAND, and in February, 1807, he started for Hartford with the results. Only one whole township was sub-divided into lots for the purpose of equalization, but several of the fractional ones on the lake shore, were. No person then lived on the tract, as Mr. TAPPEN expresses it "white, red or black."

In 1805 the Government concluded to have this coast open no longer to free trade with Canada. A collection district was established for the south shore of the lake, called the "District of Erie," and JOHN WALWORTH, of Painesville, was appointed collector. The mouth of the Cuyahoga was made a port of entry; and in 1806 Mr. WALWORTH became a resident of Cleveland with his family. His first clearance was issued to the schooner "Good Intent," which was soon after lost on Long Point together with cargo and crew. Up to this time, the more healthy settlement at Painesville, had taken the lead of the sickly city of Cleveland. The mouth of Grand river presented a much better natural harbor than the Cuyahoga. A State road had been surveyed from the forks of the Muskingum (near Coshocton) to the lake, which terminated at Grand river. Cleveland had hitherto been on the verge of the settlements.

On the west bank of the Cuyahoga, within the cast of a stone from the houses under the hill, the Indian tribes had claimed the territory as their own, indefinitely westward, and the claim had been respected. They had the acknowledged right to establish their lodges in any number, within half rifle range of the principal residents of Cleveland, from whence, at any time, they might instantly destroy the settlement, by a concerted discharge of their guns. This state of affairs was now ended, and the Indians were here only on sufferance and good behavior.

The Cuyahoga had one advantage which Grand river had not. Its boatable waters approached those of the Tuscarawas, having a portage of only seven miles, to reach indefinite canoe navigation connecting with the Ohio river. This route began again to be regarded as important, expecting through it to obtain commercial intercourse of much value. A scheme for improving the rivers and portages was already under discussion.

1807.

Nothing of special interest occurred at Cleveland in 1807, except the excitement caused by the murder of NICKSAU or NICKSHAW. The late THOMAS D. WEBB, of Warren came here in the fall, and thus describes the town and its society:

"I first saw Cleveland in October, 1807. I put up for a day or two with Major AMOS SPAFFORD, who kept a tavern. Having a letter of introduction to Governor HUNTINGTON, (then, however, a Judge,) I called at his house, and as he was absent on the circuit of the Supreme Court, I presented it to his wife and induced her to board me for a short time. I remained about three weeks, I think, and then left Cleveland. Gov. HUNTINGTON then lived in a log house, standing a little south of Superior street, not far from the site of the American House. He had a frame barn, in size thirty feet by forty, near by. In his barn-yard I saw wild turkies for the first time. At that time the family of Governor HUNTINGTON was composed of his wife, children, the number I do not recollect, and one female domestic, PATTY RYAN, who came with him from Connecticut, another, a Miss COBB, who also came with him, had returned. All the families on the city or ten acre lots, or the lands adjoining, at that time, that I recollect, and I think that I recollect all, were, AMOS SPAFFORD, —— GILBERT, NATHAN PERRY, LORENZO CARTER, SAMUEL HUNTINGTON, JOHN WALWORTH, and an Irish family I have forgotten. SAMUEL DODGE had lived on a ten acre lot, but had at that time taken up his residence at Euclid; other families had resided there also, but at the time I arrived, had removed. There were the remains of some two or three buildings along the bank of the river, one of which I was told had been occupied as a store by a Scotchman, by the name of ALEX. CAMPBELL.

"Those buildings were all occupied at that time. When I was at Gov. HUNTINGTON'S, there was a social party at his house, so far as I recollect, all females, except myself. There were several married ladies, I recollect particularly but two, Mrs. WALWORTH and Mrs. HUNTINGTON. We had all, or nearly all, the young ladies in the place. I think there could not have been more than one absent; those present were she that is now Mrs. LONG, Mrs. MATHEWS, of Painesville, and a daughter of Mr.

CARTER, afterwards Mrs. MILES and subsequently Mrs. STRONG."

What transpired in reference to the demise of NICKSHAW, is well set forth in a letter from General ELIJAH WADSWORTH, dated at Canfield, February 5th, 1807, to Judge HUNTINGTON, and his reply.

"Judge HUNTINGTON, Cleveland,

"*Dear Sir*:—Since I last wrote you, we have had information from your quarter that NICKSHAW was killed instead of JOHN MOHAWK. If this be true, as MOHAWK was the one who shot Mr. DIVER, ought not MOHAWK to be demanded of their chief, and delivered up for trial?"

ELIJAH WADSWORTH.

"CLEVELAND, February 10th, 1807.

"General ELIJAH WADSWORTH, Canfield,

"*Dear Sir*:—Yours of the 21st came to hand on Saturday last, and that of the 5th yesterday. I had, previous to the receipt of the first letter, seen SENECA and others of his tribe, also OGONTZ and fifteen of his people who came here at the request of SENECA.

"As the deceased was not one of OGONTZ' nation, he said he should not like to lead in obtaining redress, but would be satisfied with what SENECA agreed to.

"SENECA said all he wanted was that the same measure of justice should be dealt out to Indians and white men. He said he was not content to see all the exertions of our civil authority, used against those who had shot the white man while we were *asleep*, as to the murder of an innocent Indian. He concluded by saying, he should be satisfied if both the Indian and the white agressors, could have a fair and equal trial.

"I gave him assurances that the law would be put in force equally against both, and persuaded him to wait peaceably until the Court should meet at Warren. My expectation was, and still is, that the Court of Common Pleas would issue a Bench warrant for the apprehension of DARROW and WILLIAMS.

"It is said the magistrates of Hudson have been deterred by threats, from taking measures to secure the offenders. I hope for the honor of Hudson, that the majority of the people do not countenance such atrocities, and that some of the civil authorities will have firmness enough to put the law in force.

"Mr. ALLEN GAYLORD told me, that the first man who attempted to arrest DARROW and WILLIAMS would be shot, and that the constables dare not execute a warrant against them, and that if the Indians wanted war they were ready for them. * * *

"I had also called on Major CARTER, who agrees with me that the best way to give the Indians satisfaction is to do them justice, that since our talk with them, there was no immediate danger, and no necessity of a further conference as to what course would be pursued against our offenders. On the same day I saw SENECA again, who said he had been threatened by some Hudson people. He did not wish for war, and would engage to deliver JOHN MOHAWK when required to do it, voluntarily, when DARROW and WILLIAMS were secured for trial.

"He and Major CARTER and Mr. CAMPBELL agree in their story. They went up to the place where NICKSHAW was killed and buried him. There was no appearance on the snow, of a fight or scuffle and no club near. NICKSHAW appears to have been shot in the back as he was running, and fell dead in his tracks.

"SENECA observed that the Indians might lie and that white men might lie, but the snow could tell no lies. He is well convinced that it was an unnecessary murder, and is willing it should be ascertained by trial. Under this conviction, justice demands, and our own interests require, that he should be gratified.

"In case it should be necessary to demand the delivery of JOHN MOHAWK under the treaty, the regular course is to get affidavits to the necessary facts, transmit them to the Governor, and request him to make the demand. But I believe this to be unnecessary. * * I have no doubt that SENECA will freely deliver JOHN MOHAWK, when I assure him that legal steps have been taken against DARROW and WILLIAMS. Meanwhile, I think that you may assure your friends, that for the present none of the Seneca nation among us, will harm our citizens and their property.

"I am, sir, respectfully yours,

SAM'L HUNTINGTON."

SENECA, who, according to Mr. CARTER'S statement, was a brother of BIG SON, is well spoken of by all the early settlers. The late EDWARD PAINE, of Chardon, was the companion of the STILES family during the dreary and severe winter of 1796–7. After setting forth the conduct and character of the Indians who frequented the Cuyahoga, he says, "That they are capable of disinterested benevolence, and confer favors when none are expected, cannot be doubted by any one acquainted with SENECA, or as his tribe called him, "STIGWANISH." This in English means "Standing Stone." In him there was the dignity of the Roman, the honesty of Aristides, and the benevolence of PENN. He was never known to ask a donation, but would accept one as he ought, but not suffer it to rest here. An appropriate return was soon to be made. He was so much of a tetotaler as to abjure ardent spirits, since in a drunken spree, he had aimed a blow at his wife with a tomahawk, and split the head of his child which was on her back." His home was in Seneca county, Ohio, from whom it was probably named. He also came to a violent death in 1816, at the hands of JACOB AMMOND, of Holmes county, Ohio. AMMOND claims that it was done in self-defence, SENECA having first fired upon him.

During this year the great scheme for opening communication between lake Erie and the Ohio river was put before the public. Resolutions had been offered by Joshua Forman in the New York Legislature, for a survey for a canal to connect Hudson river with lake Erie.

The improvement of the Cuyahoga and Tuscarawas was then the great idea, of this part of the country and of Ohio.

It was thought if twelve thousand dollars could by some means be raised, the channels of those streams could be cleared of logs and trees, and the Portage path made passable for loaded wagons. Thus goods might ascend the Cuyahoga in boats to the Old Portage, be hauled seven miles to the Tuscarawas, near New Portage, and thence descend that stream in batteaux. This great object excited so much attention, that the Legislature authorized a lottery to raise the money. A copy of the scheme, and one of the tickets is here given.

Q No. 11441.

CUYAHOGA AND MUSKINGUM NAVIGATION LOTTERY.

THIS ticket entitles the bearer to such Prize as shall be drawn against its number (if called for within twelve months after the drawing is completed,) subject to a deduction of 12½ per cent.

No. 11441.

J. WALWORTH, { *Agent for the Board of Commissioners.*

SCHEME
OF A
LOTTERY
FOR
IMPROVING THE NAVIGATION
BETWEEN LAKE ERIE AND THE RIVER OHIO, THROUGH THE
CUYAHOGA AND MUSKINGUM.

THE Legislature of the State of Ohio, having at their last Session, granted a Lottery to raise the sum of Twelve Thousand Dollars, for the above mentioned purpose, and appointed the subscribers Commissioners to carry the same into effect—They offer the following SCHEME to the Public.

FIRST CLASS.

12,800 Tickets at $5 each,....$64,000

1	Prize of	$5,000	is	$5,000
2	do.	2,500		5,000
5	do.	1,000		5,000
10	do.	500		5,000
50	do.	100		5,000
100	do.	50		5,000
3400	do.	10		34,000
3568				$64,000

Prizes subject to a deduction of twelve and a half per cent.

The drawing of the First Class will commence at Cleveland on the first Monday of January, 1808, or as soon as three-fourths of the Tickets shall be sold; and the Prizes will be paid in sixty days after the drawing is completed.

Holders of Tickets, drawing Prizes of Ten Dollars, may, at their election, receive the money, or two Tickets of Five Dollars each in the Second Class.

For the convenience of the owners of fortunate numbers, Persons will be appointed in Boston, Hartford, New York and Albany, to pay Prizes. Their names, together with a List of Prizes, will be published in some Newspaper printed in each of those places, and in three of the Newspapers printed in the State of Ohio. Persons will also be designated to pay Prizes in Zanesville and Steubenville.

The subscribers have taken the Oath and given the Bonds required by Law, for the faithful discharge of their trust, and they flatter themselves that an object of such extensive importance, will not fail to attract the attention and patronage of many, who are not allured by the advantageous prospects held out in the Scheme.

JOHN WALWORTH, Esq., of Cleveland, is appointed Agent of the Commissioners, to sign the Tickets, and transact the business of the Board in their recess.

SAMUEL HUNTINGTON, ZACCHEUS A. BEATTY,
BEZALEEL WELLS, LORENZO CARTER,
JONATHAN CASS, JOHN SHORB,
SETH ADAMS, JAMES KINGSBURY,
AMOS SPAFFORD, TURHAND KIRTLAND,
JOHN WALWORTH, TIMOTHY DOANE,

Board of Commissioners.

CLEVELAND, May 23d, 1807.

CRAMER, PRINTER.

The drawing never came off. Those who had purchased tickets, many years afterwards received their money back without interest. LEONARD CASE remembered when he was the sole owner of one of those tickets.

From a receipt of STEPHEN OVIATT, of Hudson, it also appears that he possessed one, the price of which was $5.00. It reads thus:

HUDSON, 29th Jan'y, 1811.

Received of Heman Oviatt a Ticket of Cuyahoga and Muskingum Lottery, to account with him or the Managers, on or before the Drawing of said Lottery. No. 7775, Letter K.

$5,00. STEPHEN OVIATT.

The paper on which the copy of Judge WALWORTH'S letter is written, is of the old fashioned coarse brown sort, made by hand. It bears the name OHIO, C. B. &. B., in water lines, and was made within the State.

Judge HUNTINGTON was elected Governor of Ohio, succeeding EDWARD TIFFIN, who became a member of the United States Senate. Another large draft took place April 2d, 1807, including most of the Company's land west of the Cuyahoga.

1808.

"STEPHEN GILBERT, JOSEPH PLUMB, ADOLPHUS SPAFFORD, a son of AMOS, and Mr. GILMORE, started early in the spring for Maumee river. They were in a Mackinaw boat, with provisions and goods which NATHAN PERRY, senior, was sending to his son NATHAN, at Black river. A young woman named MARY BILLINGER, was a passenger for Black river. Mr. WHITE, of Newburg, and two sons of Mr. PLUMB, were too late for the boat. They were to go by land along the Indian trail, to overtake the party at the river, where young PERRY had a store. When about half way there, they observed a wrecked boat on the beach, and hallooing as loud as they could, had a response from Mr. PLUMB the elder. He was on the beach, below a cliff sixty or seventy feet high, benumbed with cold and very much injured.

"They soon learned from him that a squall had struck their craft about a mile from shore, capsizing it, and that all but himself were drowned.

"They were unable to reach him, down the steep rocks. Mr. WHITE and one of his sons started off rapidly for Black river. The son who remained, getting out upon an ironwood sapling, bent it down with his weight, and dropping twenty feet or more, reached his father at the foot of the cliff. During the night Mr. WHITE returned with QUINTUS F. ATKINS, and Mr. PERRY. They all managed to haul Mr. PLUMB up to the top of the bank. As he was a corpulent man, of two hundred to two hundred and fifty pounds weight, and quite helpless from exhaustion, this was no small undertaking. It was done after midnight, by the light of torches. The bodies of GILBERT, SPAFFORD and GILMORE, were near by, and were taken to Cleveland by Major PERRY, who came along there with his boat. They were all good swimmers, except Mr. PLUMB, who held fast to the boat after it upset, and was thus driven ashore. GILBERT told his fellows to rid themselves of their clothing, and thus they swam towards the shore."

"Had the weather and water been warm, they would probably have reached it. The corpse of the hired girl MARY, was found afterwards on the shore west of the wreck, and was buried at Black river.

"Of eighteen deaths which had occurred within this settlement, during the twelve years of its existence, *eleven* were by drowning. There had been no physicians nearer than Hudson and Austinburg up to this time."—(BARR.)

1809.

"This year JOEL THORP built a small schooner of five or six tons, and called her the 'Sally,' and ALEX. SIMPSON built one of about the same size, christened the 'Dove.' LEVI JOHNSON (now living, 1866,) and his brothers, SAMUEL and JONATHAN became residents of the place. AMOS SPAFFORD was elected Representative in the Lower House from this place, then embraced in the County of Geauga. He was soon after appointed collector of the new

28

port of entry, established at Maumee, and in the spring of 1810 removed to Perrysburg. The county of Cuyahoga being organized, NATHAN PERRY, Sr., AUGUSTUS E. GILBERT and NATHANIEL DOAN were elected Associate Judges, all residents of Cleveland Township, as it then was."—(BARR.)

Although the project of connecting the lakes and the Ohio river with the sum of twelve thousand dollars had failed, Cleveland was attracting attention. STANLEY GRISWOLD, of Connecticut, had been appointed Secretary for the territory of Michigan in 1805, under Governor HULL, and Collector of the port of Detroit. On account of official difficulties he resigned, and took up his abode in this township, at Doan's Corners. A vacancy occurred in the Senate by the unexpected resignation of Mr. TIFFIN. Governor HUNTINGTON appointed his friend GRISWOLD to the vacancy, and on his way to Washington he addressed a letter to Judge JAMES WITHERELL, of the District Court of Michigan, in which he sets forth the condition and prospects of Cleveland.

"SOMERSET, PA., May 28th, 1809.

Hon. JAMES WITHERELL, now at Fair Haven, Vt.

Dear Sir:—Passing in the stage to the Federal City, I improve a little leisure to acknowledge your letter from Jefferson, Ohio, of the 16th instant. In reference to your inquiry (for a place for Doctor ELIJAH COLEMAN,) I have consulted the principal characters, particularly Judge Walworth, who concurs with me, that Cleveland would be an excellent place for a young physician, and cannot long remain unoccupied. This is based more on what the place is expected to be, than what it is. Even now a physician of eminence would command great practice, from being called to ride over a large country, say fifty miles each way. There is now none of eminent or ordinary character in that extent. But settlements are scattered, and roads new and bad, which would make it a painful practice. Within a few weeks Cleveland has been fixed upon by a committee of the Legislature as the seat of justice for Cuyahoga county. Several respectable characters will remove to that town. The country around bids fair to increase rapidly in population. A young physician of the qualifications described by you, will be certain to succeed, but for a short time, if without means, must keep school, for which there is a good chance in winter, till a piece of ground, bring on a few goods, (for which it is a good stand,) or do something else in connection with his practice. I should be happy to see your friend. I am on my way to the Federal City, to take a seat in the Senate in place of Mr. Tiffin, who has recently resigned.

Very truly your obedient servant,

Stanley Griswold."

According to Collector Walworth's report to the Treasury Department, the amount of goods, wares and merchandise exported to foreign countries, (Canada) from April to October, 1809, was *fifty dollars.*

At the fourth draft of April 2d, 1807, Samuel P. Lord and others drew the township of Brooklyn, No. 7, in Range 13. It was surveyed under their direction by Ezekiel Hover, in 1809, the interior lines of which were ran with a variation of two degrees east. The fifth and final division of the Land Company's property took place at Hartford, on the 5th of January of this year, at which the unsold lots in Cleveland were included.

LETTER FROM JOHN HARMON.

Ravenna, June 11, 1860.

Charles Whittlesy, Esq., Cleveland,

Dear Sir:—I thank you for your kind invitation to attend the pioneer meeting at Newburg on the 13th.

You suggest if I could not attend, that I should put something on paper for the occasion. I fear I can scarcely add anything of interest to what I some time since wrote you. I first visited Cleveland, that part now called Newburg, in August, 1806, a boy of sixteen and a half years, and spent some ten days, perhaps more, in the family of W. W. Williams. During my stay there, I formed some acquaintance with those of the neighborhood, especially with those young men or youths of my age, among whom were the Williams', the Hamiltons, the Plumbs and KINGSBURYS, the BURKS and the GUNS. The MILES' had not then arrived. We attended meetings in a log barn at Doan's Corners once or twice, to hear the announcement of a new sect, by one DANIEL PARKER, who preached what he called Halcyonism—since, I believe, it has become extinct. We bathed together under the fall of Mill Creek, gathered cranberries in the marshes westward of the EDWARD's place, and danced to the music of Major SAMUEL JONES' violin at his house, afterwards the residence of my old friend, Captain ALLEN GAYLORD, Judge HUNTINGTON, afterwards Governor, lived then, I believe, at the place afterwards occupied by DEXTER or ERASTUS MILES. Newburg street was opened previously, from the mill north to Doan's Corners, and was then lined with cultivated fields on both sides, nearly the whole distance from Judge KINGSBURY's to the mill. But much dead timber remained on the fields. There were some orchards of apple trees on some of the farms, and Judge KINGSBURY's orchard bore a few apples that season, which was probably the first season of bearing. The Judge had a small nursery of apple trees, and there was a larger nursery of smaller trees on Mr. WILLIAMS' place.

In May, 1809, when I first saw Cleveland city, as it was called even then, there were but few families there—Major SPAFFORD, Major CARTER, Judge PERRY, Governor HUNTINGTON, and Judge WALWORTH,

I remember; and there may, perhaps, have been one or two more. DAVID CLARK and ELISHA NORTON, who had lived there, had left the city. SPAFFORD and CARTER kept taverns. PERRY had a store.

June 17th we had a military election at the house of Judge GRISWOLD, to elect an officer—I believe an ensign—of the company that included what is now Cleveland, Newburg and Euclid. It was a spirited contest, and it resulted in the election of ALLEN GAYLORD.

Judge GRISWOLD was absent from home at the time. It was understood he was attending a session of Congress. His wife was there, and appeared to be a very accomplished woman.

Your friend,

JOHN HARMON.

1810.

"GEORGE WALLACE bought out AMOS SPAFFORD, who lived and kept tavern on the MERWIN lot, where the old 'Mansion House' recently stood, at the corner of Vineyard lane, and Superior street. ALFRED KELLEY, the first lawyer, and DAVID LONG, first doctor of the place, came here this year, both becoming useful and honorable members of their respective professions.

"LORENZO CARTER built the schooner 'Zephyr' of thirty tons, which was commanded by captain STOW.

It was built on Superior lane, and launched at the foot of the street on the river. This was the first craft of vessel proportions built within the city. ELIAS and HARVEY MURRAY, who were the first regular merchants, opened a store near WILLIAMSONS on Water street."—[BARR.]

The organization of the county was perfected on the 1st of May, and the machinery of a county court put in motion, on the 5th of June. On that day the Court of Common Pleas held its first session, which was in the store of ELIAS and HARVEY MURRAY, and of which, in 1855, the following notice appeared in a city paper:

"The old house lately torn down, which stood next to the Forest City Block on Superior street, was the oldest frame building in Cleveland. It was built in 1810 by HARVEY and ELIAS MURRAY, and by them occupied as a store until the surrender of HULL at Detroit in 1812; many sick and wounded soldiers being brought to this place, this store was converted into a hospital and so used as occasion demanded during the war of 1812–14. Since that time it has been used as a store, hotel, bakery, dwelling house mechanics shop and other uses until now, it has gone, with other relics of Cleveland's early years."

Presiding Judge.—BENJAMIN RUGGLES.

Associate Judges.—NATHAN PERRY, Sen., AUGUSTUS GILBERT, TIMOTHY DOAN.

Clerk.—JOHN WALWORTH.

Sheriff.—SMITH S. BALDWIN.

The grand jury found a bill for petit larceny, and several against persons for selling whisky to Indians, or selling foreign goods without license.

Cleveland was now for the first time in full possession of civil tribunals, civil law and order. Since the organization of Geauga county in 1806, their county seat at Chardon, was nearly as inaccessible as all the previous ones had been, but now, after fourteen years, the administration of justice became a fixed and local institution. The "respectable characters" referred to by Mr. GRISWOLD, began to make their appearance.

The year 1811 was barren of local incidents. During this year, the valley of the Mississippi was shaken by earthquakes, which extended to the shores of lake Erie, with diminished force. With these tremblings of the earth, there were ominious events transpiring in the Indian wigwams, along the frontier. The British government had never relinquished the hope of regaining the lost colonies. It had kept possession of the lake country, fourteen years after our independence was an admitted fact, in the expectation that the Indians would extirpate the western settlements. With British encouragement they had again become aroused, and were preparing to commence another frontier war; when the United States, prefering an open enemy to a secret one, declared war against Great Britain.

I do not propose to go into the details of what followed from 1812 to 1815. Cleveland became an important military station. A small stockade was built on the lake shore near the foot of Seneca street, called "Fort Huntington," after the recent governor, who acted as district paymaster during the war. It was commanded by Major JESSUP of the U. S. Army, but used more as a place of imprisonment for soldiers under arrest, than for the defence of the post.

Cleveland was the rendezvous of the country militia, who entered the service as a body, following the example of their revolutionary fathers, leaving their homes and farms; to the care of the old men, women and children. Many good precepts are wasted and lost, a good example never. The patriotic conduct of the soldiers of 1812, was not forgotten by their sons of our times when they were called upon to take arms, against the internal foes of the nation.

Much of what transpired during the war will be found in the statement of persons who witnessed those events, and which are here presented.

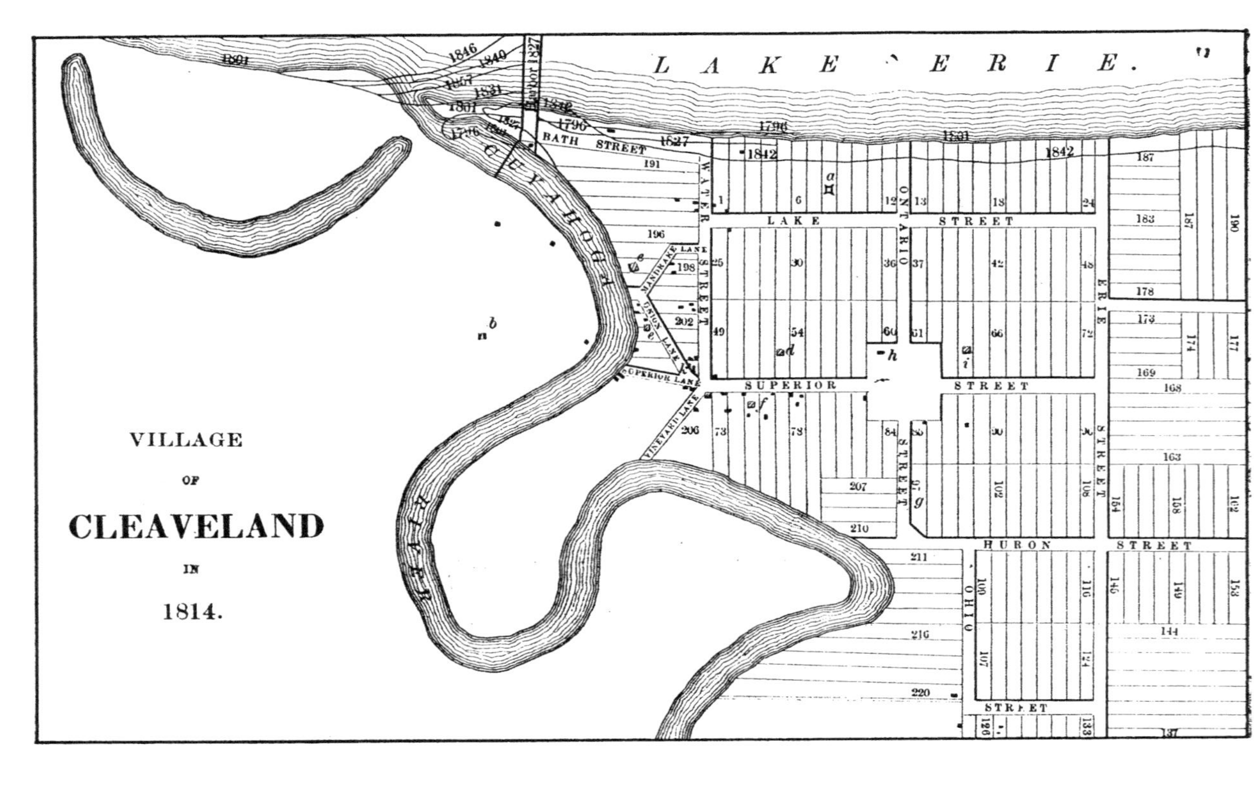

VILLAGE
OF
CLEAVELAND
IN
1814.
LAKE ERIE.
CUYAHOGA RIVER
BATH STREET
WATER STREET
LAKE STREET
ONTARIO STREET
SUPERIOR STREET
ERIE STREET
HURON STREET
OHIO STREET
MANDRAKE LANE
UNION LANE
SUPERIOR LANE
VINEYARD LANE

MAP OF CLEVELAND IN 1814.

This is a reduced copy of AMOS SPAFFORD's map of 1801, copied by the late ALFRED KELLEY, Esq. It was informally put upon record, and has been used more than any other map to determine the original streets and lots. Mr. KELLEY put on all the buildings in existence in 1814, which are indicated in black. I have added the harbor and the various shore lines, together with buildings of an earlier date than the record of this map. The different positions of the shore lines are shown by the dates of the surveys, thus, 1796, 1801, 1827, 1831, 1842, &c.

■—Buildings in 1814.

□—Buildings of an earlier date.

a—Fort Huntington, 1813.

b—Trading house of 1786,

c—CARTERS first cabin, 1797.

d—JOB P. STILES' first cabin, 1796,

e—Surveyors first cabin, 1796.

f—Surveyors cabin on the hill, 1797.

g—Cemetery lot, 1797,

h—Jail and Court House, 1812.

i—KINGSBURY'S first cabin, 1797.

k—CARTER'S house on the hill, 1803.

This reputed copy of SPAFFORD's map differs from the one heretofore given, and from the PEASE map in some particulars, but has a general identity. Maiden street, which is upon the HOLLEY and PEASE plat, is omitted from this, and Superior lane is added. Miami street is merged in Ohio, which here covers both, making a right angle in its course. Soon after the village corporation came into existence, in the year 1816, Euclid street was laid out, from the square to its intersection with Huron, the Euclid road having been surveyed in 1797, through the ten acre lots. Bond, Wood and St. Clair streets, were laid out at the same time, also a street around the public square.

STATEMENT OF SETH DOAN, 1841.

"OMIC was a fine looking young Indian, about twenty-one, and was hung upon the Public Square in this city, in the north-west corner, near where the old Court House and jail were then being erected. He was convicted of the murder of two trappers, BUEL and GIBBS, while they were asleep, in the night, near Sandusky city, for their traps and furs. Two other Indians, one older, the other a boy of fifteen were concerned with him, the older being taken near Carrying river, in the Maumee swamp, seized a musket from one of the party who arrested him, and putting the muzzle under his chin, pulled the trigger with his foot and shot himself dead. The boy was considered as forced into participation by the others and was suffered to escape, and lived to be the ring-leader of two others, in the murder of JOHN

WOOD and GEORGE BISHOP, west of Carrying river in 1816, for which they were all executed in Huron county. The family of the murdered JOHN WOOD, are now, (1841) resident in this city. The skeleton of OMIC is in possession of Dr. ISAAC TOWN, of Hudson, Portage county.

"One of the first nurseries of apple trees in this vicinity was from seeds saved by me and my brother, TIMOTHY, Jr., from a basket of apples brought from Detroit; which we bought at two dollars. Some of the finest orchards in Euclid, and the neighboring townships have their origin from these seeds."

EXECUTION OF O'MIC, JUNE 24th, 1812.

BY THE HON. E. WHITTLESEY.

I was present at the execution, and as distinctly recollect the facts I shall narrate, as I did the night of the day they occurred. I was not at the trial, but understood that PETER HITCHCOCK was assigned as counsel for the accused. The custody of the prisoner was assigned to LORENZO CARTER (there being no jail) because he was a man of uncommon energy, and because he had more influence over the Indians than any other man in the west, or at least in Cuyahoga county. Mr. CARTER's house was on the high ground near the bank, to the right of the road that descended the hill to the ferry across the river, and to the left of the street that leads to where the Light

House now stands. The prisoner was confined in a chamber of Mr. CARTER's house. Strong irons were above his ancles, with which was connected a staple that was driven into a joist that supported the floor, so that the prisoner could not go to any window. Probably I should have said with more accuracy, that a chain was attached to the fetters, and a staple was attached to the other end, which was driven into the joist, &c. After his conviction, O'MIC told Mr. CARTER and Sheriff BALDWIN, (who was from Danbury,) that he would let the pale faces see how an Indian could die; that they need not tie his arms, but when the time came he would jump off from the gallows.

Before Mr. CARTER's house, in the direction of Superior street, was an open space somewhat extensive, and covered with grass. The religious exercises were held there. Several clergymen were present, and I think the sermon was delivered by the Rev. Mr. DARROW, of Vienna, Trumbull county. The military were commanded by Major JONES, a fine looking officer in full uniform, but he was in the condition that Captain McGUFFY, of Coitsville, said he was when he was commanded to perform an evolution by his company and could not do it. His explanation was, "I know Baron STEUBEN perfectly well, but I cannot commit him to practice."

O'MIC sat on his coffin in a wagon painted for the occasion. He was a fine looking young Indian, and watched everything that occurred with much anxiety. The gallows was erected on the Public Square in in front of where the old Court House was erected. After the religious services were over, Major JONES endeavored to form a hollow square, so that the prisoner should be guarded on all sides. He rode backwarks and forwards with drawn sword, epaulets, and scabbard flying, but he did not know what order to give. The wagon with O'MIC moved ahead and stopped; but as the Sheriff doubted whether he was to be aided by the military, he proceeded onward. Major JONES finally took the suggestion of of some one, who told him to ride to the head of the line, and double it round until the front and rear of the line met. Arriving at the gallows, Mr. CARTER, the Sheriff and O'MIC ascended to the platform by a ladder. The arms of the prisoner were loosely pinioned. A rope was around his neck with a loop in the end. Another was let down through a hole in the top piece, on which was a hook to attach to the rope around the neck. The rope with the hook was brought over to one of the posts, and fastened to it near the ground.

After some little time Mr. CARTER came down, leaving O'MIC and Sheriff BALDWIN on the platform. As the Sheriff drew down the cap, O'MIC was the most terrified being, rational or irrational, I ever saw, and seizing the cap with his right hand, which he could reach by bending his head and inclining his neck in that direction, he stepped to one of the posts and put his arm around it. The Sheriff approached him to loose his hold, and for a moment it was doubtful whether O'MIC would not throw him to the ground. Mr. CARTER ascended to the platform and a negotiation in regular diplomatic style was had. It was in the native tongue, as I understood at the time. Mr. CARTER appealed to O'MIC to display his courage, narrating what he had said about showing pale faces how an Indian could die, but it had no effect. Finally O'MIC made a proposition, that if Mr. CARTER would give him half a pint of whisky he would consent to die. The whisky was soon on hand, in a large glass tumbler, real old Monongahela, for which an old settler would almost be willing to be hung, if he could now obtain the like. The glass was given to O'MIC and he drank the whisky, in as little time as he could have turned it out of the glass. Mr. CARTER again came down, and the Sheriff again drew down the cap and the same scene was re-enacted, O'MIC expressing the same terror. Mr. CARTER again ascended to the platform, and O'MIC gave him the honor of an Indian, in pledge that he would not longer resist the sentence of the court, if he should have another half pint of whisky. Mr. CARTER, representing the people of Ohio and the dignity of the laws, thought the terms were reasonable, and the whisky was forthcoming on short order. The tumbler was not given to O'MIC, but it was held to his mouth, and as he sucked the whisky out, Sheriff BALDWIN drew the rope that pinioned his arms more tight, and the rope was drawn down to prevent the prisoner from going to the post, and to prevent him from pulling off his cap. The platform was immediately cleared of all but O'MIC, who run the ends of his fingers on his right hand, between the rope and his neck. The rope that held up one end of the platform was cut, and the body swung in a straight line towards the lake, as far as the rope permitted and returned, and after swinging forth and backward several times, and the weight being about to be suspended perpendicular under the center of the top of the gallows, the body turned in a circle and finally rested still.

At that time a terrific storm appeared and came up from the north north-west with great rapidity, to avoid which, and it being doubtful whether the neck was broken, and to accomplish so necessary part of a hanging, the rope was drawn down with the design of raising the body, so that, by a sudden relaxing of the rope, the body would fall several feet, and thereby dislocate the neck beyond any doubt, but when the body fell, the rope broke as readily as a tow string and fell upon the ground. The coffin and grave were near the gallows and the body was picked up, put into the coffin, and the coffin immediately put into the grave. The storm was heavy and all scampered but O'MIC.

The report was, at the time, that the surgeons at dusk raised the body, and when it lay on the dissecting table, it was easier to restore life than to prevent it.
ELISHA WHITTLESEY.

Another old settler who remembers this execution, has said, that the old flint lock muskets and rifles, which the militia escort under Major JONES carried that day, were so thoroughly wet, by the storm, that the Indians would have had no difficulty in capturing the place, if they had made the attempt.

In 1812 when real dangers began to gather around the settlement, Mr. KELLEY states that other officers were elected. The Muster Roll of the Cleveland company, during the war has not yet been recovered.

FROM A LETTER OF CAPTAIN STANTON SHOLES, (AGED 87.)

COLUMBUS, July, 1858.

JOHN BARR, Sec'y Cuyahoga Co., Historical Society:

Sir:—With a trembling hand I will state to the Society, that about the 3d of May, 1813, I received orders from the War Department, to march my company (then at Beavertown, Pennsylvania) to Cleveland, Ohio, to aid in the defence of this frontier and to establish a military post. On the 10th, I, with my company, arrived at Cleveland, and found Major JESSUP and two or three companies of militia, called out some months before. I halted my company between Major CARTER'S and WALLACE'S. I was here met by Governor MEIGS, who gave me a most cordial welcome, as did all the citizens. The Governor took me to a place, where my company could pitch their tents. I found no place of defense, no hospital, and a forest of large timber, (mostly chestnut) between the lake, and the lake road. There was a road that turned off between Mr. PERRY's and Major CARTER's that went to the point, which was the only place that the lake could be seen from the buildings. This little cluster of buildings was all of wood, I think none painted. There were a few houses further back from the lake road. The widow WALWORTH kept the post office, or ASHBEL, her son. Mr. L. JOHNSON, Judge KINGSBURY, Major CARTER, N. PERRY, GEO. WALLACE, and a few others were there. At my arrival I found a number of sick and wounded who were of HULL's surrender, sent here from Detroit, and more coming. These were crowded into a log cabin, and no one to care for them. I sent one or two of my soldiers to take care of them, as they had no friends. I had two or three good carpenters in my company, and set them to work to build a hospital. I very soon got up a good one, thirty by twenty feet, smoothly and tightly covered, and floored with chestnut bark, with two tier of bunks around the walls, with doors and windows, and not a nail, a screw, or iron latch or hinge about the building. Its cost to the Government was a few extra rations. In a short time I had all the bunks well strawed, and the sick and wounded good and clean, to their great joy and comfort, but some had fallen asleep. I next went to work and built a small fort, about fifty yards from the bank of the lake, in the forest. This fort finished, I set the men to felling the timber along and near the bank of the lake, rolling the logs and brush near the brink of the bank, to serve as a breastwork. On the 19th of June, a part of the British fleet appeared off our harbor, with the apparent design to land. When they got within one and a half miles of our harbor it became a perfect calm, and they lay there till after noon, when a most terrible thunder storm came up, and drove them from our coast. We saw them no more as enemies. Their object was to destroy the public or government boats, then built and building, in the Cuyahoga river, and other government stores at that place. About the middle of July General Harrison and suite paid a visit to this station. While here he made his head quarters at Major Carter's. His staff were, Col. Samuel Huntington, Paymaster of of the army, and ex-Governor of this State, and Majors George Tod and Jessup, and one or two more. Col. Wood, who was shortly after killed in battle at Fort Erie was a brave officer. General Harrison during his stay, took great care to scrutinize everything that had been done for its defense. After three days stay the General and suite left

Cleveland as he found it, to return to the army, then lying at the mouth of the Maumee river.

After General HARRISON left there was nothing worthy of note. One thing I ought to have mentioned, that the General was very kindly received on his arrival at this place, and not a few came from different parts of the country to see WM. H. HARRISON, commander-in-chief of the north-western army. Citizens and soldiers were hand in hand. There is a debt of gratitude I owe the then citizens of Cleveland, for their kindness to me and my company officers, the few months we were stationed among them. Some time in July, I was attacked with the fever, and as Doctor LONG lived in a small house, about half way from Major CARTER's to the point, near to my camp; I stepped to the Doctor's, he was not at home, and Mrs. LONG seeing me shake, requested me to lie down. I was soon up the stairs stripped of my coat and boots, and fell on the bed. When I awoke and came a little to myself I smelt something very sickening. Turning my face to the wall, my face partly over the bed, I was struck almost senseless, by an object on the floor between me and the wall, my face partly over it. It was a human skeleton, every bone in its place, the flesh mostly gone. I gazed at these bones till I verily thought I was dead, and that they had buried me by the side of some one that had gone before me. I felt very sick which roused from my legarthy and I found that I was alive, and had been sleeping alongside a dead man. As soon as I recalled where I was, I reached the lower floor in quickstep, giving Mrs. LONG a fright, to see me come down in such haste. She very politely apologized for her forgetfulness. The season before, there had been an Indian hung for the murder of a white man, and I had the luck to sleep side by side with his frame, not fully cleaned. I do not remember the death of any citizen while I was encamped with them.

STATEMENT OF MRS. JULIANNA LONG.

JUNE 14TH, 1866.

I first came to Cleveland in 1804, and stayed at Judge HUNTINGTON'S. My father, JOHN WALWORTH, moved to Cleveland from Painesville in April, 1806; we came up in an open boat which was wrecked, and my father came near being drowned. He was so weak when he came out of the water that he could barely crawl on his hands and knees. My mother's name was JULIANNA MORGAN, who was born at Groton, Connecticut, Dec. 31st, 1769, and died in Cleveland, March 2d, 1853. My father died here Sept. 10th, 1812. He was born at Groton, Connecticut, June 10th, 1765.

I remember EZEKIEL HAWLEY, of Cleveland, who removed to Newburg at a very early day. His wife LUCY, was a sister of LORENZO CARTER.

When Judge WALWORTH came here there were the following families in Cleveland: Judge HUNTINGTON, Major SPAFFORD, DAVID CLARK, and PIERRE MELOCHE, a Frenchman.

ABRAM HICKOX came here in 1808. His blacksmith shop was on the north side of Superior street, where the Johnson House is now.

NATHAN PERRY, senior, who was generally called Major PERRY, came to Cleveland in the summer of 1807. His son, HORACE PERRY, came the next spring, and NATHAN PERRY, junior, the following fall. Afterwards NATHAN PERRY, senior, removed to Black river, and died there, but he was buried at Cleveland. [He died Oct. 28th, 1813, in his fifty-third year.]

MELOCHE left here, and returned to Detroit about 1808, and ALEXANDER CAMPBELL, the trader, left the place in 1808 or 1809.

ELIAS and HARVEY MURRAY took CAMPBELL'S store under the hill.

The first Postmaster was ELISHA NORTON, appointed October 22d, 1805. He afterwards removed to Mantua, in Portage county, and my father took his place. Doctor DAVID LONG emigrated from Hebron, New York, in June, 1810, and we were married April 7th, 1811.

ASHBEL W. WALWORTH, my brother, was made deputy Postmaster Sept. 9th, 1809.

When the war broke out, the following families were in Cleveland:

GEORGE WALLACE,	HARVEY MURRAY,
SAMUEL WILLIAMSON,	ABRAM HICKOX,
HEZEKIAH KING,	LEVI JOHNSON,
ELIAS MURRAY,	DAVID HICKOX, who called himself HENDERSON,
RICHARD BAILEY,	Maj. SAMUEL JONES,
AMASA BAILEY,	
HIRAM HANCHETT.	

Also without families:

Mr. BEAVER,	ALFRED KELLEY,
JAMES ROOT,	MATTHEW WILLIAMSON.

Mr. STEPHEN KING, a brother to HEZEKIAH KING, died here in the winter following. Mr. BEAVER returned to Pennsylvania. I knew JOHN O'MIC and his father very well. JOHN was not a bad Indian towards the whites. When we were children at Painesville, we used to play together on the banks of the Grand river, at my father's old residence, which we called Bloomingdale. This was the place where Governor HUNTINGTON lived and died. O'MIC's father came to our house, on Water street, a short time before the execution. We were very much afraid of the Indians then. I was alone, and my babe, (Mrs. SEVERANCE,) was sleeping in the cradle. He took up a gun which was in the room, in order to show me how SEMO killed himself, after he had been arrested. I thought he was going to kill me or my baby, in revenge for his son. I seized the child and ran up Water street towards Mr. WILLIAMSON'S, screaming pretty hard, I suppose. O'MIC followed after me, trying to explain what he meant. Mr. WILLIAMSON caught the child, and we all went to Major CARTER'S house, which was on the corner of Superior street and Union lane. Major CARTER had a short talk with O'MIC, who explained what he meant, and we all had a hearty laugh. O'MIC had lived near Painesville. I was in the crowd on the square when O'MIC was to be hung, and I suddenly thought, "why should I wish to see my old play-fellow die?" I got out of the crowd as quick as possible and went home. All the people from the Western Reserve seemed to be there, particularly the doctors. I remember several of them who stayed at our house. Among them was Dr. ALLEN, who recently died at Trumbull county, Dr. COLEMAN, of Ashtabula county, Dr. JOHNSON, of Conneaut, and Dr. HAWLEY, of Austintown. When O'MIC was swung off the rope broke, and they were not sure that he was dead, but there was a storm coming on and he was hurried into the grave near the gallows. The Public Square was only partly cleared then, and had many stumps and bushes on it. At night the doctors went for the body, with the tacit consent of the Sheriff. O'MIC was about twenty-one years of age, and was very fat and heavy. Dr. LONG did not think one man could carry him, but Dr. ALLEN, who was very stout, thought he could. He was put upon Dr. ALLEN's back, who soon fell over a stump and O'MIC on the top of him. The doctors dare not laugh aloud, for fear they might be discovered, but some of them were obliged to lie down on the ground and roll around there, before they came to the relief of Dr. ALLEN."

On the 3d of July, 1866, the following announcement was made in the public prints of Cleveland: "Died, on the 2d inst., at her late residence, 394 Kinsman street, Mrs. JULIANNA LONG, widow of the late Dr. DAVID LONG, aged 71 years, 9 months."

In a letter of the late Hon. ALFRED KELLEY, speaking of the panic caused by HULL's surrender, he makes the following statement:

"Information was received at Cleveland, through a scout from Huron, that a large number of British troops and Indians were seen from the shore, in boats, proceeding down the lake, and that they would probably reach Cleveland in the course of the ensuing night. This information spread rapidly through the surrounding settlements. A large proportion of the families in Cleveland, Newburg, (then part of Cleveland,) and Euclid, immediately on the receipt of this news, took such necessary articles of food, clothing and utensils as they could carry, and started for the more populous and less exposed parts of the interior. About thirty men only remained, determined to meet the enemy if they should come, and, if possible, prevent their landing.

They determined at least to do all in their power to allay the panic, and prevent the depopulation of the country."

"Several ladies of Cleveland, among whom were Mrs. GEORGE WALLACE, Mrs. JOHN WALWORTH and Mrs. Dr. LONG, resolved not to desert their husbands and friends. When Mrs. LONG was told that she could not fight or forcibly oppose the enemy, she replied that she 'could nurse the sick or wounded—encourage and comfort those who could fight; at any rate she would not, by her example, encourage disgraceful flight.'"

JOHN WALWORTH.

JOHN WALWORTH, though not among the earliest, was one of the most prominent settlers of the Western Reserve. He came from Aurora, New York, near Cayuga lake, to Mentor in 1799, and remaining there through the winter returned to New York in the spring for his family. WALWORTH was born in 1765 at Groton, New London Co., Connecticut. Like most young men who lived near salt water, he spent several years at sea, and visited the South American States. He came to settle at Cayuga lake in 1792. They reached their new home at Painesville on the 8th of April, 1800. He was small in stature, of very active habits, and had a pleasing countenance. There is in the family a paper-cut profile of his face, the lower part of which has an excellent expression, indicating kindness, coupled with intelligence. The upper part of the profile is concealed by the hair, which is brought down over the forehead according to the fashion, seventy years since. Mr. WALWORTH could not have been selected to fill so many offices, in the organization of the new government, if he had not been worthy of them. In those days professional office hunters, seldom became the successful candidates. Men were selected because they were qualified, not because they were anxious to obtain places.

A portion of the appointments he was called upon to accept have already been given. He was commissioned by ARTHUR ST. CLAIR, territorial Governor of Ohio, as Justice of the Peace for Trumbull county, July 4th, 1802; as an Associate Judge by Governor TIFFIN, April 14th, 1803; as Postmaster at Painesville, Nov. 14th, 1804; Inspector of the Port of Cuyahoga, by THOMAS JEFFERSON, June 12th, 1805; Collector of the district of Erie, July 17th, 1806; Associate Judge of Geauga county, Jan. 23d, 1806; Postmaster at Cleveland, May —, 1806. When the county of Cuyahoga was organized he became County Clerk and Recorder.

It was no small part of Mr. WALWORTH's good fortune, that he had a wife well suited to the circumstances, by which they were surrounded. Miss JULIANNA MORGAN was born at Groton, Connecticut,

December 31st, 1769. She was therefore at the mature age of thirty-one years, when they encountered the trials of pioneer life at the extreme west. Their previous residence at Aurora, New York, was not far from the verge of civilization, but this was a movement three hundred miles further into the western wilds.

Mrs. WALWORTH is remembered as a kind, dignified, judicious woman, spoken of with respect and kindness, by all those who shared her society or her hospitality.

When the stampede occurred at Cleveland, on the occasion of HULL'S surrender, she was one of the three ladies who refused to leave the place. She rode a horse, not merely as a graceful exercise, but took long journeys in company with her husband. In 1810 she crossed the mountains in this manner, by way of Pittsburg and Philadelphia, to the eastern States.

With such training, a vigorous physique, and a cheerful disposition, it is not strange that she survived three generations ; long enough to witness the results of her husbands expectations. She died at Cleveland, March 2d, 1853.

There were three sons, JOHN PERIANDER, now living, HORACE, who died recently in Louisiana, and ASHBEL W., who succeeded his father as Collector, dying at Cleveland, Aug. 24th, 1844, at the age of fifty-four years. The daughters were Mrs. Dr. LONG and Mrs. Dr. STRICKLAND.

Mr. WALWORTH did not live to realize the brilliant hopes he had formed of this city and county. He died in the dark days of the war, on the 10th of September, 1812. Had he survived another year he would have heard on that day, the boom of PERRY's victorious guns. But the character of such men has an influence beyond the grave. Their characteristics are impressed upon new communities, long after they are personally forgotten.

RECORD OF THE EARLY SETTLERS.

1796.

Job P. Stiles and Tabitha Cumi Stiles, his wife; Edward Paine.

1797.

Lorenzo Carter and Rebecca Carter, (ne Aikin;) Alonzo, Henry, Laura, (Mrs. Stong,) Mercy, (Mrs. Abell,) and Betsey, (Mrs. Cathan,) their children; Miss Chloe Inches, (Mrs. Clement;) James Kingsbury and Eunice Kingsbury, (ne Waldo,) with three children, Amos S., Almon, and Abigail, (Mrs. Sherman;) Ezekiel Hawley and Lucy Hawley, (ne Carter,) and one child; Elijah Gun and Anna Gun, and one child; Pierre Meloche; Peleg Washburne, who died the same season.

1798.

Nathaniel Doan and Mary Doan, (ne Carey,) Job, and three daughters, afterwards Mrs. R. H. Blin, Mrs. Eddy, and Mrs. Baldwin; Samuel Dodge, Rodolphus Edwards, Nathan Chapman, Stephen Gilbert, Joseph Landon.

1799.

Richard H. Blin, William Wheeler Williams, Mr. Gallup, Major Wyatt.

1800.

Amos Spafford wife and family, Alexander Campbell, David Clark and wife, Mason, Martin, James, Margaret and Lucy, their children, David Bryant, Gilman Bryant and Samuel Jones.

1801.

Samuel Huntington and wife, Miss Margaret Cobb, Julius C. and Colburn, sons of Mr. Huntington, Timothy Doan and Polly Doan, Timothy, Jr., Seth, John, Deborah, (Mrs. Crocker,) Mrs. Samuel Dodge, and Mrs. Bronson, their children; Elisha Norton and family.

INCREASE OF POPULATION.

1796,		4		
1797,		15		
1800,		7		
1810,		57		
1820,	about	150		
1825,	about	500		
1830, U. S. Census,		1,075		
1832,	about	1,500		
1833,	"	1,900		
1834, City Census,		3,323		
1835, " "		5,080		
1840, U. S. Census,		6,071	Ohio City, 1,577	7,648
1845, City "		9,573	" " 2,462	12,035
1846, " "		10,135		
1850, U. S. "		17,034	Ohio City ab't 3,950	20,984
1851, City "		21,140		
1852, " "		25,670		
1860, U. S. "		43,838	two cities united.	
1866, City "		67,500		

Some useful deductions may be drawn from these figures, in regard to the future population of this city. We have here the number of people on both sides of the river since 1840 with a reasonable approach to accuracy. The rate of increase in five years, from 1840 to 1845, is 58 per cent., from 1845 to 1850 is 74 per cent., 1850 to 1860, ten years, by the government census 109 per cent., and from 1860 to 1866, six years, 76 per cent. Our present numbers, January, 1867, are computed at 70,000.

From 1840 to 1850 the increase exceeded 10 per cent. per annum, compounded annually. On the east side, in the two succeeding years it reached 21 and 24 per cent. per annum.

The best ascertained average increase of the five year periods, for the past twenty-five years, is nearly 62 per cent. At this rate the census of 1870 should give about 100,000, of 1875, 162,000, and of 1880, 262,000.

COLLECTORS AT CLEVELAND.

JOHN WALWORTH, January 17th, 1806; died in office, September 10, 1812.
ASHBEL W. WALWORTH, 1812; removed 1829.
SAMUEL STARKWEATHER, 1829; resigned 1840.
GEORGE B. MERWIN, 1840.
WILLIAM MILFORD, 1841,
SMITH INGLEHART, 1845.
C. L. RUSSELL, 1849.
ROBERT PARKS, 1853; died in office August 30th, 1860.
B. BROWNELL, 1860.
CHARLES L. BALLARD, April 1861.
JOHN C. GRANNIS, April, 1865.

EARLY LAKE CRAFT.

1679—Schooner Griffin, (French,) built at Cayuga creek, near Tonawanda.

1761-3—The Schooner Gladwyn, (British,) and a French vessel burnt on the Niagara river.

1785-6—Schooners Beaver and Mackinaw, belonging to the North West Fur Company.

A vague tradition of a shipwreck which occurred near the mouth of the Cuyahoga has long been current here.

It was probably one of the above named vessels which was lost. While the Moravians were at Pilgerruh, Captain THORN, who commanded the schooner, speaks of visiting them and procuring provisions, where he saw for the first time the kittens of a wild cat. There was at the same time a trader at Rocky river. Mr. CARTER saw the wreck of the schooner in his boyhood, 1797-8. Captain GAYLORD, who came to Cleveland in 1800, knew Capt. THORN very well, and often had from him the details, of the lonely winter he passed here after the shipwreck. It occurred late in the fall or early in winter, probably in December. The name of the vessel has been lost. According to Capt. GAYLORD's recollection, she was in company with another schooner, both of which were seeking for the mouth of the Cuyahoga, perhaps as a shelter from the coming storm. They were on their way up the lake with supplies for the British garrisons. Capt. THORN's vessel had on board some brass pieces for the Fort at Detroit, but the number of the guns is not well known, different accounts varying from one to three.

It was near night when they were enveloped in a snow storm, and were close in with the land. In he darkness of the night, driven by a furious winter storm, Capt. THORN'S vessel soon came ashore, not far from Johnson's run, which enters the lake near the Marine Hospital. The crew got safely ashore, and concluded to pass the winter on the spot. They built a cabin on the bank, near the corner of Clinton and Wilson streets, the remains of which were there in 1800 and in subsequent years. The guns were taken from the hold, and carried partly up the bank, wrapped in a sail, well greased, securely plugged, and buried beneath a leaning tree on one of the benches, or slips, of the shore.

When the first settlers came here, and even as late as 1830, there were evidences of the clearing which Captain THORN made around this cabin, in old stumps and in the second growth of timber. Capt. LORENZO CARTER, father of ALONZO, procured from the wreck, in the year 1807, the irons for the rudder of his new schooner the Zephyr.

Capt. LEVI JOHNSON says he procured spikes and bolts for one of his first vessels from the same place. A piece of iron from Capt. THORN'S schooner is still to be seen forming the hinges, of Mr. CARTER'S gate at his homestead at Newburg.

The guns were frequently sought after by the early settlers, but no trace of them has yet been found. No doubt the encroachment of the lake has left them long since beneath its waters, deep sunk in the quicksands of this shore.

Captain THORN was a Canadian, who in the war

of 1812, took part with us, and afterwards lived to be a very old man at Point au Chene, on the St. Clair River, not far above lake St. Clair.

1796—Two British armed vessels.

1797—Schooner of sixty tons, Erie Pa., called the Washington. Cleared from Cuyahoga in the spring of 1806 and was never heard of afterwards.

1800—Schooner Harlequin, of Erie, lost in October of the same year, and twenty persons, being all who were on board of her. Also the schooner Good Intent, 50 tons, which was lost off Point Abino in 1806.

1801—Schooner Adams, 150 tons, United States vessel built at River Rouge, near Detroit. Also the Tracy, of 70 tons, U. S. transport, wrecked on Bird Island reef, 1809.

Schooner Wilkinson, 80 tons, Detroit.

1804—Contractor, sloop, 50 tons, Black Rock, purchased by the United States in 1812; took part in the battle of Lake Erie under the name of the Trip. Cuyahoga Packet, sloop, 20 tons, Chagrin river. Schooner Lark, 20 tons, Grand river, Canada.

1805—A Government sloop of 60 tons, Cayuga creek, where the Griffin was built in 1679. Ranger, of 50 tons, St. Clair river.

1807—Schooner Mary, 120 tons, burnt by General Proctor in the Thames, 1813.

1808—Zephyr, Cleveland, burnt at Conjocketa creek, near Black rock.

1809—Schooner Catharine, 80 tons, Black Rock. In PERRY's battle, 1813, as the Somers. Charlotte, schooner, 90 tons, built some years previous; captured at Mackinaw, 1812, as the Salina. Became ice locked among the islands in the winter of 1812–13, and floating down opposite Erie, was stripped and burned.

1810—Schooner Ohio, 60 tons, Cleveland; became a part of PERRY's fleet.

EARLY RIVER MEN.

As early as 1749 the Cuyahoga was regarded by geographers a point destined to be of commercial importance. [DOUGLASS's summary.] FRANKLIN pointed to its future value in 1765, recommending that it be occupied for military purposes. WASHINGTON foresaw its consequence, while discussing a project for water communications between the lakes and Chesapeake Bay.

POWNALL and EVANS only knew of five rivers on the south shore of lake Erie, but they had the sagacity to discuss the project of a canal, allowing batteaux to pass into the waters of the Shenango and Mahoning from "Cherage," (Conneaut) and from the Cuyahoga river.—[POWNALL's account, 1756.]

It was this idea which FRANKLIN and WASHINGTON enlarged upon, as the mode, and the route, of the future inland commerce of the west. Batteaux once transferred, from the waters of lake Erie to those of the Ohio, were to be forced up its upper branches as far as possible into the mountains, and property thus transferred to the Atlantic rivers.

When the State of New York, began to agitate the plan of a rival route by way of Oswego river and the Mohawk, in 1793–4, the discussions of POWNALL, FRANKLIN, and WASHINGTON were renewed.

But we know of no permanent occupation for the usual purposes of trade, prior to 1786; when the British, although in a state of quasi war, drew their supplies from the United States. Their posts held on our own soil, in violation of the treaty of 1783, obtained provisions from Pennsylvania through this place.—[HILLMAN's letter.]

From 1760 to this time, the French and British traders in furs were probably here, as there was no part of the country they did not penetrate. From 1786 to 1795, flour and beef were furnished to the military posts on the lakes, British and American, by way of Erie and Cleveland. DUNCAN & WILSON of Pittsburg, were the first forwarders who did business here, packing flour in bags upon horses, along the time-worn trails of the Indians.

When Gen. WAYNE overcame the north-western tribes at the Maumee rapids, in 1794, the enterprising merchants of Pittsburg and Beaver, contracted to furnish supplies on the Maumee, by way of the Cuyahoga. The old Indian highway from Beaver to this place, became a notable thoroughfare along which ninety horses and thirty men, were continually passing. From this place goods and provisions were taken, sometimes in vessels or in batteaux, to the Maumee or Detroit, and sometimes through by land on horses.

The commercial importance of the mouth of the Cuyahoga was thus foreshadowed from the earliest days. It was on a nearer route from the valley of the Monongahela and the Potomac to the head of lake Erie, than the one by the Allegheny river and Presque Isle or Erie. The Muskingum and the Cuyahoga came so near together at Akron, that a portage of only seven miles was to be made with a light canoe, and then an almost interminable navigation might be pursued in all directions. These great natural routes being known to the early geographers and statesmen, led them to think of improvements here, and to predict great things for the future.

When the city was laid out, its future business was provided for by the landings intended for batteaux, by which it was expected the principal transportation would be effected. The "upper landing," at the foot of Vineyard lane, was for the up river business, and the "lower landing," where Mandrake and Union streets came to the river, now St. Clair street, was for the lake trade. General CLEAVELAND and the surveyors well knew that large vessels could not enter the river. Until 1827, when a harbor was constructed by the General Government, lake craft of all sizes worthy the name of a vessel, came to anchor outside and were unloaded by lighters. LORENZO CARTER engrossed most of this business in the early days of the settlement. In 1805 the mouth of the Cuyahoga was made a port of entry. Most of the traffic, prior to this time, was made in open boats, coasting along the shore. The surveyors' old cabin, CARTER's log shanty, and CAMPBELL's store, afforded more than warehouse room enough for the business. Those staunch, well-built batteaux, appear to have been capable of weathering the terrific gales of the lakes as bravely, as the sloops, schooners and steamers of later times. Accidents were no more common than they are now. The scheme for improving the Cuyahoga by means of a lottery, got up in 1807 has already been noticed. With all its disadvantages, this route crossing by land to the Tuscarawas and to the Mahoning, down those rivers, up the Ohio and its branches to the Potomac, and down it to the ocean, was thought to be a competitor with the one by way of Niagara, Oswego, Fort Stanwix and the Mohawk.

In 1808, Mr. CARTER built the "Zephyr," of 30 tons, intended particularly for the trade of this place. Salt, iron, leather, groceries and dry goods were the principal needs of the settlers, in return for which they collected furs and made grindstones, to be sent east in payment. MURRAY & BIXBY built the Ohio, of 60 tons, in 1810, which was launched near the warehouse of PETTIT & HOLLAND. About this time CARTER built a log warehouse on the bank of the lake between Meadow and Spring streets, where he received and discharged property until after the war of 1812, when it was undermined by a rise in the waters of the lake. The brothers ELIAS and HARVEY MURRAY erected another in 1811, which stood within the point on the river bank, where the new channel or harbor is now. Not far from this time, some person not yet identified, built a small log house for storage on the east bank, a short distance south of Superior street. LEVI JOHNSON built the Pilot in 1813. About the year 1816 the first frame warehouse was built by LEONARD CASE and Capt. WILLIAM GAYLORD. It stood a little north of St. Clair street, on the river. In 1817 or 1818 LEVI JOHNSON and Dr. DAVID LONG put up another, a short distance lower on this shore, northward of CASE & GAYLORD, and soon after a third was erected near them by JOHN BLAIR. Of these early and enterprising forwarders, JOHNSON and BLAIR still survive. From BLAIR's warehouse down the river, to the point of ground on which the MURRAY's built, was then an impassable marsh. ALONZO CARTER purchased land on the West Side, soon after the township of Brooklyn came into market. He built a tavern and a small warehouse on that side, opposite Superior street. The ferry crossed at this street which was kept by CHRISTOPHER GUN.

In 1816 an attempt was made to build a pier on the open lake. For this purpose an act of incorporation was procured and an association formed under the name and style of the "Cleveland Pier Company," as follows:

We, the undersigned, hereby covenant and agree to associate and form ourselves into a company, to be known and distinguished by the name and title of the "Cleveland Pier Company," for the purpose of erecting a pier at, or near the village of Cleveland, for the accommodation of vessels navigating lake Erie. Agreeable to an act of the Legislature of the of the State of Ohio, passed at their session in 1815 -16, authorizing the incorporating of a company for the aforesaid purposes.

ALONZO CARTER,	GEORGE WALLACE,
A. W. WALWORTH,	DARIUS E. HENDERSON,
DAVID LONG,	SAM'L WILLIAMSON, Sen.,
ALFRED KELLEY,	IRAD KELLEY,
DATUS KELLEY,	JAMES KINGSBURY,
EBEN HOSMER,	HORACE PERRY,
DANIEL KELLEY,	LEVI JOHNSON.

Something was done towards this pier, principally by Mr. KELLEY. These slight works, based upon quicksand, and constructed without the aid of pile drivers, withstood the fury of the lake storms but a short time. About this time the late CHAS. M. GIDDINGS became an importer of salt, from his home at Onondaga to the western lakes. After a few years he became a citizen of Cleveland, where he pursued a business career of surprising activity, so long as his health allowed him to participate in business.

In February, 1816, NOBLE H. MERWIN, with his family, arrived at Cleveland, direct from Connecticut He purchasedt he tavern stand of GEORGE WALLACE, on the corner of Superior street and Vineyard lane, and a tract between Superior and Vineyard lanes, extending to Division street, now Center street. He occupied his hotel, afterwards known as the "Mansion House," but became extensively interested in vessel stock, transportation, army contracts, and commercial business generally. A log warehouse had been erected on his property, near the foot of Superior street, which he continued to occupy for the purpose of storage and forwarding. When the Ohio canal was made navigable to Akron, the two lower locks were incomplete. Mr. MERWIN had the canal packet "Pioneer," brought from Buffalo, and taking her up the river, near where the stone mills are now, hauled her up the bank into the canal. On this boat the Cleveland party went to meet Gov. TRIMBLE, and the party from Akron, consisting of the Canal Commissioners and other celebrities on the boat "Allen Trimble." Mr. MERWIN died at St. Thomas, West Indies, in October, 1829, leaving his first purchase unimpaired to his heirs.

The site of the old log warehouse has became traditional in the commerce of Cleveland. GIDINGS & MERWIN, GIDINGS & BALDWIN, GIDINGS, BALDWIN &

PEASE, and GRIFFITH, PEASE & Co., were firms whose names appeared successively upon the sides of the warehouses located there. A fire which occurred about 1854 destroyed the entire row of buildings from Superior street to the canal.

In 1819, JOHN BLAIR became a river man, competing with GIDINGS & MERWIN, in the purchase of wheat.

In those days wheat, pork, flour, potash, and in fact, all the merchantable produce of the country was brought in by four or six horse teams, laboring slowly onward, through roads that would now be regarded impassible, the owners encamping by the road side, wherever night found them. When the Ohio Canal was projected our citizens, and particularly the produce dealers, indulged in the gloomiest anticipations. No more Pennsylvania teams with their sturdy horses, and covered wagons, would enliven the streets of Cleveland. If Painesville, Black River or Sandusky wanted a canal, they were welcome to it.

Mr. BLAIR and LEVI JOHNSON are the only survivors of those early forwarders, who viewed the approach of a Conestoga wagon with so much interest. When experience had shown that the canal did not prove to be the ruin of the place, they turned their enterprise into new channels. The General Government constructed a harbor while the State was excavating the canal. Sail vessels, steamboats and canal boats, became more plenty than the wagons had ever been. A race of active young men succeeded the pioneers on the dock. Such of the original members of the Land Company as survived, at last witnessed in the decline of life, the success of the projects of their youth.

PRESIDENTS OF THE VILLAGE OF CLEVELAND.

Under the charter incorporating the village of Cleveland, dated December 23d, 1814, the first election took place on the first Monday in June, 1815. There were twelve votes cast at this election, which were given unanimously for the following officers:

President—ALFRED KELLEY.
Recorder—HORACE PERRY.
Treasurer—ALONZO CARTER.
Marshal—JOHN A. ACKLEY.
Assessors—GEORGE WALLACE and JOHN RIDDLE.
Trustees—SAM'L WILLIAMSON, DAVID LONG and NATHAN PERRY, junior.

On the 19th of March, 1816, ALFRED KELLEY resigned his position as President of the corporation, and his father, DANIEL KELLEY, was appointed in his place. At the annual election, on the first Monday in June, 1816, DANIEL KELLEY was elected President by the unanimous voice of twelve voters, and was continued in the office through the years 1817, 1818, and 1819.

The names of those who participated in this election were as follows:

A. W. Walworth,	Irad Kelley,
Thomas Rummage,	George Wallace,
Alonzo Carter,	Samuel Williamson,
Levi Johnson,	D. C. Henderson,
S. A. Ackley,	Amasa A. Bailey,
George Pease,	Daniel Kelley.

The total assessed value of real estate within the city in 1816, which includes the entire plat surveyed 1796, was $21,065. At the election in the year 1820 Horace Perry was made President, and Reuben Wood, Recorder, who rose to the Presidency in the following year.

From the year 1821 to 1825, Leonard Case was regularly elected President of the corporation, but neglecting to qualify in the latter year, the Recorder, E. Waterman, became President, ex-officio. Here the records are defective until the year 1828, when it appears Mr. Waterman received the double office of President and Recorder. On account of ill health he resigned, and on the 30th day of May the trustees appointed Oirson Cathan, President, and D. H. Beardsley, Recorder. At the annual election, June, 1829, Dr. David Long was elected President, and a fire engine was purchased. Forty-eight votes were cast at this election. For the years 1830 and 1831, President, Richard Hilliard. For the years 1832, 1833, 1834 and 1835, John W. Allen; at this last election there were one hundred and six votes cast.

POSTMASTERS AT CLEVELAND.

Elisha Norton, October 2d, 1805.

John Walworth, May, 1806. Died in office, September 10th, 1812.

Ashbel W. Walworth, 1812. Resigned, 1816.

Daniel Kelley, 1816. Resigned same year.

Irad Kelley, 1816. Removed, 1830.

Daniel Worley, 1830. Resigned, May, 1840.

Aaron Barker, May, 1840, to October 1841.

Benjamin Andrews, October, 1841, to April, 1845.

Timothy P. Spencer, April, 1845, to 1849.

Dan. M. Haskell, 1849.

J. W. Gray, 1853.

Benjamin Harrington, 1857.

E. Cowles, 1861.

Geo. A. Benedict, 1865.

LOCATION OF POST OFFICE.

Judge Walworth at first occupied the upper part of a frame building on the north side of Superior street, near Water street. When his family moved from this building, to their house on the Walworth farm, Pittsburg street; a small frame office was erected south of Superior street, where the American house now stands. During Judge Walworth's life, this office contained the combined authority of the, city, the county, and the federal governments.

Mr. Kelley states that in 1810, Mr. Walworth was Recorder, Clerk of the Common Pleas and Supreme Court; Postmaster and Collector of the Cuyahoga district. The same office accommodated Mr. Kelley, the only attorney in the place, and Dr. Long, the only physician. During the first quarter of 1806 the receipts at the post office amounted to *two dollars and eighty-three cents.*

Probably the post office remained at the same place while Ashbel W. Walworth was Postmaster. When Irad Kelley succeeded to that place it was removed to his brick store, on the south side of Superior street, opposite Bank street. The receipts for a year were about five hundred dollars, of which one-fourth belonged to the Postmaster, as compensation, which included rent, fuel and clerk hire. All letters written by the Postmaster could be franked by him, which, to a man of business was of more value than his per centage on receipts. The postage in those days was never less than five cents, and for distances exceeding three hundred miles, it was twenty-five cents.

Under Postmaster Worley, the delivery office was removed to the north side of Superior street, at Millers block, between Seneca and Bank streets, and afterwards to a store where the Johnson House is now, the rear of which was occupied as the Custom House. Mr. Haskell removed it to the Herald building, on Bank street. When Mr. Gray received the appointment, the office was transferred to his building on Waters treet, west side, near St. Clair.

While Mr. Harrington was postmaster the government building on the Public Square was completed, and thus the place of delivery became fixed.

THE FIRST COURT HOUSE.

While O'MIC was dangling upon the gallows on the north west quarter of the Public Square, the assembled multitude sat upon the timbers, which LEVI JOHNSON had collected for the erection of a Court House. It was of the composite order. The lower story was divided in two parts, one of which was the jail, and the other the residence of the jailer. The apartment designed for criminals, was constructed of blocks of square timber three feet long, placed endwise and bolted together. Over all, in the second story, was a Court room, equal in size to the ground plan of the building, the position of which is given on the map of 1814. Mr. E. WATERMAN officiated as jailer, President of the village corporation, and Recorder.

In 1828 the citizens became able, and spirited enough to have a new Court House, and a separate jail.

It was a fine building for those times, of which a faithful sketch by Professor BRAINERD is given on the next page.

It stood upon the south-west quarter of the Square, facing towards the lake. Here justice was administered thirty years, until it became wholly insufficient for want of room, and unsafe for the public records. The present edifice for the Courts, and other public offices, was erected in 1858. H. L. NOBLE, one of our early and honest mechanics, had the contract for

building the brick Court House represented above. When it was taken down it was found to be sound and good as new, and except in the exposed wood work, was capable of enduring at least another century. The old stone jail, oftener called the "Blue Jug," stood opposite the Court House, on the south, fronting the Square. Of these twin institutions, where an entire generation received the administration of justice, where so many judges sat, and lawyers labored; where sheriff's and bailiff's executed the decisions of the courts, or the findings of juries, upon troops of unlucky culprits, not a relic now remains. In WHELPLYS views of Cleveland, the old Court House is a conspicuous object. But for these pictorial representations, the next generation would have lost all traces, of what constituted the public buildings of the county, during the active life of the present.

OHIO CITY.

On the west side of the river, opposite St. Clair street, where the Indians had a ferry, a trail led out across the marshy ground, up the hill past the old log trading house, where there were springs of water, to an opening in the forest, near the crossing of Pearl and Detroit streets. In this pleasant space the savages practised their games, held their pow wows, and when whisky could be procured, enjoyed themselves while it lasted. The trail continued thence westerly to Rocky River and Sandusky. Another one, less frequented, led off southerly up the river to the old French trading post, where MAGENIS was found in 1786, near Brighton; and thence, near the river bank, to Tinkers creek, and probably to the old Portage path. A less frequented trail, existed from the Indian villages of Tawas or Ottawas and Mingoes, at Tinkers creek, by a shorter route, direct to the crossing of the Cuyahoga at the "Standing Stone," near Kent. The packhorsemen, who transported goods and flour to the northwest from 1786 to 1795, followed this trail, crossing the Cuyahoga at Tinkers creek.

SAMUEL P. LORD drew a considerable part of the township of Brooklyn, whose son, the late RICHARD

LORD, and the late JOSIAH BARBER, became very early, if not the earliest settlers. The CARTERS, father and son, purchased the land at the mouth of the river, on the west side soon after the survey. ALONZO occupied this tract, living and keeping tavern in the "Red House," opposite Superior lane. In 1831 the spirit of speculation crossed the river. Lots on the west side began to command high prices. The Buffalo Company purchased the CARTER farm, where a rival city was expected to arise, covering the low ground with warehouses, and the bluffs with stores and residences. In 1834–35, water lots on the old river bed, commanded higher prices than they do now. In the flush times of 1836–37, land contracts on long time, became a kind of circulating medium, on both sides of the river, daily passing from hand to hand, by indorsement; the speculation accruing to each successive holder, being realized in cash; or in promises to pay. The company excavated a short ship canal from the Cuyahoga to the old river bed, at the east end, and the waters being high, a steamboat passed into the lake, through a natural channel at the west end. On the 3d of March, 1836, the village of Brooklyn became an incorporated city. Soon after, the city made a canal, from the Cuyahoga river opposite the extremity of the Ohio canal, through the marsh, into the old river bed, above the ship channel. The bridge, represented among the lithographs at the beginning of this book, which stood at the foot of Columbus street, was built by the late James S. Clark, and an excavation made through the bluff, on the south side, at great expense.

City rivalry ran so high, that a regular battle occurred on this bridge in 1837, between the citizens and the city authorities on the west side, and those on the east. A field piece was posted on the low ground, on the Cleveland side, to rake the bridge, very much as the Austrians did at Lodi, and crow-bars, clubs, stones, pistols, and guns were freely used on both sides.

Men were wounded of both parties, three of them seriously. The draw was cut away, the middle pier, and the western abutment partially blown down, and the field piece spiked, by the west siders. But the sheriff, and the city marshal of Cleveland, soon obtained possession of the dilapidated bridge, which had been donated to the city. Some of the actors were confined in the county jail. The bridge question thus got into court, and was finally settled by the civil tribunals. In 1855, (June 6th,) all jealousies and all rivalry between interests, that had never been in reality opposite, were hapily terminated, by an union which did away with the arbitrary and unreal line of separation.

The following list of gentlemen filled the office of Mayor, during the existence of the Ohio City charter.

1836—Josiah Barber.
1837—Francis A. Burrows.
1838-9—Norman C. Baldwin.
1840-41—Needham M. Standart.
1842—Francis A. Burrows.
1843—Richard Lord.
1844-45-46—D. H. Lamb.
1847—David Griffith.
1848—John Beverlin.
1849—Thomas Burnham.
1850-51-52—Benjamin Sheldon.
1853—Wm. B. Castle.

FLUCTUATIONS IN THE LEVEL OF LAKE ERIE.

When the early emigrants arrived at Buffalo creek they were at the end of roads. From Canandaigua to lake Erie, there was only a summer trail for horses, along which sleighs and sleds could be moved, on the snow in winter. West of Buffalo there was nothing resembling a road, except an ancient trail of the savages, not much used by them, except in their warlike expeditions. Fortunately at the beginning of this century, the lake was low, causing a beach of clean sand at the margin of the water. Some of the streams were difficult to ford, but many of them were so much choked with sand, at their mouths, that teams could cross. Not far outside of the shore line there is deposited a changeable sand bar, which forms at the debouche of all streams, where the force of the current is lost in the still water.

In the transparent waters of our northern lakes this bank is easily found. The emigrants thus made a passage of the streams by leaving the land, and driving their teams, apparently into the lake. If the water was rough, the waves breaking over the beach, they made a comfortable camp, above the bluffs in the woods near the shore, and waited patiently for better weather.

A few years afterwards, they were surprised to see this natural road submerged, by the waters of the lake. This alternate appearance and disappearance, of the lake beach, has been a standing mystery to the pioneers and their descendants. It is a change due to the most simple and natural causes. The lakes are large ponds or reservoirs, through which the waters of many united rivers flow to the ocean. All rivers are affected by the seasons, but it is more noticeable in large ones like the Mississippi, the Ganges and the Amazon. A year or two of drought in the country about their main branches, always produces low water.

When other meteorological conditions occur, and one or more rainy seasons follow each other, the rivers are high. The Straits connecting our northern lakes, are short rivers, not having capacity enough to discharge the surplus waters at once. This chain of lakes and their connecting outlets may be regarded as one great river, from tide water at Quebec, to the sources of the St. Louis river, in Minnesota. Like all large rivers, there is a spring rise and a winter fall; except in lake Superior, where the rise occurs in August or September.

This annual rise, occurs in June or July, about the time of the annual flood of the Missouri and the Mississippi rivers. It is much less in quantity, being only from twelve to sixteen inches; owing to the expansions, which act as reservoirs that must be filled; and which when full, require some months for their discharge. In the fall the surfaces of the lakes decline, simultaneously, as they rose. A smaller supply of rain, and increased evaporation, together with a continual discharge towards the ocean, disposes of the surplus water of the spring rains. When winter sets in, the supply from the streams is diminished by frost, and the lowest stage is reached in February or March.

These results have been obtained by long continued measurements, of the changes of level on all the lakes, during the past fifty years.

The annual rise and fall, is only one of the fluctuations, to which the lakes are subject. There is a sudden flux and reflux, which is completed in a few seconds, or few minutes; sometimes due to distant storms, but more often cannot be traced to a visible cause. Those oscillations are not yet explained. They occur on all the lakes, and upon other bodies of water; causing a rush into the mouths of the rivers, generally of a few inches in height, but sometimes of several feet. They have the form of a low undulation coming in from the offing, parallel with the shore. I have known them to continue many hours, and even days, with unbroken regularity, the interval from flood to flood, varying from five to eight minutes. Besides the annual and the sudden fluctuations, there is another which is more important, and which is called, the "Secular fluctuation." It occupies a cycle of years, which is not equal in duration. For a series of years the water is observed to settle away at the end of the annual decline, lower than it was the previous year at the same time.

Then it is seen to be higher and higher every year, till it reaches the maximum height. Reckoning from the highest annual rise, to the lowest, as at present known; the difference is six feet nine inches; a change which has an important influence, upon all harbors and docks. The lowest known stage of water occurred in February, 1819. From that date, there was a regular rise until June, 1838, when it flooded warehouses in this city, to the depth of one foot. At the mouth of Conneaut creek, the people were obliged to use boats, in order to pass along the streets, from house to house.

The remarkable rise of June, 1838, attracted the attention of every resident, on the shores of lake Erie. In the other lakes there was a conspicuous elevation about the same time. The members of the geological surveys of Ohio and Michigan, made observations upon this flood in the lakes, and procured what information it was possible to find, in reference to previous years.

Since the settlement of Detroit, in 1701, it is probable there had been no water as high as that of 1838. Timber which had grown to maturity on low lands, having an age of from one to two hundred years, was killed by this flood. From 1788 to 1790, lake Erie is reported to have been very high. The old French inhabitants affirm, that a road which had long before been in use on the Detroit river, was rendered useless by high water in 1802, which agrees with the statements of early settlers in Ohio. In 1814, and from thence to 1820, Col. HENRY WHITING, of the U. S. army, made measurements, upon the surface fluctuations in Detroit river, which disclosed the lowest known state of the water to be in February, 1819. In more recent times some of the United States officers, connected with the construction of harbors on the lakes, kept water registers, some of them daily or three times a day. Of these were Capt. MACOMB, (now Colonel,) Lieut. JUDSON, Col. J. B. STOCKTON, and Lieut. Col. KEARNY. The head of the Topographical Bureau at Washington, Col. ABERT, refused all aid and countenance, to these observations, although they showed a change of level, which rendered their reported soundings to be erroneous by several feet; for want of a fixed or mean plane of reference. It was not until Capt. (now General) MEADE took charge of the lake survey, that regular daily water registers, were officially kept on the lakes. Prior to this time, many persons at different places on lake Michigan, lake Erie, and lake Ontario, had had established points of reference, made frequent measurements, and kept a register of the same. Among these are JOHN LOTHROP, civil engineer, Buffalo, N. Y., I. A. LAPHAM, Milwaukee, GEORGE C. DAVIES, GEORGE TIEBOUT, and I. N. PILLSBURY, at Cleveland, Dr. DOUGLASS HOUGHTON, A. E. HATHAN, and JACOB HOUGHTON, Detroit, EDWARD GIDDINGS, Niagara, T. P. SPENCER, Rochester, and M. P. HATCH, Oswego.

From these sources and from my own observations, in all numbering some thousands, I have constructed a table of elevations, going back as far as there is any reliable information. The diagram which is here presented, expresses for lake Erie, in a condensed form, addressed to the eye, such of these recorded measurements as were made once a day or oftener, and were continued long enough to cover three or more consecutive months. They are all referred to a common zero, which is the Mitre sill, or bottom, of the enlarged Erie canal.

The curves are determined by an average of the observations for each month, expressed in feet and decimals; thus fixing a point in the middle of the column of months. Through each of these points a curve is drawn, representing a year or part of a year. Where there are blanks in the readings, the curves are continued by dotted lines which are conjectural. This diagram is on a vertical scale of four feet to

DIAGRAM

showing by curves the mean monthly elevation of the water in LAKE ERIE so far as determined by daily measurements embracing all the records prior to 1853, reduced to the depth of water on the mitre sill at Buffalo, N.Y.

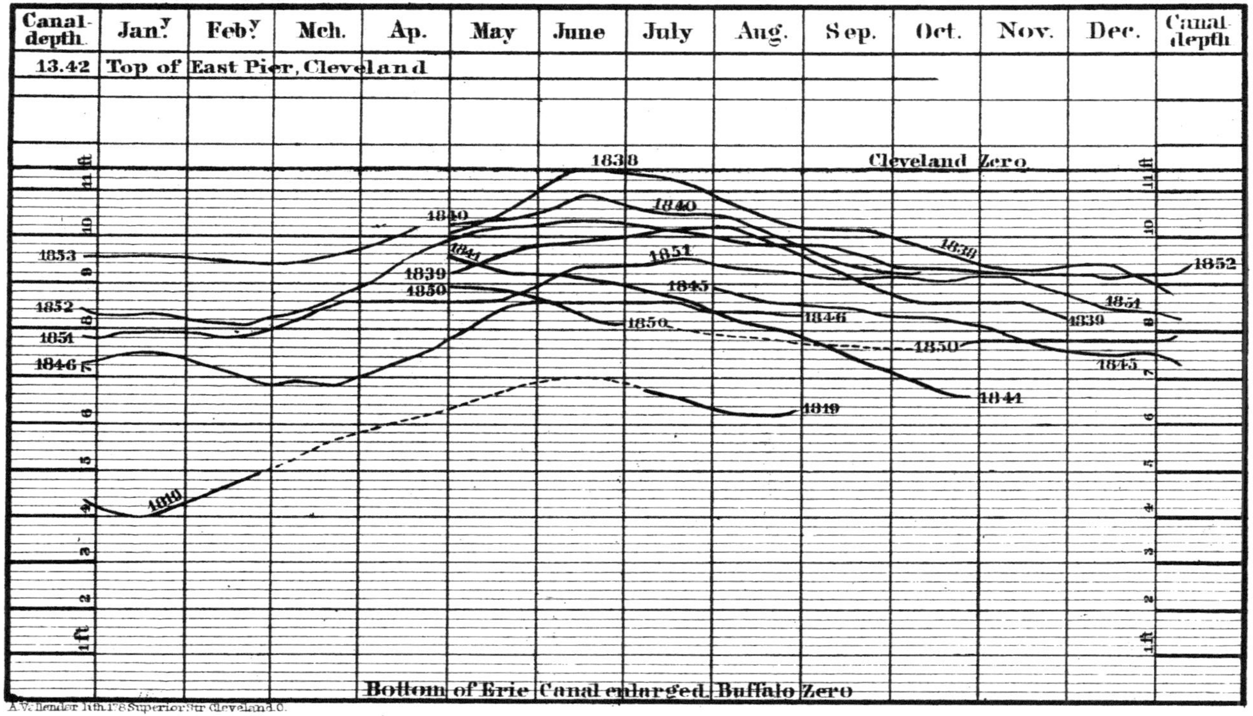

A. Vallendar lith. 178 Superior Str Cleveland O.

the inch, a quarter of an inch representing one foot, which is divided by finer lines, into fifths or two-tenths of a foot. Each place where registers were kept, had a zero, or point of reference of its own, but these are reduced by means of consecutive readings to the one at Buffalo, as the most permanent. At Cleveland, we used the high water line of June, 1838, counting downwards. Several marks were made on the piers and warehouses at that time, all of which have disappeared, except one, on the wing wall of the canal lock, at the river. The plane of reference however, has been preserved by adopting it as the city zero, for engineering work, and multiplying bench marks in different parts of the town. Capt. B. STANNARD has kept the registers here, for the lake survey since 1854.

A similar diagram might now be made for the years; taking the mean height of each period of twelve months as the ordinate, instead of one month, and thus show at a glance, the secular fluctuations. For the three best determined years, in my tables, the difference is as follows, counting downwards; the lake being on a declining stage of the water.

1839,	below	1838, ...	1.25 feet.
1840,	"	1839, ...	1.25 "
1841,	"	1840, ...	1.65 "
		Total decline in three years,	4.15 "

An examination of the curves at once demonstrates what I have already stated; that there is an annual spring rise, and a winter fall in the surface of the lakes, like that of our large rivers. This annual difference between the highest and lowest months, is not precisely the same at all places.

At Cleveland, the average of 16 years is	1 ft.	3	in.
At Detroit, " " " " "	1 "	$2\frac{1}{2}$	"
At Buffalo, " " " " "	0 "	$10\frac{1}{2}$	"
Average of these three stations,	1 ft.	$1\frac{1}{2}$	in.

These observations dispel the popular belief, derived from the Indians; that the lakes rise seven years and decline seven years. This could not be the case, unless the seasons should repeat themselves in every particular, in that period. In these tables there is no case of a change at seven, or at fourteen years.

From 1819 to 1838, there was a continual rise; a period of nineteen years. From 1838 to 1841, a decline; in 1841 a slight rise, and from 1842 to 1851, eight years, a regular decline. In 1853–54 there was a high stage; in the latter year for a short period fully up to the line of 1838. Since 1853, we can rely upon the water registers of the lake survey, for which an effort is now being made before Congress to have them published. By these it was discovered, after many thousands of observations on lake Michigan, by Lieut. Col. GRAHAM and Prof.

Lapham, that there is a slight lunar tide on the lakes. It is too small for direct cognizance, being for ordinary tide at Chicago, only $\frac{153}{1000}$ of a foot or 1 inch $\frac{84}{100}$, for the spring tides $\frac{254}{1000}$ or 3 inches $\frac{48}{100}$.

www.ingramcontent.com/pod-product-compliance
Lightning Source LLC
LaVergne TN
LVHW020917110826
845150LV00004B/704
9781425555047